Medieval
Yorkshire
Towns

Medieval *Yorkshire* Towns

People, Buildings and Spaces

GEORGE SHEERAN

EDINBURGH
University Press

© George Sheeran, 1998

Edinburgh University Press
22 George Square, Edinburgh

Typeset in Palatino Light
by Pioneer Associates, Perthshire, and
printed and bound in Great Britain by
Redwood Books, Trowbridge, Wilts

A CIP record for this book is available
from the British Library

ISBN 1 85331 242 8

The right of George Sheeran to be identified as
author of this work has been asserted in
accordance with the Copyright, Designs and
Patents Act 1988

Contents

Acknowledgements

IN WRITING THIS BOOK I have drawn on the help and advice of a number of people, none more so than Jane Grenville of the Department of Archaeology, York University; Steve Moorhouse; Richard Morris, Council for British Archaeology; and Yanina Sheeran. Their suggestions and comments have been truly helpful. I also wish to thank colleagues at Bradford University for their advice and support in this project.

I further wish to thank York Archaeological Trust for allowing me to publish the photograph of St Mary's Abbey sewer.

List of Abbreviations

BCL	Bradford Central Library: Local Studies
BCMSS	Beverley Corporation Manuscripts, Humberside Record Office, Beverley
BIHR	Borthwick Institute of Historical Research, York
BMC	Bradford Manor Court Rolls, vols I–IV, at BCL
CBA	Council for British Archaeology
HCR	Hull Corporation Records, Hull City Record Office
HMC	Historical Manuscripts Commission
PRO	Public Record Office
RCHME	Royal Commission on Historical Monuments England
SURTEES	Publications of the Surtees Society
TRANSHAS	*Transactions of the Halifax Antiquarian Society*
VCH	Victoria County History
YAJ	*Yorkshire Archaeological Journal*
YASRS	Yorkshire Archaeological Society Record Series

CHAPTER ONE

Constructing and Deconstructing the Town

TAKE THE WORD TOWN. It occurs in the title of this book, and readers no doubt understand what is meant by the word. Yet, if asked to describe what makes a town a town, there would be different explanations, and if asked to list Yorkshire towns, we might expect to find a fair amount of agreement but some disagreement too. How then are we to define a town? We might think of a town as characterised by the numbers of people making their living by trade or commerce or industry; religious or civil administration might also be important. In other words, there should be a significant number of non-agricultural occupations – and more than just this, it should be possible to observe a variety of occupations. Towns should not be dependent on one industry or way of trading, as for instance are single-industry pit or fishing villages. Basic to the functioning of a medieval town was a market place for this was the centre of exchange. Size or perhaps scale might also be regarded a striking feature of towns or cities, since some contained the largest congregations of people in one settled place, either within a region or within a nation. Yet they should not contain people all, or nearly all, of the same social standing, as in large peasant villages. Thus, both occupational and social heterogeneity become the marks of a town. Towns also have their own social institutions with legal and administrative structures. If these have their counterparts in villages, they are, nevertheless, different from them.

We might add that this gives rise to special physical identities over the centuries, agglomerations of built features which we do not associate with villages – walls, market places, shops, warehouses, great churches, town halls and so on. However, we must be careful here not to slip into a fallacy by describing what are the outcomes of social processes. It is people – their occupations, the positions they maintain in the social hierarchy and the ways in which social groups interact – which give rise to the physical aspect of towns. To use urban architecture as the defining characteristic of a town begs the question, since we must first show the existence of the social processes.

This is a trap that some archaeologists have fallen into. Biddle (1976/86), in accepting Heighway's (1972) suggestion that occupational heterogeneity may be characteristic of a town, also accepts without question the latter's contention that such physical features as planned street systems and defences are equally valid parts of the definition. Objections can be raised to this along the lines that such features can also be observed in some villages, but a more important objection concerns the question-begging logic of the argument. The clearest expression of the error lies in Biddle's and Heighway's statement that towns should contain plots and houses of an urban type, the very conclusion they wish to establish. What is more, while it may be of use to archaeologists and architectural historians to be able to recognise what were urban building types, they should realise that they have been classified as such because they have resulted from a certain way of living within a particular society and not because they possess some kind of peculiar urban essence.

If definition proves tricky today leaving areas over which we might haggle, it is more difficult trying to negotiate in the foreign tongue of the past. For in a foreign country they speak a foreign language, and unfortunately for us we can never learn this language from native speakers. Thus, misconstructions arise not only from an inability ever to recover the force of meaning of some language, but also from a naive assumption that people of the past always used words with accuracy and consistency and perfect understanding.

Study of a variety of medieval documents dealing with the legal status of towns highlights this point. The word used for a borough in medieval Latin was *burgus*. However, at times even a chartered borough was not referred to as a *burgus* but as a *villa*, *villata* or simply a *vill*, a term that might equally well be applied to a village or, confusingly, that area of jurisdiction that might be called in English a township. Hedon, for example, was granted a charter making it a borough between 1154 and 1173, yet an assize roll of between 1202 and 1208 refers to the 'vill of Hedun'. An assize roll of around 1260 refers to Scarborough both as a borough and a vill, the terms being interchanged, apparently, without distinction of meaning (YASRS 44: 27, 118–19). Examples in a different context occur in the Nomina Villarum, the list of cities, towns and villages drawn up for Edward II by his sheriffs in 1316 to settle the question of borough taxation. This document appears to reveal confusion between one county and another as well as within a county as to what might indeed constitute a borough. While some of the principal towns of Yorkshire – Hull or Northallerton, for instance – were written down as *burgi*, even a large, well-attested chartered borough like Pontefract went down as a vill. To suggest that this was an attempt to avoid urban taxation or parliamentary representation is again naive, since Pontefract was a well-known and populous town.

The point is that terms changed and became modified, and niceties of distinction were forgotten or tailored to suit new circumstances, as perhaps in the Nomina Villarum. While lawyers might well attempt to give exact definition to such legal terms, historians should be wary of them. Academic theory was not necessarily the same thing as practice or common usage in provincial courts or by seigneurial, county or town officials.

The legal history of towns is, indeed, an important though potentially confusing area. Some sort of legal status – a charter, evidence of burgage tenure – would seem to be the sure mark of a town and has been held to be the defining characteristic by some historians. But this is again unreliable. Borough need not imply a town, and in early medieval England the term was probably used as much to suggest a fortified settlement. If by the fourteenth century it had come to mean a town, technically speaking, it might imply no more than burgage tenure and associated privileges – the legal oil on the wheels of trade and commerce – in an attempt to set up a town. Whether this led to the establishment of a flourishing town is a different question. Moreover, charters cannot be relied on to tell us what such a town was, for they never really define the concept of a town and are usually no more than recognition or affirmation of rights and privileges which in themselves varied from place to place. Nor can the granting of a charter be used to pinpoint the date at which a town came into being. While it is true to say that some towns were entirely new creations, at other places charters perhaps did no more than consolidate or extend a state of affairs that had existed for years.

The interpretation of burgage tenure in particular needs careful handling. Historians have been too keen to seize on mentions of burgages in documents as an indication of a town, since, so the argument goes, burgages could not be found outside boroughs. While burgage tenure was common in boroughs, we should recognise that this was a form of tenure only. It is likely that there was a certain amount of burgage tenure in places which had no pretensions to becoming boroughs, as Ballard and Tait (1923) have argued or as Palliser (1992) has suggested in relation to South Dalton, a village in the east of Yorkshire. Thus, with terms such as *burgus* and vill, borough and burgage, we have entered a medieval hall of mirrors, and the reflected image is here magnified and there diminished. Such terms should certainly be regarded as an important indicator of urban status, but not its defining characteristic.

So far we have been examining words which historians and others have taken to mean *town*, at least in a legal/administrative sense. There are further ideas connected with the social concept of a town – community, neighbourhood, urbanism, for instance. All present problems and are not to be used lightly, although they have become inextricably a part of the concept of a town. *Neighbourhood*, for example, might imply a geographical area, a socially cohesive unit or an area defined by class or ethnic origin. *Community* might similarly be used, as well as having a wealth of other meanings (Hillery 1955). Such words have ideas to communicate if used accurately, but their meanings are rarely pinned down and they seem to be forever shifting.

The problem, however, is greater than a semantic lack of discipline, although this is where it might originate. While *community*, for example, may have several meanings, it must surely include among them certain specialised meanings which are sociological and historical. It might be used to denote areas defined by ethnicity or religion; it might also imply the sharing of traditions and customs, or the acceptance of certain norms and social controls. It might even imply a social system partly or wholly complete in itself. But an unproblematised, undefined usage of the term community has become dominant today, having its origins in a liberal ideology. In this sense it might be linked either to a rural past – a concept which Williams (1973) has effectively disposed of – or with working-class districts of cities. It also incorporates qualitative notions of caring, co-operation, the familial, the supportive; yet it is never closely defined. Indeed, because the word remains undefined, it can be applied to a range

of social situations, and can be used to legitimate or condemn them by virtue of its qualitative overtones.

We should take care that this view of community does not colour the term when we apply it to the medieval town or city. There are difficulties anyway in trying to analyse the medieval town in this way because sources of information are relatively scarce and unyielding. From what little we do know, it seems that a city like York had some things in common with nineteenth-century cities and characteristics which some sociologists have regarded as inimical to community – specialisation of labour, contractual relationships, a high rate of population replacement. Moreover, in matters of trade, commerce or city administration there were frequent disputes between social groups and occupational groups. Although citizens may have come together in civic ceremony – the mystery plays at Corpus Christi, for instance – this was perhaps as much from a sense of rivalry between occupational groups as from deeply held convictions about a shared civic culture, for disputes between the parties were common.

If we accept these as features of York life in the high Middle Ages, then it is difficult to find examples that concur with cosy ideas about community. On the other hand, it is perhaps possible to argue for and identify some of the characteristics of community that I have suggested above among craft, religious or fraternal guilds in some parts of the city. Fraternal or religious guilds in particular were concerned with the welfare of their members and members' families; they held common worship and vigils; they met together to enjoy fraternal conviviality. Rosser (1984) has argued thus using the vill of Westminster as his example. However, where such arrangements existed over wide geographical areas – whole towns in Rosser's argument – then it perhaps represented temporary associations over single issues, self-interest or simply charity rather than community.

There may have been exceptions. Many York butchers, for example, lived around Shambles and streets leading off where they carried on their trade. They had a guildhall close by, and many worshipped at and left bequests to the neighbouring Christ Church where several were buried, or St Crux church which contained a butchers' chapel. Family residence, common trade and fraternal links as well as common places of worship could all be found within a compact area. It is probably also correct to consider the members of a religious house such as a monastery as a community, since the acceptance of religious and social norms and the sharing of common work routines took place within the confines of the monastic precinct, although occasional conflicts between abbot or prior and the religious body might lead to the breakdown of community. The point about this is that whatever view one takes, *community* in a sociological sense implies more than a group of houses and people, or common trade interests, ethnic origins or associations spread through a wider population.

There is also another way in which community can be applied to the medieval town or city. The Latin *communio* or *communitas* can be found in documents relating to the award of urban privileges or to describe the people of towns. *Communio, communia* or *commune* might be translated as 'commune' meaning a sworn association of townsmen. It may possibly have carried with it political overtones, since some associations may well have sought independence from seigneurs, such as the attempt – and its suppression – to form a commune by some townsmen of York in 1173–4 during King Henry's rebellion. Similarly *communitas*, usually translated as 'community', should be taken as something akin to the residents or commonalty of a town, as a town body from whom leaders might be elected or, in the late Middle Ages, a town corporation. In these senses no objections can be raised to the terms. However, one has to be careful that one does not ascribe to the body – the community – of a town notions of democracy engendered by the ideological sense of community described above, a notion absent from medieval concepts of government. To avoid such confusions, then, it would be better if 'community' were restricted to technical uses, or possibly even abandoned altogether, since it has

been invaded and settled by a twentieth-century social construct of dubious value.

A further problem concerns the notion of urbanism. The idea that towns are different from villages in several ways sometimes leads to the view that there are different value systems at work, that townsfolk are different from country folk, and, more pertinent to the argument, that this is a result of a quality, a certain 'urban-ness', resident in the town itself. Of course there are differences between living in towns or cities and villages – differences of occupation, of labour relations, of habitation, of ceremony and customs, to name a few. But to suggest that this translates into some kind of urban quality, the essence, as it were, of urban living, itself resident in the urban environment is a reification. In considering the differences between town and village one should recognise that this is at heart a question of social and occupational differences and not a tangible quality, the mysterious physical embodiment of a process. As Abrams (1978) – one of the few writers to have got to grips with the problem – has argued, we should not be considering the town as an urban entity capable of development in itself, but as the outcome of particular ways of life expressive of the struggle for dominance of particular social groups.

A related way of looking at the town is as a physically separate place isolated from the countryside, rural society and its economy. It is easy to see how such ideas might arise when considering medieval towns which were indeed physically separated from the countryside and villages. In towns people were gathered together in relatively dense accumulations and sometimes surrounded by town walls or other defences. But if these differences were real and given physical expression, there were also many links between town and countryside, town and village – markets for agricultural produce, agricultural occupations within towns, town fields, family links between village and town-dwellers, migration to the towns from the countryside. What is more, as Rubin (1992) has pointed out, there were some similarities between cultural and religious activities in town and country. Also, the culture and ceremony of towns might well become a spectacle on some feast days to be shared by countryfolk – Corpus Christi and its urban mystery cycles is one well-known example. If towns, or rather townspeople, did operate within a different culture, an urban culture, it was neither so separate nor so alien that those living outside towns could not understand it.

It has been argued, however, that different social and economic structures found in towns together with generally different forms of tenure and privileges did in one sense make towns separate entities – as Postan (1972) put it, 'non-feudal islands in the feudal seas'. Postan's metaphor, however, lacks accuracy, since it would appear to suggest that there was such a thing as a feudal economy *and* a non-feudal economy operating independently of each other. This is difficult to conceptualise, for the feudal economy would be reliant to some extent on the economic activities of townspeople, since towns and their markets were important centres of exchange for both locally produced goods or foodstuffs and those imported from outside a region.

Perhaps what Postan and some others mean to suggest is that, freed from seigneurial obligations, men might move freely between urban centres pursuing a life of trade and were no longer tied to manors. What one has to reflect on here is not so much whiggish notions of free burgesses and their seeming struggle to create independent towns, but how such towns served regional or national interests in the shape of monarchs or seigneurs. For instance, when Edward I created the royal borough of Kingston upon Hull in 1299 he did so after acquiring a non-burghal town from the monks of Meaux Abbey. This was not in an attempt to set up a social and economic laboratory, as it were, in which one sort of society would be transmuted into another by some strange regal alchemy, but to bind and strengthen an already flourishing town which might further contribute to the Treasury, and to acquire a strategically significant port on the Humber which might be used as a base for military campaigns against the Scots. Hull is a remarkably clear example of how civic freedoms might intersect with the interests of the monarch.

There were also more complex ties that bound the town to superior authority. Despite the liberties that charters might bring, the authority of the monarch and of seigneurs continued to exert an influence. The presence of a castle in a town was symbolic of this. In seigneurial boroughs attendance at the court baron of the manor rather than a borough court was sometimes the rule, the seigneurial relationship continuing as it did for other kinds of tenant such as villeins or agricultural tenants who might also be living in or adjacent to the town. In large towns there might be more than one area of jurisdiction, as at York where jurisdictional territories ranged from the liberty of St Mary's Abbey to the tiny liberty of Davy Hall, the residence of a minor royal official. In addition to this there were broad high-roads of authority, rights and duties that cut across local boundaries – the authority of the church, the obligation to pay national taxes, the duty of some boroughs to return members to the House of Commons. What we find in the medieval town is an intricate gearing of power and authority where the civic cogs were in constant mesh with the larger wheels of church, state and monarchy.

The above comments touch on some of the chief social and economic issues raised in considering the concept of a town: heterogeneity, community, the town as urban entity, towns in society. One other important contribution to the concept of a town is made by its shape and physical appearance. As stated previously, the architecture of the town is not the architecture of the village. But to understand how this has come about, how the buildings have got there and why they are arranged in particular spatial relationships necessitates an understanding of the relationships in urban society. Their importance to the physical appearance of towns cannot be overemphasised, for it is patterns of living which, to use Philip Abrams's (1978) phrase, towns 'restlessly express'.

CHAPTER TWO

People in Towns

THE THEORETICAL BACKGROUND

AT FIRST SIGHT IT seems reasonable to assume that the social systems of the medieval town and country were different, given differences of occupation, administration or culture. On the other hand, another interpretation might present the town as a subsystem of society, and while it might be contrasted with rural society, it might also be regarded as part of a broader social order. Already we have two different views, and it is the purpose of this chapter to review some of theories of society which might be brought to bear on the Middle Ages as a background against which people in towns might be placed.

The most important nineteenth-century commentator to deal with medieval society was Karl Marx. Marx was important because he placed medieval society for the first time within the context of a grand social and economic analysis. The Marxist perspective stresses that the most important factor in determining social position is relationship to the means of production. In medieval England most people were engaged in a largely agrarian economy where land was held from landowners by service or rents or a mixture of both – the feudal mode of production. Moreover, further tolls, levies or fines might be due to landlords for the use of mills and ovens, for trading in a market place or for entry onto lands. Essentially Marx introduced a perspective of conflict into social and economic relations between landlords and tenants, an interpretation which provides insights into economic class relations and explains some of the different forms of relationship and labour organisation that could be found in towns. However, one of the problems with the Marxist approach lies in the basing of social relations entirely on the relations of production. This does not allow for the effects of, say, new religious or political ideas. Moreover, in a strictly economic theory of social change, non-economic coercion poses a further problem.

A major contribution to the study of pre-industrial urban societies – and one which ran counter to Marxist theory – was made by Gideon Sjöberg (1960). His purpose was to compare such societies across time and culture, elucidating their common structural features. Since his work eschewed the ethnocentricity and fixedness in time or period that characterise most historical studies, his researches cannot and are not meant to be applied with precision to a particular place and society. Rather his analysis is useful in pointing up common societal characteristics. In terms of social stratification Sjöberg has argued that city-dwellers can generally be divided into two classes: an aristocratic upper class and a lower class ranked by occupation and social honour, together with an outcast group. Such a class formation, he maintains, however composed, is characteristic of all pre-industrial urban societies, including medieval Europe.

Perhaps what Sjöberg's work illustrates as much as anything is what was for much of the 1950s and 1960s an alternative theoretical perspective to Marxism: structural functionalism. This placed less of an emphasis on conflict or economic relationships but argued instead that societies maintained themselves through cooperation between classes or social groups. The problem with functionalist theories is their tendency to structure society into a hierarchy of social groups seen as essential to its functioning. In this way academic constructs become reality: society is seen as having real structures and 'knows' how to fulfil its needs, needs that are best served by harmonious social interaction.

Another view of English pre-industrial society is that proposed by Laslett (1965) who has argued that an aristocratic elite, occupying the upper ranks of a hierarchy of social groupings, directed society. Although Laslett was analysing sixteenth- and seventeenth-century society which he described as one-class, his views, nevertheless, have implications for the society of the Middle Ages. We might, for example, take the view that the central and later Middle Ages also had some of the characteristics associated with a power elite. The elite itself could be seen as a broadly based establishment of prelates and aristocracy with the monarch as *primus inter pares*, aided when considered necessary by the foremost commercial and mercantile houses.

It is no accident that all of these groups came from similar social backgrounds or had similar economic interests. To begin with, there were strong links of kinship between many top families. If, on the other hand, the church can be considered the most open of medieval social institutions in terms of recruitment, numbers of prelates even so came from aristocratic families, while lesser men destined to rise might be inculcated into their role through administrative service to bishops or the crown. Where the help of outside commercial interests was needed then the king might ennoble the blood of commoners as a reward for service and as an extension of the aristocratic embrace. Outside of this elite, society might be ranked in similar ways to those which Laslett has suggested, although a more basic division would have to be made between a clerical order on the one hand and a lay order on the other. Also, if such an elite was an alliance of magnates, it was a loose alliance troubled at times by rivalries and contained cliques and factions with individuals who pursued self-interest and career, while at the same time all parties acted their roles as clerics, seigneurs or merchants.

Objections might also be made on the grounds that this is not so much a theory of society but of how society is governed, or is an exploration of the locus of power. But it is a tempting analysis, since some other forms of administration reflected this form of government. Town corporations and similar urban bodies, for example, were very often structured as self-perpetuating assemblies of elite urban families which, if in theory ruling in consultation with and on behalf of the majority of townspeople, had a tendency towards closed government and oligarchy.

Recently Rigby (1995) has published a comprehensive work on later medieval society. While accepting the insights that Marxism can provide, he also takes into account factors other than purely economic ones, although he rejects the functionalist perspective, turning instead to the work of Max Weber. Class, religion, gender, status group and the effectiveness of some status groups in restricting entry to that group form part of Rigby's powerful analysis.

So far this review has concentrated on nineteenth- and twentieth-century theoretical perspectives, but we might also examine the ways in which medieval thinkers themselves conceptualised society. We might try to see whether their theories of the society in which they lived were similar to or differed from modern theories, and we might try to understand at what sort of level they operated – did commentators seek to provide an objective analysis, for example, or were their theories the construction of an ideal, expressed through an ideology?

By the late ninth century a threefold social categorisation had emerged – those who pray, those who fight and those who labour. The problem with this model is that it made no reference to those who lived by trade or industry other than by the assumption that they should be included with those who laboured. Le Goff (1977: 57), however, has argued that the Latin *laboratores*, usually translated as those who labour, suggested not mere labourers, but producers: that is, an economic order. Other threefold divisions, which continued to be used in the later Middle Ages, were less specific – *maiores*, *mediocres, minores*, for example. A vaguely defined social model of this sort would seem to imply that merchants and burgesses generally could be fitted somewhere into the middle, the *mediocres*.

But by the thirteenth and fourteenth centuries more sophisticated models of society had been developed. Berthold von Regensburg, a German Franciscan friar of the mid-thirteenth century, divided society into a hierarchy based on the nine choirs of angels: the earthly hierarchy thus reflected the celestial. The levels consisted of, first, the pope and priests, second monks and third kings and seigneurs or lay judges. The remaining six levels consisted of merchants, physicians, craftsmen in iron, craftsmen who made shoes and clothing, victuallers and peasants. These latter categories, however, although inferior to those above them, were ranked not hierarchically but side by side with one another for all were equal in the eyes of God, as they should also be in the exercise of lay justice. This was at heart a division of society into three orders – clerical, aristocratic and those who worked. John Gower, a contemporary of Chaucer, in his poems 'Confessio Amantis' and 'Mirour de L'Omme', divided society in a similar way, except that his inferior order was ranked hierarchically. Books of courtesy of the fourteenth and fifteenth centuries (Furnival 1868, for example) tend to imply similar stratification, or social honour at least, in their instructions for the ordering of formal entertainments – who should be ranked above whom in seating arrangements, and so on.

The church's part in all this should be emphasised. From the pulpit and through the preaching of friars in market places the church disseminated ideas about the three orders of society, their divine origin and the mortal dangers of failing to play one's allotted part. Although some of the more radical friars may have preached about the equality of man and the misdeeds of those highly placed in society, one must take care before ascribing to them a proto-communist ideology. As Owst (1961: Chapter 9) has argued, it was not the paradigm that was under attack but common abuses.

Most medieval teaching, then, propagated this view of society. Moreover, the threefold division has been accepted by several present-day historians (Keen 1990, for example) who have argued that, although such models of society might be viewed as tendentious and seeking to legitimate the power of clerical and aristocratic orders, nevertheless they were a fair approximation to divisions which existed within early and central medieval society, social divisions which persisted until the late Middle Ages. While this may indeed have been the paradigm engendered by all medieval discourse on society, it does not mean that we have to accept it as an accurate analysis, but simply recognise it and recognise its importance.

The paradigm is open to a number of objections – it could be regarded more as ideology than social analysis, for example – and the sorts of criticisms levelled at functionalist social theory generally can be brought to bear here also, for medieval social models of this sort are essentially functionalist. Nowhere is this more clearly seen, perhaps, than in Thomas Wimbledon's sermon 'Redde racionem villicacionis tue' preached in 1388. Wimbledon is concerned with perhaps two things: the god-given nature of what he sees as the structure of society, and the sinfulness and folly of men reaching beyond or neglecting the duties of their station in life. He sees society as composed of priests, knights and labourers – priests to give moral and spiritual guidance, knights to uphold the law and defend the realm, labourers to provide sustenance. This is the balance of society, and if it were disturbed:

> . . . gif presthod lackede, the puple for defaute of knowynge of Goddis Lawe shulde wexe wilde on vices and deie gostly. And gif the knythod lackid and men to reule the puple by lawe and hardnesse, theves and enemies shoden so encresse that no man sholde lyven in pes. And gif laboreris weren not, bothe prestis and knygtis mosten bicome acremen and heerdis and ellis they sholde for defaute of bodily sustenaunce deie. (Owen 1966: 179)

Thus, the smooth functioning of society relies on cooperation between the orders, a state justified by Wimbledon's appeal during the course of his sermon to the authority of the New Testament.

Rigby (1995: 189–91) makes a further cogent criticism of such threefold categorisations. While we might well distinguish between a clerical order set apart by religion and an aristocratic order distinguished by landholding and military service, the third order of those who laboured was set apart by very little else other than that they worked. Le Goff's suggestion that they represented an economic order is not a strong enough justification, for, to quote Rigby, 'the third estate was little more than a residual category consisting of those excluded from the other estates.' Moreover, although the clerical order was set apart from the aristocratic order by its control of religion, yet how different really were the top levels of the clerical order from aristocracy? Prelates, by their management of church estates, were in effect great landowners, prelates and aristocracy became entangled in the affairs of state, and although the clerical order was often placed above the aristocratic order, is it really feasible to accept that a parish priest in a humble living held more power or status than a rich earl? But the problem becomes clearer by considering the model, once again, as the expression of an ideology rather than as a twentieth-century sociological analysis. The intention is to justify the supremacy of church and aristocracy over the mass of people excluded from these orders.

This section began by stating that we could view the people who lived in medieval towns from different theoretical perspectives. Thus, whatever social groups we may wish to study, they should be read against the sort of theoretical contexts outlined above: each provides its own insights, inconsistencies and problems. For whether we look at the work of twentieth-century academics or medieval social commentators, not one of them can be considered an unproblematic social analysis.

TOWNS AND THE SOCIAL ORDERS

The most striking social difference that can be found in the medieval town is not so much between extremes of wealth, power or status, but between the towns themselves. This is a theme that will re-emerge in other parts of the book: the differences between large towns and small towns. It was in the large towns that not only greater numbers of people, but also a more heterogeneous mixture of clergy and laity could be found. All the social orders and a great variety of both occupational and status groups were to be seen in a city like York, for example. Within the clerical order there were abbots, the dean and chapter of the minster, monks, friars, parish priests, chaplains – everyone from the archbishop to boy choristers.

There was a similar heterogeneity when we come to consider the aristocracy. If their numbers were far smaller and their ranks not as wide, nevertheless the highest and the lowest of the aristocratic order were represented. As England's second city for much of the Middle Ages, monarchs visited and resided at York, brought the court there and held parliaments there. On occasion armies had been marshalled at York which brought further members of the aristocracy to the city. Some aristocratic families had houses in York – fewer almost certainly than in the seventeenth and succeeding centuries, but Raine (1955: 108) notes the residences of the Neville and Percy families in Walmgate, for example.

Since York was also a centre of administration, a further, lower level of gentle families could be added, gentlemen bureaucrats as they have been designated by Storey (1982), the lawyers and town officials who, by the fifteenth century, were often the sons of gentle families from surrounding districts.

Looking at the third order of those who worked, York without doubt had the largest numbers and the greatest variation of occupations in commerce, trade or craftwork. If a good deal of York's prosperity had been based on wool in the fourteenth century and on the manufacture and export of woollen cloth from the late fourteenth century, there was far more to the city than wool merchants or weavers. Lead, hides, wine, spices as well as wool and cloth were all merchanted through York. There was a trade in luxury goods, whether in precious metals or furs, together with industries such as tanning, founding or the production of leather goods. There was also a large service sector supplying food and drink – butchers, fishmongers, bakers or saucers – and there was a well-developed building industry, not just masons working on the many churches but carpenters, tilers and plasterers erecting or rebuilding houses and shops.

Finally, as an important market centre, administrative centre, inland port, the scene of cultural events and a place of pilgrimage, York attracted large numbers of visitors from England and abroad. There was thus not only a diverse resident population, but also a diverse transient population.

Contrast this with a town like Skipton, a small market town in Airedale. Although we can identify representatives of the three medieval orders as at York, nevertheless their numbers are much smaller and the diversity of occupational and status groups much diminished. The clerical order, for example, was represented largely by the parish priest and two chantry priests, although there was a further small chapel in the town and a private chapel in the castle. The aristocracy was represented by the seigneurs of the castle – the Romilles, Aumales, Forzes and by 1310 the Cliffords, the latter being resident at the castle the longest. Some property does seem to have been owned by local gentlemen, but not as their town houses, rather as investments, and by the fifteenth century, if not before, there was at least one resident professional family and probably one or two others.

There was *some* diversity in the occupational profile of Skipton, much more so than in a village. However, by the fourteenth and fifteenth centuries a fair proportion of those not employed in agriculture were employed in the clothing industry either as weavers or in one of the related branches such as dyeing or fulling. Having said that, there were also butchers, drapers, merchants

and glovers, together with the sorts of craftsmen one would expect to find in villages – smiths and carpenters, for instance.

Skipton probably also attracted a transient population through its resident aristocracy and their guests, its administrative business as the centre of an honour and its markets and fairs. But, again, such crowds were not of the same frequency or diversity as those that might have been experienced at York. We might thus conclude that while towns like Skipton have several social and structural similarities with cities like York, both scale and heterogeneity are greatly reduced.

As small towns go, however, Skipton was probably an active, even a busy place. Towns at the bottom of the urban league possessed even less evidence of social and occupational heterogeneity than Skipton which is what puts them on the margins of town and village. Bradford, for example, had a small population employed mostly in agriculture and the clothing industry in the later Middle Ages. A greater number of agricultural occupations is a salient feature of the populations of such towns. But there *was* a market at Bradford and there *were* other occupations, trades and crafts. What is more, its population appears to have been sizeable enough to justify a town chapel separate from the parish church. However, there were no resident aristocracy, and local gentle families lived outside the town. Bradford's fourteenth-century seigneurs, the earls of Lincoln, seem rarely, if ever, to have visited, and before 1432 the seigneurial residence had been subdivided and tenanted (James 1967: 81).

Between these two extremes were the regional centres, places like Doncaster or Malton, which display greater diversity. The populations of some of these towns were exceptional for their size. Howden, for example, the urban centre of Howdenshire in the east of the county, had a collegiate church with residences for its canons. As the Bishop of Durham's town it had a palace built there which was on occasion visited by members of the royal family. Its occupations were remarkably diverse for a town of around 300 taxpayers in 1377. Besides the sorts of occupations that one might expect – weavers, smiths, butchers, alewives – there were also tradesmen and women such as barbers, chandlers, spicers and wimple-makers.

What seems to create the social differences between medieval towns is not so simple as at first appears. Size of town is obviously an important factor, but it is not the only one. How well the social orders were represented is another, but only if taking into account the range of people that could be found within the orders. The greater the range and heterogeneity of population a town possessed the more it tended towards an urban centre; the less, and the more it tended towards a market village.

SOCIAL GROUP AND FORMATION

It was only in the large towns that the clerical order was represented in anything like its great variety, for it was there that the clergy performed duties other than ministration or pastoral care. Ecclesiastical law and administration created a church bureaucracy especially at centres like York. At the courts of the archbishops or the dean and chapter, for example, probates on estates in Yorkshire and some other parts of the church's northern province were registered. Churches and religious houses also owned much urban property, while some prelates and religious houses might dominate towns very much like lay seigneurs. The Archbishop of York or the Bishop of Durham, for instance, held seigneurial rights in Ripon and Northallerton respectively; the abbots of Selby and Whitby controlled the towns in which those abbeys were located. It is difficult to see, therefore, at first sight how prelates differed from the aristocracy, but they did so in two important respects. First, their wealth was not personal wealth but the corporate wealth of the church. Second, unlike the aristocracy, they had a religious mission to fulfil.

When we come to consider the clergy's religious duties, we need to be aware that rankings and the roles pertaining to them had been carefully drawn up and demarcated within a hierarchy of authority and command. One basic division which should be made was between the secular clergy – bishops or priests, for example – and the regular clergy – members of the religious orders such as monks, friars or nuns. All were subject to the authority of the pope, secular clergy to the authority of archbishops and bishops, regular clergy to the authority of the heads of their orders, although the Augustinians and Benedictines submitted to bishops. We can add to the secular and regular clergy those taking their first steps towards the religious life, although many might never progress beyond this humble clerical position, serving instead minor roles about the church – acolyte or doorkeeper, for instance.

The clerical order was thus differentiated from the lay orders by its religious duties and by a hierarchy enshrined in religious law and tradition. It was in itself almost a complete social system. At York the religious formation of the secular clergy was represented by the archbishop, the dean and chapter of the minster, colleges of priests, parish priests, chaplains and priests attached to almshouses. On the regular side there were four monasteries including the nunnery at Clementhorpe, and four friaries. Something of this formation can be observed at other large towns such as Hull, Beverley or Scarborough. All had a variety of secular clergy, and regular clergy were also present in religious houses within or around the towns. To a somewhat lesser extent this held good for the regional centres – Malton, Pontefract, Richmond or Yarm, for example. One category of regular clergy, the friars, had a specifically urban locus because of their mission which was to preach and beg for their living, actions which they could carry out most effectively where there were large concentrations of people.

Although duties and jurisdictions between these various clergy were well delineated, nevertheless it did not stop disputes from occurring. Tensions were felt between the archbishop and the dean and chapter of the minster at York; there was competition between monks and friars; social differences were evident between priests in prosperous livings and those in poor livings; clergy from other parts of the county or the country might possess urban estates within

Yorkshire towns, a further point of resentment and dispute over rights. To complicate matters, relations between religious institutions and burgesses were often far from harmonious and occasionally boiled over into violence, as happened in the disputes between Whitby Abbey and the burgesses of the town or St Mary's Abbey and the burgesses of York (see pp. 21 and 46 below).

It is tempting to think that in the smaller towns with fewer priests and perhaps no regular clergy, relations were more harmonious because the opportunities for conflict were less. However, a list of incidents could be compiled which seems to suggest otherwise. There were inter-clerical disputes such as that between the Prior of Kirkham, who had been granted Helmsley church, and the Archbishop of York who in 1253 founded a chapel in Helmsley castle to the annoyance of the prior who complained that his rights in Helmsley were being infringed (VCH 1914: 504). There were poor relations between some seigneurs and the church such as on the occasion when Sir Edmund Hastings sued the vicar of Pickering for failing in his duties to provide a chaplain for a chapel at nearby Kingthorpe (VCH 1923: 475). Other disputes affected towns more directly. Thus at Knaresborough in 1510 the chancel of the town church, which was the responsibility of the rector to maintain, was found to be in poor repair with water running down the walls internally and parts of the choir roof on the floor of the vestry (Jennings 1969: 115). There was also conflict between town authorities and the church, such as that between the Bradford court and the vicar of Bradford in 1411 over the right to dig for stones in the highway opposite the church (BMC IV: 28). Finally, there were crimes committed by individual members of the clergy. Robert de Lellia, for example, was the priest of Tadcaster church, and had three times pleaded guilty to bloodshed in the lay courts and proceedings were ordered against him in the ecclesiastical courts for having had three wives (Speight 1902: 269). These are not isolated occurrences but several taken at random from large numbers of

minor and some major disputes in small towns which occurred over the centuries.

Despite disputes and occasional lawlessness, the place of the clergy in the authority structure of the town was, nevertheless, an important one. Besides the spiritual and legal authority that the clergy wielded they had a further educational authority. Their control of education both through the grammar schools and the universities is well known. While some historians have suggested that lay endowment of schools in the later Middle Ages points to a greater involvement of the laity in education, the important thing to realise is that the church's authority over the curriculum was never in much doubt.

Rigby (1996: Chapter 6) and others have suggested that the clerical order was the least exclusive, that mobility within the order was possible and that even its highest levels could be penetrated by men of humble background. While this is true in terms of stark fact, a steady stream of aristocratic families nevertheless continued to fill the topmost ranks of archbishops, bishops and abbots. There were twenty-six archbishops of York between 1181 and 1530. Of twenty-four whose origins can be ascertained twelve were of aristocratic background and seven of these twelve were drawn from the highest ranks of the aristocracy, the Arundels, Nevilles or Plantagenets, for example. The rest were from the humbler ranks of the clergy but had not progressed to the high office they eventually gained without first passing through a period of training and socialisation as administrators in either the royal or episcopal households. One might well ask, therefore, that if the clerical order was the most open of the orders where lesser clergy might rise, what significant changes did this bring about? The answer is none, for the process by which men rose ensured a continuity of established ideas and authority.

A further question to be raised in this respect is why the clerical order should be relatively open. Part of the reason is perhaps because the esoteric and specialised religious knowledge necessary for advancement could be acquired through education, and progress through the order bears some resemblance to progress through the twentieth-century civil service. But a further reason suggested by Sjöberg (1960: 260) is that celibacy among the clergy did not permit the building up of religious dynasties, hence recruitment from below was needed to replace higher levels as circumstance demanded.

Far less open was the aristocratic order. Defining aristocracy in the period after the eleventh century and up to the sixteenth century is not as easy as it appears owing to its changing nature. We cannot view it as a static and carefully graded sequence from dukes to barons, from baronets to gentlemen as we might view eighteenth-century aristocracy (although there are problems here, too). Perhaps the basic distinction to be made before the fourteenth century was that between those entitled to bear arms (literally) and the rest. However, by the fourteenth and fifteenth centuries aristocratic titles were becoming more clearly codified, and we can see the emergence of one group – the *bones gentz*, gentle gents or gentils – which can be identified with the group which were to become known collectively as gentry.

More important for our purposes is the position of the aristocracy with regard to the towns. Aristocrats have long been considered by historians as a social group whose interests were essentially rural – a landed group or social order. Sjöberg (1960: Chapter 5), however, has argued that the aristocracy was essentially an urban elite. If Sjöberg's argument is too generalised to apply in specific ways to medieval European aristocracies, it is nevertheless a useful antidote to interpretations that locate European aristocracy firmly in the country. To begin with it is somewhat naive to conceptualise aristocrats as living solely in castles or large houses in the country. Major and even some lesser aristocracy might possess several houses as well as enjoy regular visits to London or York – as we have seen, Raine (1955) has identified some aristocratic houses in York. Other residences were urban castles or fortified houses, and in addition to these, urban estates were held by many

families which contributed varying amounts to family revenues – as little as 12 per cent of the Earl of Albemarle's Yorkshire estates in the thirteenth century, but as much as 50 per cent of the Earl of Lincoln's Yorkshire estates in the fourteenth.[1] We should argue, therefore, that aristocratic families were indeed landed families, but significant amounts of their land might be urban land, including urban residences.

By the fourteenth and fifteenth centuries we can observe a lower aristocratic group emerging within the towns, an urban gentry occupying a grey area between aristocracy and merchants. Both Storey (1982) and Horrox (1988) have argued that the styles *esquire*, *gentleman* and *mister* began to be applied at these dates to men from either merchant families or minor rural aristocratic families who were pursuing careers in the towns through the law, medicine or administration. The latter might have been attached to one of the great aristocratic houses or been in the monarch's service. Horrox, for instance, outlines the career of John Ferriby, son of a minor landed family who had become valet to the crown and received property in Beverley where he had become resident in the mid-fifteenth century. Other members of the family appear to have been merchants at York. Miles Metcalfe, gentleman of York, was a member of a minor landed family of the North Riding. He had taken up residence in York where he had become recorder; he also served as member of parliament for the city three times in the later fifteenth century. He died at York and was buried in the Minster (SURTEES 53: 9).

The Coppandales of Beverley were wealthy merchants. While earlier generations styled themselves *merchant*, later generations used the styles *gentleman* and *esquire*. They had married with the Hothams, an important landed family of east Yorkshire, and had been engaged as commissioners of the array and supervisors of boat-building operations for Edward III in his Scottish campaigns of the 1330s.

However, one or two caveats should be added. If gentle styles appear to have been emerging strongly in the fifteenth century, it may be that they became more visible after the Statute of Additions of 1413 which required that 'additions shall be made of their estate, or degree or mystery' for every person going to law. If the style of gentleman were taken up by some merchants and members of the professions, these groups also seem to have been content to have been styled by their callings. Moreover, gentlemanly styles might quickly be dropped or denied by some when it was politic. Thus in 1419/20 the monarch required the aid of all gentlemen eligible for military service. The bailiff of Beverley could find only two gentlemen in the town – one was a Coppandale – and the bailiffs of Hull replied that:

> They have warned Thomas Constable of halsham dwellyng in thaire bailly to be forthe[,] and uthire Gentilmen they knaw none there, but men that lyves be theire merchaundise and be thaire shippes. (Goodman 1981: 242)

The point is that for a good many townsmen *gentleman* or *esquire* was an aspirational style, and if using it posed a threat or a burden, then the occupational style of merchant, doctor of law or whatever was invoked.

Merchants and the professions formed the top stratum of the third order of medieval society. This order might be grouped or stratified in different ways: as a series of vertical rankings by occupation, wealth and status, or by broader social groupings where status might be dependent upon urban privileges – burgesses and non-burgesses. The problem with the latter is that it relies on only one legally defined concept of a town and does not recognise the non-burghal town.

Looking at the town in terms of occupational group then the observations made above about the differences between large and small towns can again be applied. It was also at the large towns that the greatest numbers of merchants could be found, especially at the coastal and inland ports. Merchants are often thought to be, characteristically, the wealthiest of townspeople. While this is to some extent true, we should realise that many people that we would recognise

today as shopkeepers or small wholesalers might have been called merchants in medieval towns. Moreover, although there were large and successful dealers in single commodities in medieval towns, such merchants were perhaps in a minority compared with those who dealt in several commodities and engaged in other enterprises – finance or transport, for example. Successful merchants might be regarded as part of the upper ranks of townsfolk among whom we should include other large and prosperous traders – mercers, pewterers or goldsmiths – trades which might require more than modest start-up capital.

At the other end of the scale were the poor tradesmen, especially some of the tailoring or building trades – tilers and plasterers, for instance. Among the poorer tradesmen and craftsmen secondary occupations seem to have been common. Poverty was almost certainly the cause of people engaging in more than one occupation, especially victualling, in order to make ends meet. Trade or craft status acquired through a properly supervised apprenticeship seems to have been retained as the master occupation, however, while other occupations remained secondary.

In manufacturing the productive unit was the family, although wives might possibly engage in secondary or related occupations as detailed below. However, the familial unit of production should be thought of as encompassing not just kin but apprentices and servants, arrangements which are sometimes hinted at in wills or other documents. Thus, when Richard King of Sheffield died in 1547 he left to Otwell Cutler, his servant, an anvil and tools (BIHR vol. 13, fol. 434). Similarly John Rodes, a York fishmonger, made bequests to his servant Agnes Monkton and his apprentice Thomas Dawson in 1457 (SURTEES 30: 209), while in 1458 John Snayth, a bow-maker of Doncaster, left his apprentice Richard de la Stede forty shillings and some tools 'for his trade' (SURTEES 30: 218).

By the fifteenth and sixteenth centuries we can also see the beginnings of the organisation of industrial labour by merchants and master manufacturers, especially in clothing and edge-tool production, suggestive of a more regimented use of family productive units or even the marshalling of a workforce. In Sheffield, for instance, there would appear to have been numbers of master cutlers or makers of edge-tools such as scythes who had placed work and tools with other craftsmen in the vicinity of the town. Hugh Sponer's will of 1539 lists six people in the Sheffield area to whom he had granted bellows and anvils in the pursuit of trade. The putting out of woollen cloth-weaving by clothiers and merchants might be similarly organised, especially in the Halifax area where around the beginning of the sixteenth century the Hodgkin family had erected a hand-weaving factory (Cooke Taylor 1891: 53). However, we should also heed Braudel's (1983: 372) warning that while such structuring of labour and the activities of merchants in pre-industrial Europe may well herald capitalism, the organisers were not characteristically specialist entrepreneurs and were usually active in other spheres, connected, as Braudel puts it, by long chains of commerce to perhaps several related activities.

Nor were all trades and crafts held in the same social esteem. Some were regarded as low or troublesome – butchers and innkeepers, for example, who in York were excluded from government, a government almost exclusively composed of mercantile interests and wealthier tradesmen during the central Middle Ages. But if it was from among the top strata of townsmen that municipal government was drawn in large towns, matters were different in small towns. As Swanson (1989: Chapter 1) has again argued, tradesmen such as butchers or tanners might be regarded with suspicion in the major urban centres, but might be a mainstay of government in small towns and occasionally in the larger towns, especially in periods of economic depression or demographic crisis when councillors could not be replaced from the usual sources of recruitment. However, in large towns it was usually as aldermen and councillors that the higher ranks of the townsmen sought to control the activities of lesser burgesses, craftsmen or tradesmen, or even to exclude them from government. One means of doing this was through craft guilds whose formation and ordinances might be vetted and approved by town councils.

While lesser burgesses may have shared some common urban privileges with those above them, they were removed, often far removed, from them in terms of wealth and with probably little in the way of surplus profits even in good years. It was this accumulation of capital that led to such significant differences between poorer and wealthier burgesses, not only in the obvious things such as attire, luxury goods and lifestyle generally, but also in the investment of profits in land and property. This enabled some merchants, no doubt, to marry into aristocratic or prosperous agricultural families, providing a further route to landownership. Probably fair numbers of the wealthier burgesses owned urban property or small agricultural estates or both. The Langton and Selby families of York, for example, were of merchant origins, and during the fourteenth and fifteenth centuries acquired both urban and rural estates (VCH 1961: 70–1). At Beverley in 1425 the merchant Thomas Kelk founded a chantry in St Mary's church to be endowed with six houses and fourteen cottages together with three acres of land and seven acres of meadow (HMC 1900: 150). The Whitby merchant Thomas Husey made bequests of property in Flowergate, Grape Lane and Kirkgate in his will of 1456 (BIHR vol. 2, fol. 337). Even a small town such as Helmsley had its wealthier burgesses. Thomas Brown, a mercer who died in 1441, besides making bequests to friaries and abbeys and leaving forty stones of lead to St Peter's at York, left a small urban estate in Helmsley (BIHR vol. 2, fol. 25).

From this review it is clear that throughout the Middle Ages there were several potential causes of conflict within the body of burgesses, causes largely grounded in municipal control and economic organisation. There were also noticeable differences of wealth and status. However, one thing that all shared in common was that they were burgesses and freemen of towns and enjoyed similar urban privileges. A large group of people below them did not. This did not usually mean that such people were unable to trade within towns but that they could lay claim to few, if any, privileges and were restricted in the trades that they could carry on. Many were what might be described as hucksters, petty traders employed mostly in the victualling trades and possibly dealing in second-hand goods. Many were women. The frequent mentions of alewives in medieval documents points to a typical occupation. While historians have tended to concentrate their efforts on mercantile and burgess wealth, yet as Hilton (1982a) has observed the huckster was probably a ubiquitous figure in medieval urban society.

This brings us to the people who made up the lowest strata of the lay orders: labourers, the poor of various sorts, vagrants and criminals. Living in perhaps relative poverty were labourers and household servants with no better prospects, although some would have been in better circumstances than others. Semi-skilled labourers in the employ of a good master and possibly housed within the master's household were almost certainly better off in overall terms than those existing on perhaps day labour eked out with the produce of their garden and living in a tumbledown cottage on the edge of town. But the poverty of such people was relative to that endured by those with no means of support: old widows, the sick, the infirm or those plunged into poverty by sudden, crippling accidents. People in these conditions might be housed or maintained at the town's expense or, in the later Middle Ages, at the parish's expense. A major form of charitable aid were the hospitals or almshouses founded by wealthy clerics and laymen. Usually the recipients of such charity were under the obligation to pray for the souls of founders and perhaps their families.

It is at this point that we cross a great divide in the medieval world. The people discussed so far all had occupations or, at least, roles. Either they were clergy or aristocracy or by productive labour they contributed to the common good and thus maintained the balance of society. By the later Middle Ages, the merchant, an unproductive occupation regarded with suspicion in the earlier Middle Ages, had also come to be seen as serving a useful purpose in distributing goods or making available goods that might otherwise

have been unobtainable. Even the poor had their role in that they provided an object of charity for the rich and in turn prayed daily for the salvation of their benefactors. These, however, were the deserving poor. But sturdy beggars who placed themselves in a condition of poverty through their idleness or those who actively pursued a life of crime forfeited all rights to be part of the common orders of man as divinely ordained. Far from being productive members of society they were plunderers and wasters.

Again, we must be careful in such assessments. Some activities that we would today consider crimes might come to be looked upon, especially by the later Middle Ages, with toleration if not exactly moral approval. Prostitution was tolerated in some towns since prostitutes performed a service, curbed men's desires and directed them away from virtuous women, they had their uses in cases of proving non-consummation of marriages by impotence, and they even provided an outlet for the sexual desires of the clergy – Goldberg (1992: 153–4) has shown how brothels and bawdy houses might be situated near to ecclesiastical establishments in places such as York, for example. Thus, if prostitution was a sinful occupation, male attitudes were ambivalent. At Hull during the late fifteenth century prostitutes received municipal recognition and were allowed to ply their trade by the town gate, on the town walls and in the towers, paying the corporation between three and eight pounds yearly for the privilege (VCH 1969: 75).

Persistent crime and wilful beggary was different. It consumed the charity of the deserving poor and, if allowed to go unchecked, would overturn society. Most towns where records exist seem to have had a criminal element either resident within the town or attracted to it from neighbouring areas. Many towns also seem to have had continual trouble. Of several examples that might be quoted, nowhere is the medieval attitude of mind to incorrigible criminals better displayed than in the Bradford Manor Court Rolls of the early fifteenth century. In 1411, for example, John Tomlynson, who lived in the nearby manor of Idle, came into Bradford several times to commit crimes and to act as a hired thug. He was, in the words of the court of Bradford:

> continually within this town [and] goes armed, to wit, with a doublet de Fens,[2] wyrhatt,[3] Karlelehax[4] and other unlawful arms to the grave damage of the common people of the lord King. And likewise the said John who has nothing whereby he can live goes well apparelled and will not work, but is awake in the nights and asleep in the days. Therefore it is commanded to attach him . . . (BMC IV: 23)

Here is wayward criminality and the rejection of social norms: it is the world turned topsy-turvy. One might indeed raise the question of whether unyielding criminals constituted a place in the social order at all, as some medieval commentators argued, for it was occupation and role which supplied such a place. If, therefore, legitimate occupations were rejected it was tantamount to denying society and forfeiting one's position in it. As the Dominican John Bromyard wrote:

> The Devil, however, finds a certain class, namely the slothful, who belong to no Order. They neither labour with the rustics, nor travel about with the merchants, nor fight with the knights, nor pray and chant with the clergy. Therefore they shall go with their own Abbot, of whose Order they are, namely, the Devil, where no Order exists but horror eternal. (Owst 1961: 554)

So far this review of medieval urban society has not touched on gender. Women had many roles. They were not only wives and mothers, they also engaged in trades and crafts, although subject to male-dominated urban economic and political structures. This immediately raises the question of what exactly was the position of women with regard to their own circumstances – were they able to take charge of their own lives, or were they seen in their husband's rather than in their own right, and were their life chances prescribed by men? Legally speaking, the answer to this question is the latter. In law married women were the responsibility of their husbands, daughters the responsibility of fathers. What property a woman may have possessed became her husband's on marriage: movable property belonged to him; land was in his guardianship. Even on the death of a husband, a woman had no legal right to live in the family home for much longer than a month. By the later Middle Ages, however, some towns and counties tended to vary and temper the harshness of such law and a woman's claim to a third of her husband's estate became a legal right. Nevertheless, even if some husbands or fathers behaved with generosity to female members of their families, women could not expect to be treated equally at law.

In other respects medieval women seem far less restricted. They are, indeed, highly visible to anyone who studies the Middle Ages, and are the subjects of a range of documents dealing with court business, taxation, probate and so on. Two important studies of work and of women in Yorkshire by Swanson (1989) and Goldberg (1992) respectively have shown the variety of occupations in which women were engaged. Overwhelmingly women found employment in the victualling industry, especially as brewers, or in selling dairy products and poultry in markets. Many such women were hucksters, either living within the town or coming into town from its hinterland on market days. More rarely were they women who had obtained the freedom of the town in their own right, and it was more usual to acquire such right in their husbands' names.

There were also significant numbers of women who pursued a trade or craft, some of which might surprise traditionalist views of women's occupations, historically speaking. One broad area of employment comes as no surprise: that where women's domestic skills might be used or possibly redirected. Thus there were many sempstresses and laundresses in towns, along with related but more specialised crafts. In Howden, for example, in 1379 there was a female wimple-maker. There were also probably quite large numbers of women employed in the textile industry. In Beverley, Ripon or York, and the centres of production in the south and west of the county, women can be found as carders and spinners, a traditional female occupation; but there were also women weavers by the fourteenth century, several of whom can be identified in the Poll Tax returns either working in their own right or in their husbands'. Women also worked in the heavier, dirtier craft industries. At Beverley the borough records mention Margaret Limeburner (VCH 1989: 41) who seems to have worked at the limekilns in the Grovehill district, and Leach (1896: 31) mentions Agnes Tiler supplying 1,000 bricks for the building of North Bar in 1409. In Sheffield women can be found working as smiths. Richard King of Sheffield, referred to above, left his daughter his anvil, bellows, tongs and other tools, and his smithy and grinding mill to his wife and daughter (BIHR: vol. 13, fol. 434).

There were also occupations in which it was unusual to find women. Few women seem to have become merchants, for instance, although the Howden Poll Tax return of 1379 does list a woman mercer, and Goldberg (1992: 126–7) notes Emma Erle of Wakefield merchandising considerable quantities of cloth in the late fourteenth century. Other occupations were considered unsuitable for women – butchering and tanning – and women were forbidden by the York tanners' ordinances from taking up such employment unless it was to help their husbands.

This last example and one or two others above pose another question: how many of these women were employed in their own right, and how many worked under their husbands within a family business? The King will above provides an interesting example of what appears to be both wife and daughter taking over a business after the husband's death, and possibly inheriting the freedom of the borough, a circumstance which Swanson (1989: Chapter 1) found common in York, suggesting that many women worked in familial businesses yet went unrecorded as practitioners of a trade or craft until after their husbands' deaths.

It is over issues such as these that the visibility of women in the medieval urban record begins to fade. While men were usually recorded by occupation and as the heads of households, women very often appear only as wives. It is thus difficult to decide whether some women were working as part of a family unit of production or not. Similarly, how many of the women who had recorded occupations and were married pursued their occupations either in their own right or as helpmates to their husbands? Such questions are difficult if not impossible to answer with any degree of accuracy. However, where records of admissions of freedom to towns have survived very few such admissions are for women. The freedom to practise a trade or craft or the right to hold a stall in the market place was usually inherited from a husband.

Goldberg (1992) has suggested that the way we have traditionally viewed women of the late Middle Ages is in need of modification. Economic and social developments of the fourteenth and fifteenth centuries after the Black Death led to a shortage of craftsmen and tradesmen, a shortage which women were able to remedy and which in turn provided them with some small degree of economic independence and greater control over their marital condition. However, one must beware of the functionalist tendencies of this argument – that society somehow noticed a skills shortage and women were drawn in to fill the gap and restore the balance. This is not the interpretation that Marxist feminists might put on such a situation.

Arguments such as these should be placed in the broader context of the economic and political control of the town which remained male-dominated, with men tending to set the limits to female participation. Indeed, the participation of women in the craft guilds even of occupations that they followed was rare; participation in town government was almost non-existent. Thus despite a greater freedom and control over their own circumstances women of the late Middle Ages remained unequal, being discriminated against both legally and in their access to wealth and political power.

In the face of such inequality, therefore, might we assume that women of the later Middle Ages saw themselves as an oppressed group, or did class and access to wealth and power fracture any sense of sisterly solidarity?

No matter whether a woman was of aristocratic background or whether she was a huckster, all women were unequal to men in law, as we have seen. Moreover, both the church's teaching and misogynist literature represented women as inferior. However, if women could not fail to be conscious of this position, there is little evidence of any concerted action by them to reverse the situation. Furthermore women, like men, were also divided by class, status and occupation. A basic division was between aristocratic women and the rest. Another was between women married to burgesses or women who had acquired the freedom of the town, and those who had not. There were also status differences in occupations: those trades or crafts that were considered respectable, and those which were not – innkeeping and prostitution, for example, were not. Even at the lowest levels in society there were differences between women who were deserving poor and those who were indolent beggars and criminals. In other words, women should not be seen as a homogeneous body united by their sex and possessing a sense of solidarity. A woman's position in medieval society was a complex one which cannot be understood simply in terms of gender inequality, but is better understood as the intersection of gender with class, status and wealth.

CONCLUSION

This review of urban society in the later Middle Ages has adopted the medieval threefold division of society for the purpose of identifying social and occupational groups, and placing them into some sort of broader social categories. It does not imply an acceptance of the medieval paradigm, simply the appropriation of a useful social schema. Indeed, what closer observation of medieval theories of stratification tends to highlight are the problems inherent in such functionalist analysis. If harmonious interaction between social groups was the means by which society would be maintained – a position given legitimacy by the teachings of the church – then this was demonstrably untrue from what can be observed of medieval urban life. As we have seen intra- and inter-order disputes were frequent, resulting at times in individual or collective violence. Yet the societies and economies of many towns looked at as a whole from the twelfth to the fourteenth century, strengthened.

A different interpretation can be found in Marxist analysis, although such monolithic explanations tend to reduce all conflict to class conflict, or in the sort of Weberian analysis advanced by Rigby (1995) suggesting a complex interaction of social forces rather than giving causal primacy to the economic, important as this might be. Such conflict is significant for it created the sorts of unequal structures which gave towns their dynamic. This is why an understanding of people in towns advances our understanding of the physical expressions of towns. Areas of jurisdiction, trade, domicile or religious worship were often the outcomes not of a haphazard or organic growth, but of competition for space or the imposition of seigneurial authority. And this brings us back again to Abrams's (1978) observation that this is what towns 'restlessly express'. It is to the many physical expressions of town life that we now turn.

NOTES

1. Compiled from YASRS 12: 77:81 and YAJ 8 and 13. The figure for urban property held by the Earl of Albemarle may be on the low side.
2. A reinforced doublet.
3. *Possibly* a hat made of leather thongs attached to an iron framework.
4. Carlisle axe – Carlisle was well known for the production of axes.

CHAPTER THREE

The Pattern and Plan of Towns

PATTERN

IN YORKSHIRE FEW TOWNS of the post-Conquest period were entirely new creations. Many had some kind of pre-urban nucleus. Hence, continuity of settlement and function is an important issue. But how many of those early settlements can be thought of as towns, and how many of those were of Romano-British or Anglo-Scandinavian origins? Also did any continue to display features of town life? From the Romans to the Normans is a long timespan, from say the first to the eleventh century. Yet, it must be admitted, we have little more than a rudimentary knowledge concerning towns then.

The full extent of Roman urbanisation in the North has yet to be firmly established, although archaeological evidence suggests that Adel, Aldborough or Malton with Norton were more than just fortified camps (Wilson, Jones and Evans 1984: 87–8). Finds of statuary, altars and mosaic floors and traces of potteries, metal-working sites and goldsmiths' shops suggest the possibility of small towns within the vicinity of some forts, while Aldborough (Isurium Brigantium) appears to have been the civic capital of the Brigantes.

An equally tough problem is to try to determine the degree of Anglo-Saxon and Scandinavian urbanisation. Really, it is not until 1086 and the Domesday survey that wide-ranging comment becomes available. If historians have interpreted the Domesday entries correctly, then many of the known Romano-British settlements had failed to develop as towns, although a number of Anglo-Saxon and Scandinavian settlements seem to have been developing in this direction.

Two of the perhaps largest towns were in the southwest of the county: Dadsley (Tickhill) and Tanshelf (Pontefract) where relatively high numbers of burgesses were recorded. Burgesses were also recorded at Bridlington and Pocklington, and there were numbers of settlements, some of them wealthy vills, throughout the county which, if of less certain status, were the administrative centres of large manors or possessed important liberties – Beverley, Howden, Ripon, Wakefield, Whitby, for example. Thus, while it might be difficult to arrive at the exact extent of urbanisation, it is clear that the county was more than just a collection of rude villages.

Moreover, while the evidence should not be pushed too far, it is significant that, even before the Conquest, we can begin to identify a number of places which were to become or remain urban centres. Outstanding in this respect is York, one of the few places where some sort of urban continuity can be demonstrated. Although the boundaries of Roman, Anglo-Saxon and Scandinavian settlements did not exactly concur, all were close to one another and were to be encompassed by the bounds of the city in the central Middle Ages. Similarly, Doncaster would appear to show some continuity, if not from Roman to Anglo-Saxon, then certainly from pre- to post-Conquest. There are also good reasons, as we shall see in Chapter 9 (p. 155), for believing that Ripon was developing an urban identity under Anglo-Saxon influence. What this would appear to point to is a pre-Conquest date for the beginning of a medieval urbanisation of the county. While the twelfth and thirteenth centuries have traditionally been thought of as a time of borough foundation and the progress from a rural, village England to one in which towns, trade and commerce played an increasingly important part, it seems clear that in Yorkshire, at least, the onset of urbanisation was in the ninth or tenth centuries.

However, this is not to deny that the twelfth and thirteenth centuries appear to have been the vital time for the emergence or perhaps expansion of towns. From borough charters, taxation records and other documents it is possible to compile a list of above forty towns (see Table 3.1). Several points need to be made about this list. Bearing in mind the issues raised in Chapter 1, borough charters do not necessarily indicate a foundation date but may simply confirm a state of affairs that had already arisen. It is safer to say that the majority of charters were granted in the twelfth and thirteenth centuries, suggesting a period when monarchs or seigneurs were most easily persuaded to favour urban settlement and the creation of boroughs. The towns listed here as boroughs either had borough charters

granted – Beverley, for example – or, where charters are absent, they are recorded as possessing the privileges one would associate with a borough such as burgage tenure or a borough court – Skipton, for example.

However, if we define a town as more than the narrow legal conception of a borough, then it becomes clear that there were a small number of towns which, while they possessed the sort of social and occupational heterogeneity mentioned in Chapter 1, nevertheless they lacked the freedoms associated with a borough – no charters awarding the right to buy and sell property, no freedom from tolls, no self-government or borough court. Yet to deny that such settlements were towns is odd, to say the least. Rather they *were* towns, but lacked borough status – non-burghal towns. Whitby is a clear example. Here was a town which had its borough charter revoked within perhaps twenty-five years of its having been granted. The people of Whitby do not appear to have changed their

TABLE 3.1 Yorkshire towns by 1450

Boroughs		Non-burghal Towns	Failures	Problems
Bawtry	Pocklington	Bedale	Almondbury	Bingley
Beverley	Pontefract	Guisborough	Brough-on-Humber	Bridlington
Boroughbridge	Richmond	Halifax	Drax	
Bradford	Ripon	Selby	Harewood	
Doncaster	Rotherham	Snaith	Ravenserodd	
Hedon	Scarborough	Tadcaster	Skipsea	
Helmsley	Sheffield	Wetherby		
Howden	Sherburn	Whitby [a]		
Hull	Skelton			
Kirkbymoorside	Skipton			
Knaresboro'	Stokesley			
Leeds	Thirsk			
New Malton	Tickhill			
N'allerton	Wakefield			
Otley	Yarm			
Pickering	York			

[a] Borough charter of 1175–85 revoked 1201.

occupations much between 1175 and 1201, yet it was during this period that borough status was granted then taken away. While a large part of the population of Whitby may have been incensed by the revocation of their town charter and the rights and freedoms that went with it, they nevertheless continued to pursue the same sorts of occupations and lifestyles and Whitby continued to function as a town, if on less advantageous terms. Furthermore, some residents continued to think of themselves as burgesses. As late as 1463 William Manston was referred to in his will as a burgess of Whitby (YASRS 6), and even in 1530 John Ledum could be called a 'burges of Whytby' (SURTEES 79: 214).

The same can be said of the other towns in this column, except that they never seem to have been granted borough status. Two towns here, Bedale and Halifax, seem to have changed from agricultural villages into towns by the fifteenth century. Bedale is difficult to account for, since aspects of its early history are obscure. While Henry III had granted a charter for a market and fair in 1251, taxation returns suggest no more than the handful of craftsmen that many large villages possessed – carpenter, smith, tailor. But by the fifteenth century there is evidence of some mercantile activity, and Leland was certainly impressed in 1539 or 1544 describing Bedale as 'a faire market towne and next to Richemont self in the sheere' (Toulmin-Smith 1909: 30). Also, by the sixteenth century, if not before, Bedale had acquired a market house within the market place, and probably before the seventeenth century appears to have been administered by a body known as the 'four and twenty', although the exact dates/origins of these developments remains uncertain (VCH 1914: 291–300). Halifax, on the other hand, would appear to have grown in response to increasing industrial activity, becoming a centre not only of wool-textile production, but also of wool and woollen cloth marketing. But although the town possessed the right to hold a market and fair, this was by prescription rather than charter, and there was no form of separate municipal government. Yet by 1500 Halifax had become, along with Leeds and Wakefield, one of the principal towns of the area we today call West Yorkshire.

Of the towns that did possess charters, the question of who was responsible for the granting of the charter arises. Table 3.2 lists this information where a grantor is known, either because a charter exists or there are clear documentary records of other kinds, for example a record by an archbishop of York in his register. As far as Yorkshire is concerned the grantors appear to have been chiefly the crown or seigneurs, and by guesswork we might add a number of other towns to the list – Skipton, Stokesley, for example – which were almost certainly granted rights by charters from seigneurs. The archbishops of York and the bishops of Durham were responsible between them for the granting of charters to seven towns. The religious houses, on the other hand, granted only one charter at Whitby, but, as we have seen, in 1201 it was revoked and vested in the abbey. The religious houses, however, dominated the life of at least two other Yorkshire towns – Guisborough and Selby – but never granted them the liberties and freedoms associated with chartered boroughs. The Yorkshire religious houses seem to have been loath to relinquish control over their urban property.

What part was played by the inhabitants of towns, especially merchants, in obtaining charters and the freedoms associated with them is not certain. Whether they were the prime movers in petitioning the crown or seigneurs as they did in the sixteenth and seventeenth centuries is a matter of conjecture in many cases. There is, however, some slight evidence to suggest that this may have been so. The inhabitants of Wakefield appear to have payed the Earl of Warenne and his family 120 shillings in order to obtain a charter of free burgage around 1188–1202 (Clay 1949: 116–17). Then again, it may have been that some seigneurs initiated the process – the Counts of Aumale, for example, when laying out new planned units at Hedon and Skipton, or the de Vipont family when laying out Bawtry on the wastes of the manor of Austerfield. Similarly in Richmond the

TABLE 3.2 Grantors of Town Charters

Town	[Crown]	[Bishop]	[Religious House]	[Seigneur]
Bawtry				x
Beverley		x		
Brough-on-Humber		x		
Doncaster	x			
Hedon				x
Helmsley				x
Howden		x		
Hull	x			
Kirkbymoorside	x			
Knaresborough	x			
Leeds				x
New Malton	x			
Northallerton		x		
Otley		x		
Pickering	x			
Pontefract				x
Ravenserodd	x			
Richmond				x
Ripon		x		
Scarborough	x			
Sheffield				x
Sherburn-in-Elmet		x		
Thirsk				x
Wakefield				x
Whitby			x	
York	x			

Counts of Brittany seem to have built not just a castle there, but made provision for the establishment of a small settlement within the outer bailey to which they were willing to grant urban privileges (Clay 1935: 22–3, 44).

Even where there were charters and seigneurs who looked favourably on the idea of fostering trade, not all towns survived and others contracted. Hedon, for example, declined as the principal Yorkshire port on the Humber from perhaps the early fourteenth century or before as Hull began to capture the greater share of trade and shipping. It was also hit by one or two disasters – fires and the slow silting of the Haven, the chief waterway. By perhaps the end of the sixteenth century Hedon had decayed back to a smaller urban core with merchants and tradesmen abandoning parts of the new town laid out around the quays and settling nearer to the market place and church. Hedon could still be viewed as a town, however, if physically smaller than it was in the thirteenth century.

If Hedon declined it was not like a number of other towns which for one reason or another failed entirely. Perhaps two disappeared through natural disaster. The most spectacular was

Ravenserodd or Odd. The site was an island thrown up in the Humber near to Old Ravenser on Spurn Head. It was joined to the mainland by a 'sandy road scattered with round, yellow stones'. A settlement of sorts had been founded on the island by the Count of Aumale in the mid-thirteenth century and had grown to a fair-sized town – 100–200 houses at least together with market rights – by 1299 when Edward I granted a borough charter. But destruction followed in the next century. During 1356–67 the chronicle of Meaux Abbey records that after storms and floods the inhabitants left the town which was 'entirely swallowed up in a whirlpool of sea and Humber flooding' (Bond 1868: 120–1). A similar, if less dramatic, fate *may* have befallen Drax. An extent of Drax taken between 1247 and 1255 assesses both the manor and the borough, but a further inquisition of 1405 states that the manor was worth nothing since it had been flooded by the River Ouse (YASRS 12: 123–5; 59: 52–3); the borough is not mentioned, nor are there any further references to it. Was the town destroyed by flooding, or was flooding a decisive factor in the abandonment of an already declining town? It is difficult to say. The same factor may even have played a part in the disappearance of the *town* of Brough-on-Humber which was quite clearly created a borough by the Archbishop of York in 1239 and given the liberties of Beverley (SURTEES 56: 251). However, little more is heard of Brough the town, assuming it was ever established as such, and it seems to have remained a village.

Other reasons may account for the decline and disappearance of towns such as Almondbury and Harewood. The former was perhaps never a going concern, since references to the place functioning as a town are not easily found. Its location within the outer bailey of a castle situated on a ridge more than 275 metres above sea level in the Pennines probably held little attraction for merchants and tradesmen. Although there is archaeological and documentary evidence that a settlement had existed in this position before the seventeenth century, a plan of the Huddersfield district made in 1634 marks the enclosure on Castle Hill only as 'The scite of Ttowne' (Faull and Moorhouse 1981: 737–8). Harewood is more difficult to account for. It was undoubtedly functioning as a small town in the fourteenth century, yet by the sixteenth it had reverted to a village. The reason is uncertain – the chills and fevers of the late medieval economy or competition with successful neighbouring towns perhaps may have had their effects. But by 1570 James Rither of Harewood Castle could write to Lord Burghley about the 'restoring of the town of Harewood to its ancient state, having once been a market town, and fairs in it' (Jones 1859: 166).

This leaves a couple of towns that might be considered problems – Bingley and Bridlington – though they are problems in different ways. At Bingley certain properties were held by burgage tenure and there was also a market. The problem is in finding some corroborating evidence of urban function. There is little to suggest anything other than a sizeable village with market rights: occupational heterogeneity, administrative importance, municipal government – none can be substantiated. The reverse is true of Bridlington. Here was a moderately sized town with a market and three fairs. Moreover, a variety of occupations can be observed in the fourteenth and fifteenth centuries – mercers and merchants, tailors, smiths, barbers, fishermen, as well as a variety of occupations dependent upon the priory – cellerers, cooks, bakers, brewers and probably the quarrymen and masons also. The Domesday Book records burgesses at Bridlington, and it is tempting to accept this as the clinching evidence. However, as Goldberg (1994) has suggested, one should not view Bridlington as 'a nascent Domesday borough' – for one thing one cannot show any burghal continuity between the pre- and post-Conquest periods, nor is there any record of burgesses after 1086. But one cannot agree with Goldberg fully in his assumption that because of a lack of burgesses, a borough charter or institutions such as friaries that Bridlington was not a town. It is probably better to regard it as a non-burghal town under the control of the priory, rather than, as Goldberg has suggested, an 'estate village', a concept perhaps better suited to the eighteenth century.

It is also worth commenting of the relative sizes of towns in Table 3.1. Only four towns appear to have had populations of above 1,000: York (above 7,000), Beverley (above 2,500), Hull (above 1,500), Scarborough (above 1,000). These figures relate to the Poll Tax return of 1377 and are the numbers of taxpayers; in reality populations would have been higher, a good deal higher perhaps at York. Indeed, these towns represent the largest centres of population in the county, and York – the only city in the county – was one of the largest in the country after London.

A second rank of towns might also be proposed with populations of around 1,000 taxpayers or slightly less: Doncaster, Pontefract, Ripon, Selby, Tickhill, Whitby. But there is also a cluster of towns with populations of 300–500 taxpayers – Howden, Malton, Richmond, Sheffield and Wakefield. These places together form a distinctive group or type of town. Here were the important regional centres of marketing, manufacture or administration. Several of them can also be identified as the capitals of a 'pays' – Richmond in Richmondshire, for example.

Both of the above categories represent recognisable urban centres. But below them we might place a third category of town – the towns with much smaller populations, places like Bawtry, Bradford or Otley. Where the occupations of the populations of these towns can be discovered, they are less diverse than the larger towns and many have much closer ties to a rural economy rather than a mercantile one. Many were perhaps only just distinguishable from the large and prosperous village which had a market. At the same time it would be wrong to underestimate both the diversity of occupations that *might* be present and the amount of trade that even a small market might handle. Few records of the smaller towns have survived, assuming that they once existed in any coherent form, but Bradford's manor court rolls (BCL) are extant for several periods in the fourteenth and fifteenth

centuries. Both manorial and town business would appear to have been conducted at the courts of the manor. From these it is evident that while several families were engaged in agriculture, there was also a wool textile industry organised enough to require a fulling mill; that there were butchers, chapmen, dyers, innkeepers, masons, shoemakers, smiths, tanners and tailors; that coal, stone and iron ore were dug in and around the town; that on market days people came a fair distance – from the more isolated parts of the Craven district, for example – to sell their cattle and produce.

By the fourteenth century this pattern of towns in the county was almost complete. Only one or two more might be added in the fifteenth century, notably Halifax but also Bedale. The towns formed a roughly crescent-shaped array running from the south and over to the west then northeast, but with a few towns over towards the Humber (see Figure 3.1). The reasons for this are probably ease of communications and regard to the land mass: towns have been sited away from the Pennines in the west and the North York Moors in the northeast, while the marshy nature of the land in Holderness permitted few good sites for urban growth, although one important town, Beverley, is located in this area.

It is also worth remarking that the largest towns in the county were located in the east and north – Beverley, Hull and Scarborough. York occupies a roughly central position, but is connected to the Humber and thus the east coast by the River Ouse. The locations of these large towns is more than historical accident. Whatever their pre-urban origins, during the Middle Ages they were ideally situated to capture a share of the prosperous east-coast trade by being either on the coast itself or one of the arterial waterways, the Humber or the Ouse. Selby and Whitby should also be considered in this light. Even some more northerly towns might prosper for the same reasons. Yarm stands on the northern boundary of the county, yet it was probably the east-coast trade, this time along the River Tees, that was a factor in the growth of the town.

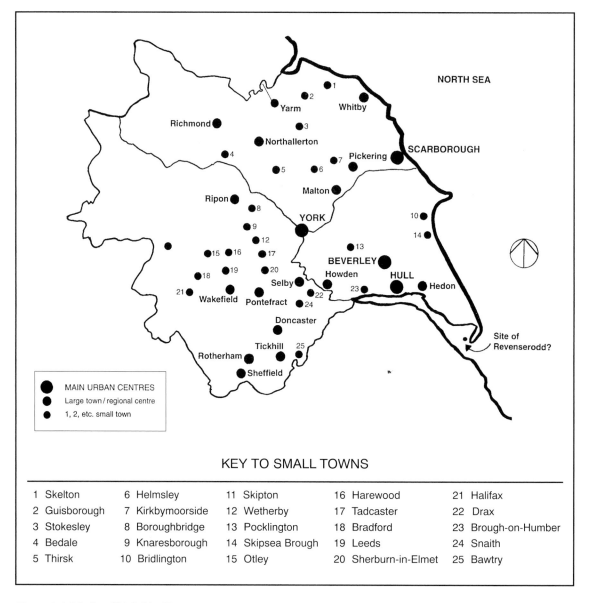

KEY TO SMALL TOWNS

1	Skelton	6	Helmsley	11	Skipton	16	Harewood	21	Halifax
2	Guisborough	7	Kirkbymoorside	12	Wetherby	17	Tadcaster	22	Drax
3	Stokesley	8	Boroughbridge	13	Pocklington	18	Bradford	23	Brough-on-Humber
4	Bedale	9	Knaresborough	14	Skipsea Brough	19	Leeds	24	Snaith
5	Thirsk	10	Bridlington	15	Otley	20	Sherburn-in-Elmet	25	Bawtry

Figure 3.1 Medieval Yorkshire Towns

However, one should be careful not to pursue such geographical determinism too far. Location is only one factor among several.

What is more remarkable in some ways is the absence of anything approaching a town in the Yorkshire Dales. Richmond and Bedale on the eastern fringes of the Dales are the nearest, although one might include perhaps a number of market villages or market centres – Middleham, for example. Similarly, the southern Pennine area lacked towns. As we have seen, Halifax became the urban focus of the Calder Valley only in the fifteenth century. But there are exceptions. Pontefract and Doncaster were among the largest towns in the West Riding, the parts of it, that is, which we call South and West Yorkshire today. However, in these and other towns like them administration was often a part of their urban function – Pontefract, for instance, was the administrative centre of the Honour of Pontefract.

Trade, access to waterways, administration and the fostering hand of a seigneur together with good fortune – all these were factors in determining which towns might prosper, grow and ultimately survive. If we can see a pattern in the spread of towns that emerged it is not one imposed by any individual. But what of the internal layouts of towns? The opposite was often true here.

PLAN

For some commentators the image of the medieval town is that conjured up by Sjöberg (1960). It consists of a jumble of narrow streets, a market place and a number of administrative and ceremonial buildings. Is this a correct picture, even given that sociologists like Sjöberg were attempting to produce a simple model for making comparisons across cultures? The problem is that it suggests a town which lacks any sophistication in planning. It tends to the view that while spatial relationships and order are important, they are subjugated to aggressive competition for space. While such models have usually been intended for the analysis of the development of cities, some authors have made of the 'jumble of streets around a market place' not a model but a stereotypical image descriptive of all medieval towns. Others have gone further, arguing as Peter Borsay (1977) has that, in England, 'provincial urban architecture' in the Middle Ages and sixteenth century 'paid little attention to questions of aesthetics and planning'. Yet there is a good deal to suggest that many medieval towns are not a fit with this stereotypical image, but had a high degree of organisation and planning which can be found in even some small towns. What is more, several distinctive urban plan-forms are identifiable, or at least can be categorised as conforming to distinctive types.

The simplest of plan-forms is the linear plan. Several Yorkshire towns were laid out like this, one of the clearest being Skipton (see Figure 3.2). The one principal street is aligned north–south and is terminated at the northern end by the church and castle. The street is broad enough to accommodate a market, and houses and shops front the street having long plots running back from them. Back lanes seem to have been developed running in line with the main street to give access to the plots. Numbers of side streets, alleyways really, connect the main street with the back lanes for further ease of access. A feature of the layout – and one typical of linear-plan towns – are the buildings located within the market place/main street. These were the market hall and probably the meat and fish shambles. The emphasis, however, is on one long, broad, main street.

Exactly when Skipton was laid out to this plan is uncertain, although references to Skipton as a borough occur from the thirteenth century (Williams 1981). A study of the plan of Skipton together with surviving documentary records suggests that the main street may have been a thirteenth-century remodelling of an existing highway, thus giving shape and form to an emerging town. Archaeological investigation tends to support this view, since the outer defences of the castle were abandoned around the thirteenth century and would have cut across the end of the main street had it existed – the earlier highway skirted around the defences. The pre-urban nucleus of Skipton may have been in the northeast quarter of the site close to the castle.

Skipton also illustrates how the linear-plan town might be expanded. The southern end of the main street is cut across by Swadford Street to the west and Newmarket Street to the east, streets probably constructed or remodelled to accommodate an expanding market, hence the name. Documentary references to these streets occur only from the fourteenth century (Williams 1981).

Other medieval linear-plan towns in Yorkshire include Kirkbymoorside and Northallerton. The plan of Northallerton is one of the things which seems to have struck visitors to the town as worthy of comment. Leland wrote in the early sixteenth century that the 'towne of Northalverton is yn one fair long streate lying by south

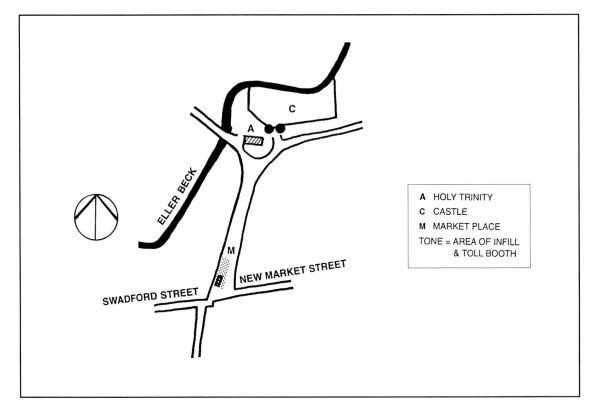

Figure 3.2 Skipton

and north' (Toulmin-Smith 1907: 67); while in 1791 Miss Crosfield, a local author, still felt obliged to comment:

> It consists of one wide street above half a mile in length . . . At about a third of its length from the south end stands the Toll-booth, an old ugly building . . . A little further stands the Market-cross . . . still more northward, are the Shambles. (Crosfield 1791: 16)

A related plan-form consists not of one, but two or three streets running side by side which are crossed by further streets – the rectilinear plan. Sometimes this is referred to as a grid plan, but that term should perhaps be reserved for towns laid out with near mathematical precision and which can be divided into at least nine and preferably more squares. Rectilinear is a term more appropriate to the plans of several towns

where streets might be straight and parallel or might wind and stray in order to accommodate a natural obstacle or follow a contour.

Rectilinear plans form the core of several Yorkshire towns – Bawtry or Hull, for example – or have been added as planned units to others – Hedon. Bawtry seems to have been laid out on the wastes of the manor of Austerfield not later than 1223, probably by Robert and Idonea de Vipont, the manorial lords (Beresford 1967: 522–3). It lies between the old Great North Road and the River Idle where a small port was developed. Two main streets were aligned north–south; the market place was to the west and the port to the east, the two streets being connected by a series of cross streets (see Figure 3.3). The market street was made wider and the Great North Road appears to have been diverted slightly to pass through it – a practice found in other towns at this period.

It is easy to misinterpret such simple recti-linear plans, especially when analysing the town plan from later maps. Decay or extension of the town in later centuries can confuse matters. At Yarm, for example, it would be easy to argue the case for a linear-plan town with one long, broad street/market place (High Street) running through the town to a crossing of the Tees at its northern end. However, archaeological investigation has established that what now appears as a quiet back lane (West Street) running parallel to High Street was once occupied, and represents a part of a more complex rectilinear plan which had developed by perhaps the thirteenth century. By the seventeenth century the importance of West Street declined, probably as a result of the port facilities being relocated on the eastern side of the town (Evans and Heslop 1985; Tann 1992).

A number of towns in the county were designed or grew up around the junction of three or four roads. Where these ran into one another a roughly triangular market place was often sited. This convergent plan – convergent because the principal streets converge on one point – is easy to see at Wakefield (see Figure 3.4). The Wakefield manor court rolls record a large market place at the junction of Kirkgate, Westgate and Northgate. Houses held mostly in burgage tenure fronted these streets, while in the market place itself stood the toll booth and gaol. Although convergent plans are typical of several small towns in the county, they could nevertheless accommodate a considerable market as at Wakefield.

Roads might converge on towns in different patterns. Where several converged on a particular feature, a castle for example, and had to pass through town walls or defences, then they might appear to radiate like spokes from a wheel. Clear examples of such radial plans persist at New Malton and Richmond (see Figures 3.5a and

---

Figure 3.3 Bawtry

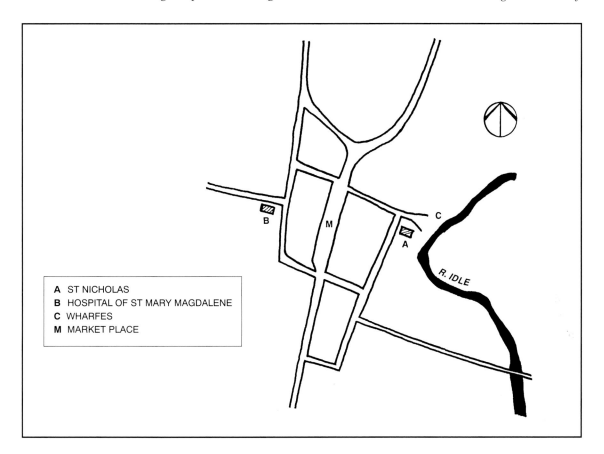

A ST NICHOLAS
B HOSPITAL OF ST MARY MAGDALENE
C WHARFES
M MARKET PLACE

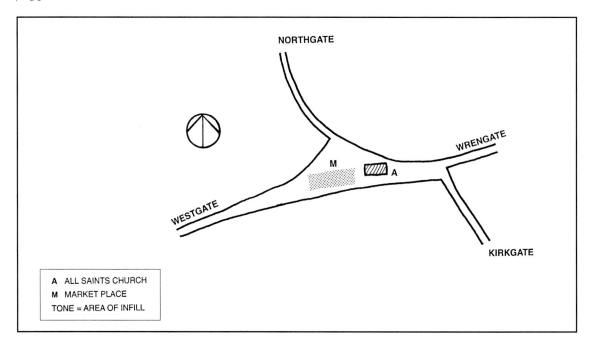

Figure 3.4 Wakefield

3.5b). In both of these towns a compact area of houses, market place and chapel were contained within the outer defences of a castle which were replaced by town walls. It is significant that in both places urban development beyond these confines became known as Newbiggen – the new building.

It was also possible for a town to grow by the addition of one or more planned units. Pontefract seems to have evolved in this way. The first urban settlement after the building of the castle in the eleventh century probably developed as a linear plan running east–west from the castle along Micklegate, but at the western end a further market place, West Cheap, had grown up and was chartered between 1255 and 1258. This converted a linear into a convergent plan, since West Cheap accommodated not only Micklegate running east–west but roads running north–south also. A related development occurred at Guisborough where the road passing the abbey and the pre-urban settlement ran approximately north–south. This was added to with a new planned linear unit running

east–west, joining the old road at the eastern end where a market place was formed.

Sometimes planned units extended a town to link it with new or developing facilities. This has been clearly demonstrated by Hayfield and Slater (1984) at Hedon where they have shown how a rectilinear planned unit was added in the twelfth century, a process that went hand in hand with the development of the port. Hedon, as Hayfield and Slater show, is a particularly complicated example, but simpler additions have survived at small towns. Leeds seems to have consisted of a linear planned unit – the present-day Briggate – added to the west of the older settlement around the parish church. The same process probably occurred at Sherburn-in-Elmet. Figure 3.6 shows Sherburn on Jefferys' map of Yorkshire published in 1772. The detached nature of the town is evident in the contrast between the tentacular form of what was probably the pre-urban settlement around the church to the west and the linear plan developed along the highway to the east. Although somewhat diagrammatic, Jefferys' representation compares well with Warburton's map of 1720 and the more detailed OS 6" sheet of 1852.

The addition of planned units to a town raises

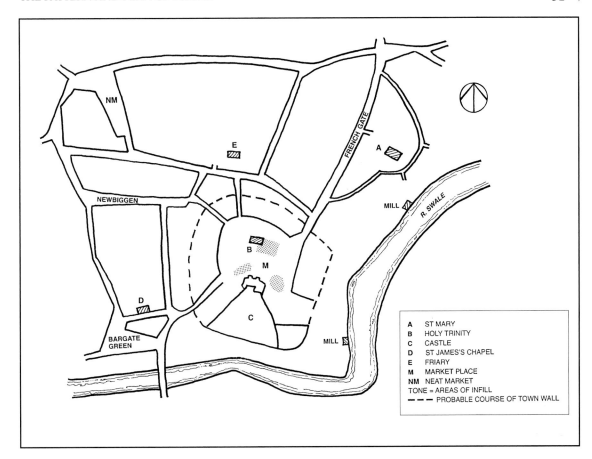

Figure 3.5a Richmond

the question of what is sometimes called the organic plan – the important exception mentioned above. The organic theory of development comes closest to substantiating the jumble-of-narrow-streets stereotype, since some towns appear to have developed by precisely the reverse of what I have been arguing here: a lack of overall planning producing no recognisable pattern of streets. A number of objections can be raised both to the term and the process it purports to describe. To begin with, the terms organic and organic growth invest the town with a being it does not possess. It is a functionalist reification suggesting that the physical environments of towns operate in their own interests, and what is more, this does not really provide us with a basis for analysis but is a bald statement that a town has somehow grown. This distracts us from other possibilities. While some towns may have developed without an overall plan,

within them they often contain small areas or units that have been well planned nevertheless. In other words the lack of a recognisable plan-form does not imply a lack of planning. What the so-called organic plan usually represents is the redevelopment of existing areas or additions over the centuries. This type of plan is much better described as an additive or agglomerative plan and is, in theory, capable of analysis.

The trouble is, however, that most towns might be said to have developed in this way: 'additive' is more the description of a process than a preconceived plan. The problem occurs partly from failing to recognise an ambiguous usage of the term plan – plan as a preconceived idea for a building campaign, and plan as a category given to several layouts that have

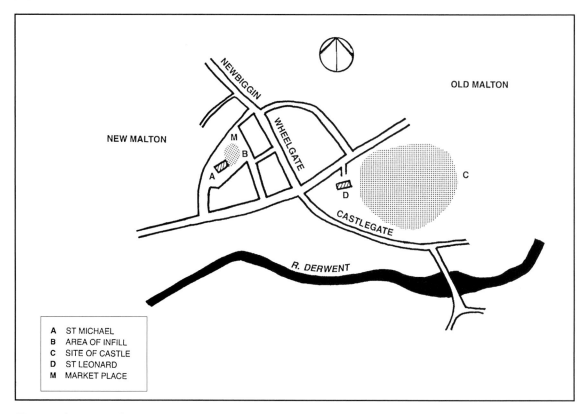

OLD MALTON

NEW MALTON

NEWBIGGIN

WHEELGATE

M
B
A
D

C

CASTLEGATE

R. DERWENT

A   ST MICHAEL
B   AREA OF INFILL
C   SITE OF CASTLE
D   ST LEONARD
M   MARKET PLACE

Figure 3.5b New Malton

similarities, although the processes by which they came into being may have been different. Thus Guisborough, Hedon or Pontefract were all extended by planned units, but these were probably not conceived of at a single point in time or were the product of one plan which was eventually brought to completion. Nevertheless, we can analyse the process and comment on the component parts.

These are relatively simple town plans to unravel. But in larger and more complex towns such as Beverley, Ripon or York, the forces which brought some areas of town into being are far less straightforward and the end-products are not simple shapes that can be neatly categorised. Hence 'organic', a nebulous word easily applied to any complicated layout, comes into its own. However, it is often possible to highlight significant features within the urban environment or to outline stages of development, even

where research towards a more detailed analysis of the overall plan proves recalcitrant. At York, for example, the Roman fort and Rivers Ouse and Foss proved perhaps the most decisive physical influences on the city's medieval layout. The development of Beverley, on the other hand, was influenced more by the marshy terrain in the early Middle Ages, since the minster and its surroundings and a settlement further to the north seem to have been located mostly on two separate islands of boulder clay. Over the centuries the land between was reclaimed, stabilised and built over. It is the cumulative effect of processes such as these that give us the complicated layouts of some towns, and it is correct to see the end result as an agglomeration of some complexity but not one that is without planning.

Aside from any overall planning of towns, a study of their internal workings and spatial relationships suggests a high degree of organisation and differentiation of functions. This will be more fully dealt with in the chapters on spaces

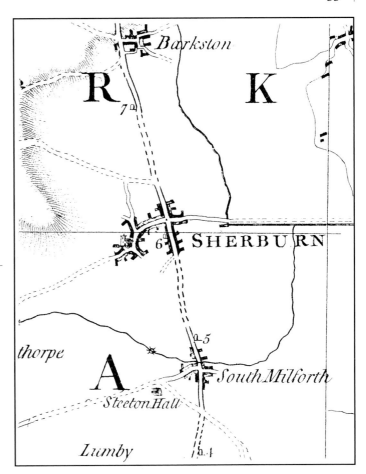

Figure 3.6 Sherburn-in-Elmet, Thos Jefferys 1772

for trade and the arrangement of some towns into commercial, agricultural and industrial areas. It is worth noting here, however, that the market place with its market cross, butter cross, shambles and possibly a toll booth or market hall was a central focus within the medieval town plan and a space that was too important to be allowed to develop in a haphazard manner. Other important foci of the plan were churches and castles and again these will be dealt with more fully in the appropriate chapters. Here it is relevant to acknowledge that the social institutions they represented might have been responsible for the promotion or development of towns or had a vital economic influence on them, and the buildings themselves often hold clues crucial to an understanding of how plans developed.

Thus at Pontefract the parish church of All Saints, of post-Conquest foundation, was situated close to a former Anglo-Saxon church, and may well indicate the location of the Anglo-Saxon town of Tanshelf adding a further reason why the Norman castle was located there apart from wider strategic considerations. But Pontefract appears to have developed westwards away from the parish church, making a chapel of ease necessary – St Giles which was built in the new market place at West Cheap. These two churches between them would seem to indicate significant stages in the growth of the town. At Knaresborough a castle was built in perhaps the twelfth-century well to the south of the church on a rocky cliff above the River Nidd. It seems likely that the church marks the site of an earlier Anglo-Saxon settlement near to a crossing of the river. During perhaps the twelfth century a town was developed around the castle, the

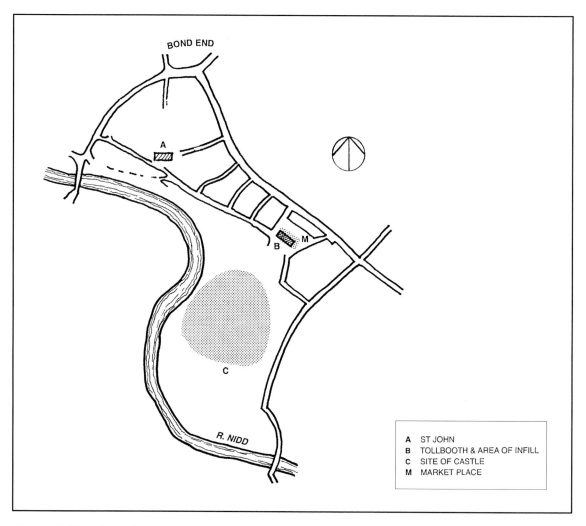

Figure 3.7 Knaresborough

church becoming isolated from the central town in the process (see Figure 3.7).

As suggested above, what always presents problems of interpretation is the agglomerative plan of a truly complex city. However, study of some of the important foci of the plan can often bring clarity to the overall picture. Take York. The problem here is a city redeveloped century on century, incorporating a Roman fort, Anglo-Scandinavian and medieval street patterns, new eighteenth-century streets and the consequences of becoming a railway centre in the nineteenth century. As medieval England's second largest

city and a busy inland port, it should come as no surprise that York lacks an overall plan, but has grown by additions and redevelopment on sites already occupied, thus giving an irregular, confusing feel to the city.

And yet despite this past, a certain order can be discerned in York's medieval plan, largely along two axes one of which had been present probably in the Anglo-Scandinavian town, while both may originally have been created in response to the River Ouse and the Roman fort (see Figure 3.8). The first runs approximately east–west from Micklegate Bar along Micklegate, across Ouse Bridge, the principal crossing of the river, and on to Pavement. As visitors approached the city by this route in the later

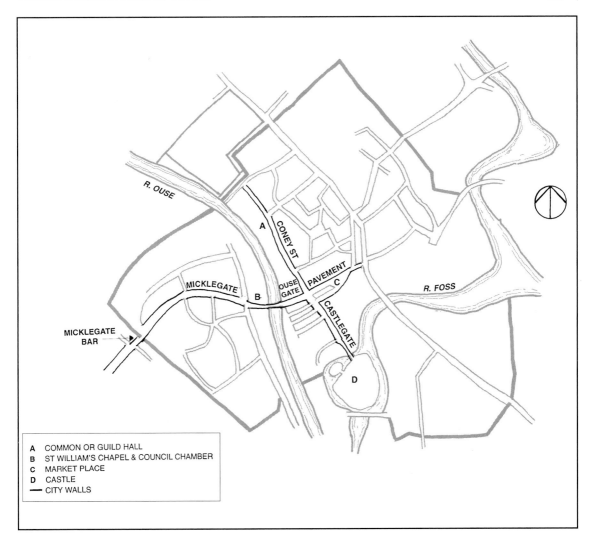

Figure 3.8 York: two routes from Drake 1736

Middle Ages they passed by St William's Chapel and the council chamber on Ouse Bridge and the city clock to enter Low Ousegate, a street lined with tall timber-framed shops and houses. They would then have passed on to High Ousegate and Pavement, a long market place also known as Market Shire and terminating in one of York's prettiest churches, All Saints, Pavement. This route ran to the southeast of the Roman fort and had probably been the commercial heart of the Anglo-Scandinavian town (Ramm 1972: 250).

The second axis ran southeast to northwest passing between the fort and the Ouse. It ran along Lendal, Coney Street, Spurriergate,

Nessgate and Castlegate: from St Leonard's Hospital in the north to York Castle in the south. Along its length were two friaries, the Ouse waterfront, the lodgings of foreign merchants, the houses of other wealthy traders, St Martin's church, the Guild or Common Hall, St Christopher's Chapel and St Helen's. The two routes intersected near Ouse Bridge and within their quadrants were many narrow streets – by the end of the Middle Ages crowded residential and trade areas in contrast to the relatively spacious streets that were their boundaries. Nevertheless, along the two axes in question there seems to have been a consistent aim to provide architecture of quality and architectural incident – notice how both the seats of civic government – the Council Chamber on Ouse Bridge and Common Hall – were located on these routes. And again it is significant that when Henry VII was received into the city in 1486, it was via Ouse Bridge and Coney Street and on to Common Hall with short pageants played out at points along the route – Ebrauke (the symbolic figure of York's foundation) presented the king with the keys of the city at Micklegate Bar; the figure of Solomon presented the king with a sceptor at Ouse Bridge; King David yielded a sword of victory to the king at Common Hall (SURTEES 85: 53–7).

Several conclusions might be drawn from this discussion of the county's medieval towns and their plans but three are worth emphasising. First, it is clear that most new or substantially new towns – Bawtry or Hedon, for example – underwent some process of planning resulting in a street layout that was systematic and far from haphazard. Whether a simple linear plan or a more complicated rectilinear plan, there was a degree of organisation. Added to this the internal workings of many towns were also planned and regulated, having specialised divisions of markets or areas devoted to certain trades. Even in large agglomerative plans order might be imposed on routes into and through the town as well as around the market place. There might be insanitary areas of housing, badly drained streets and warrens of narrow alleys and courtyards, but there was also a seigneurial or civic will to impose order.

Second, the view that where medieval planning occurred it was minimal or crude cannot be sustained. The most recent expression of this argument has come from Peter Borsay (1977, 1989), who, writing in relation to eighteenth-century towns, has suggested that medieval 'urban architecture had paid little attention to questions of aesthetics and planning', and has gone as far as to write, 'After the mid-fourteenth century urban planning virtually collapsed, and for the next three centuries remained a dormant

force. Only a trickle of new towns were founded . . .' But if on his own admission few new towns were founded after the mid-fourteenth century it is hardly correct to talk about a collapse of planning – a collapse of foundations, yes. Moreover, the argument is distorted by rather whiggish value judgements. Because medieval art and architecture did not conform to an enlightenment conceptualisation of taste, this cannot then be used to suggest the lack of a medieval urban aesthetic: the outlooks of medieval and eighteenth-century town-dwellers were simply different, and it is not a question of progress from the primitive to the sophisticated.

Third, few towns, even those planned from new, remained unaltered over the centuries. Expansion, decay or changes in the way a town functioned led to remodellings. For a variety of reasons Hedon began a slow decline in the fourteenth century resulting in a severe depression in probably the second half of the fifteenth. It was then that the earlier extensions of the town were abandoned and it shrank back to only a little more than its pre-urban nucleus, losing two or three chapels in the process. At York an important space in the Roman town and colonia had been the waterfront along the Ouse, but this became of perhaps secondary importance to a waterfront on the Foss in the Anglo-Scandinavian town. In this period a central area of marketing and trade had been around Ousegate and Pavement; while this remained an important market place, as the town expanded in the later Middle Ages, further spaces for trade were developed and the Ouse waterfront regained its prominence. In other towns the centre of focus might shift entirely, as at Thirsk where a market place in Old Thirsk was vacated to be relocated to the west in New Thirsk, probably after the building of a castle there in the twelfth century (see Figure 9.4 on p. 158).

Even where plots had been marked out in new developments there was no guarantee that they would be taken up. Thus at Hull plots to the north of the town within the walls were thinly inhabited, a reason perhaps why the De La Poles acquired and rebuilt a house in that part of town in the fourteenth century.

The abandoned market place in the borough of Old Thirsk.

So far the discussion has revolved around the social groups that promoted and lived in towns and the planned elements within medieval towns, and has suggested that, with study, these might be recovered and categorised. While this approach is a legitimate line of historical inquiry, another more difficult avenue of research is the one that leads to the individual's view of the town – the mental map that contemporaries may have carried about. The individual makes many emotional investments in a town: home, familiar territories, exclusive suburbs, the route to work, red-light districts, unknown streets and so on. This is at odds with the analysis of the town plan we attempt when we spread a map on the table in front of us, but it is an aspect of the plan to be taken account of nevertheless. As Rossiaud has commented, the medieval city may well have been 'a strange and fascinating world

for the newcomer, a world he had to explore for some time before he understood it, perhaps never succeeding totally'. It was, Rossiaud argues, a townscape continually 'remodelled by expansion or destruction . . . a tangled network of tiny winding streets, courtyards and alleys' (1990: 143–4). Since I have been arguing that a good deal of planning went into the medieval town, such statements as Rossiaud's seem to run counter to this. They do not; rather they are complimentary. The planned town was as much idea as reality and rarely took shape in one short span of time. Over the centuries it grew, decayed or simply changed, as we have just seen. In such ways the cartographic image of the town is different from the mental image. A plan is a drawing of the whole made at a fixed point in time and space. But the mental map is born out of a living world and a changing scene bounded by living and working areas experienced at eye level.

This is one aspect of the medieval town or city that is difficult, if not impossible, to recover, since few traces of such attitudes of mind have survived. Thus, while we know from town records that many immigrants came to the town from the country, settling in places like York, there the record ends. There is little or nothing to tell us how they comprehended their new urban environment. Few people possessed more than rudimentary literacy, and if letters or diaries once existed they have now been lost. We can, of course, point to religious and municipal records, and to the buildings and spaces themselves, in this way hoping to come to some understanding of people in towns, but the interpretation is always our own.

It may, however, be correct to argue that the cognitive maps of large towns – York along with Beverley and Scarborough or Hull – were far more complex than those for the smaller populations and simpler layouts of a Knaresborough or a Bawtry. Such towns might well have been comprehended in a way in which the great urban centres were not. Yet there are other mental images and attitudes, both collective and personal, which seem to have commonly occurred in all towns. Take medieval street names – while some record occupational districts, the orientation of a street or an ecclesiastical building, others retain perhaps faint traces of a way of viewing parts of the town. For instance, archaeological and documentary research suggests that the name Silver Street at York and at other places rarely denotes a street of silversmiths, but there may be a hint that property rents here were high or higher than the property merited. Grape Lane (York or Whitby) is a later polite contraction of Grapcunt Lane, thought to denote a street where a brothel was located but might more simply suggest a dark back street where sexual encounters might take place. The trader who named his probably gimcrack

tenement in Bradford market place the Belle Bothe must surely have taken a pride in his property (BMC I: 146), or was it perhaps, like all of these examples, sardonic humour?

We should also be aware of the pride some individuals felt for their urban places of birth. This occurs in different ways. Horrox (1988) has noted the desire of some people to be remembered as having town origins or origins in a particular town, often inscribed on memorials. It is also noticeable that there are some changes in the nature of charitable bequests made in late medieval wills, one such being a care for the fabric of the town. This was viewed in a favourable light by the church, for as one York bidding prayer read: 'Also ye sal pray specially . . . for thaim that brigges and stretes makes and amendes' (Simmons 1879: 65). Bequests made to such purposes could be substantial – the £20 bequeathed in 1487 by John Carre, a York draper, 'to making of ways w^{t}in the fraunches of York' (SURTEES 45: 182), or the £40 and 10 marks bequeathed by Robert Holme of Hull for improving communications in and around the town (SURTEES 53: 26), a bequest paralleled by that of Thomas Brown a mercer for the repair of the roads into and out of Helmsley in 1441 (BIHR: vol. 2, fol. 25). We could add to this the bequests to maintain bridges such as that by Thomas Wath of Bawtry for the repair of Bawtry Bridge (BIHR vol. 2, fol. 29) or Thomas Husey, a merchant of Whitby who left twenty shillings for the fabric of Whitby Bridge in 1456 (BIHR vol. 2, fol. 337). Probably the clearest and the wealthiest expression of pride in urban origins occurs in the will of Thomas Rotherham, Archbishop of York, who died in 1500. Born in Rotherham, he had in later life founded and endowed the College of Jesus in his home town on the site of the house in which he was born. His will gives a fond account of his early upbringing in there.

It could be argued, of course, that all such bequests have an ulterior motive: they are to be regarded as pious works that would expunge former sin and ill deeds. In the will of Richard Pigot (1483), Serjeant at Law of York, there is an explicit statement to this effect:

Item to be disposed for that I have been occupied in the worlde, and taken men's money, and not done so effectually for it as I ought to have done, for ther soules, and all Cristen soules, in making of heigh ways, and othre gude dedes of charitee by discrecion of my saide executores C marc. (SURTEES 45: 285–6)

The point is, however, that there were many other works of charity that testators might have, and did, bequeath money towards. The upkeep of roads, the repair of bridges, the maintenance of buildings, coloured glass windows in churches or the founding of a *maison dieu* or chapel – behind all of these were probably motives of personal aggrandisement and fear of damnation, but surely another motive was the furtherance of trade by maintaining good communications – or civic pride, a genuine feeling for the urban environment and a wish to make a positive contribution towards it? It is by these means, through religious and municipal records and especially the buildings and spaces themselves, that we may come to some better understanding of the medieval urban subject.

CHAPTER FOUR

Liberties and Precincts

THE POWER EXERCISED BY elite social groups and urban institutions gave rise to subdivisions of authority within towns. This subdivision into liberties controlled by a specific group or institution can best be seen in the major urban centres. York presents a complex but easily understandable pattern of liberties. Within the city walls were the liberties of the Mayor and Citizens of York, St Peter's (the dean and chapter), the Castle (the monarch), St Leonard's Hospital and Davy Hall (the royal forester). Outside the walls to the northwest was the liberty of St Mary's Abbey (see Figure 4.1). It is also important to realise that while important liberties existed within towns, the liberties of some institutions extended well beyond town boundaries.

Such subdivision occurred in less complex forms elsewhere. At Scarborough the principal division was between the royal authority repre-

Figure 4.1 York's liberties

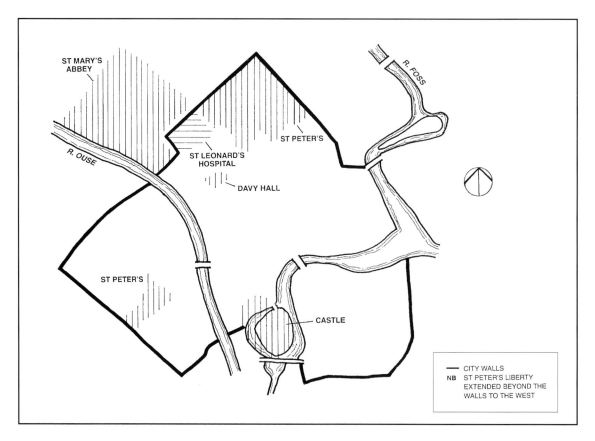

sented by the castle and the town, while at Beverley it was between the Archbishop of York's borough and the liberty of the collegiate church of St John. At Ripon there was a three-way division between the Archbishop of York's borough and manor, the liberty of the chapter and canons of the collegiate church of St Wilfred and the liberty of Fountains Abbey, although the latter did not impinge much on the town itself.

At some small seigneurial towns legal differences between agricultural tenants and burgesses might similarly be represented spatially. At Knaresborough agricultural tenants appear to have been located to the north at Bond End and burgesses to the south around the market place and castle. Similar spatial divisions may have existed in the Archbishop of York's borough of Otley where the burgesses probably lived along Boroughgate and the agricultural/manorial tenants at Bondgate. If this interpretation is correct then the same spatial separation occurred at some non-burghal towns also – Selby, for instance, has a Bondgate located to the north-west of the market place and Micklegate, in other words away from what would appear to have been the commercial centre of town, and the same is true of Snaith.

There were also religious and legal jurisdictions which created areas of authority outside the control of civic administrations. The most unusual of these (to the modern mind) was the sanctuary that some towns offered to miscreants – Beverley and Ripon, for example. At Beverley offenders on the run from the law could claim the right of sanctuary issuing from the shrine of St John of Beverley, an area of a league in all directions from the church door.

Boundaries were jealously guarded and were often marked out in some form, although little now remains. At York wall marks or posts known as stulpes were used, while stone crosses were a form of demarcation used at other places – Beverley, for example, where the boundary of sanctuary was marked by grith or sanctuary crosses.

The demarcation of territory occasionally gave rise to grander architectural expressions, such as St Peter's Gate, York, which provided the main entrance to Minster Close in St Peter's liberty where the court house was situated. The church at Ripon enclosed similar buildings once within a walled close with its own gatehouse. Most liberties had their own court houses and gaols, although little or nothing has survived. York, again, supplies the most substantial reminder in the gatehouse of St Mary's Abbey, part of a range of stone and timber-framed buildings which contained the court house, although only the rebuilt fifteenth-century gatehouse now stands.

The gatehouse of St Mary's Abbey introduces a related subject – the enclosed precincts of urban religious communities. A distinction might be made here. In some non-burghal towns such as Guisborough or Selby the abbey probably acted not only as the controlling authority, but also as an urbanising influence, the success of the town being firmly tied to the abbey. But in other places religious communities formed subdivisions, areas of autonomy closed off from the town and the sorts of jurisdiction mentioned above. St Mary's Abbey stood just outside the walls of York, having, as we have seen, its own liberty, but enclosing the precincts of the abbey itself with strong walls. Within these precincts was a church, built almost as a rival to the minster, together with claustral and other ranges that one would expect to find at any monastery. The walls of the city and the walls of the monastery almost touch at one point reinforcing the impression of extra-municipal jurisdiction, and we should remember that there were further monasteries and friaries at York forming further closed-off areas within the city, although none possessing the wide – and resented – liberties of St Mary's.

The same was true to a lesser extent at other large towns, although standing remains have rarely survived so well as at York. Beverley, Doncaster, Hedon, Hull, Pontefract and Scarborough – all attracted numbers of religious houses. So did prospering towns like Richmond and Yarm, although on a lesser scale. The areas enclosed were often large so that precinct walls must have made a considerable contribution to the townscape.

This is all that remains of one of the grith crosses at Beverley marking the boundary of sanctuary.

St Peter's Gate.

(opposite) York, stulpes at Petersgate. Although modern they mark the medieval boundary between the Liberty of St Peter and that of the Mayor and Citizens.

The walls of St Mary's Abbey, despite some reconstruction, remain the best surviving precinct walls of any urban medieval religious house in England. The fifteenth-century gateway to the left marks the northern entrance to the abbey in contrast to Bootham Bar, across the road, the entrance into the city.

Matters became more complicated still where the walled precincts of monasteries were divided within to create further areas of control or privacy. Usually this was a two-part division: an outer court where necessary dealings with the outside world took place and an inner court secluded from the world. Bridlington Priory is slightly unusual in that it probably did not have an encircling outer wall but a ditch. Within the outer court so formed was a space for worldly business, a space where the town's annual fairs were held, for example. Entrance to this outer court was controlled by a three-storey gatehouse constructed of brick and stone. Beyond the outer was an inner court around which were ranged the treasury, library, frater and dormitory (Earn-shaw 1976).

Some large abbeys like Bridlington had considerable influence over towns, supplying religious services as well as being a major source of trade and employment. Such differences, however, might be given meticulous spatial emphasis. At Selby, for example, the abbey provided a burial place within its walls for the laity, but there was a clear division even in death between the lay and clerical orders as a fifteenth century account roll of the abbey records when

A good deal patched with brick and stone, this is the gatehouse to the precinct at Bridlington Priory, an impressive structure dating from around 1388.

referring to 'a wall with a stone archway between the cemetery of the town and the cemetery of the monks' (Morrell 1867: 98). Similarly at Bridlington the canons' cemetery lay to the southeast of the priory church, the town cemetery to the northwest. This also corresponded with a division of the church: the nave had a parish altar located at the crossing, beyond which, in the chancel, was the high altar of the priory.

We have seen at Bridlington that the precinct was demarcated probably by a ditch, and we should realise that not all precincts had walls. Even where they did they were not always extensive structures soundly built, like those of the wealthy houses. At friaries in particular, since friars vowed to live in poverty, we ought to expect to find inferior buildings. To some extent this may have been true. The house of the Friars Minors at Scarborough, for instance, seems to have had precinct walls made of earth (YASRS 31: 81), possibly a ditch and rampart. But a generous patron might might make a difference. At Richmond Ralph Fitz Randal of Middleham created the Franciscan friary which subsequently enjoyed the patronage of the Earl of Richmond, Lord Scrope and Lord Raby. Only the chapel tower of the friary survives, but Harman's plan of Richmond suggests that as late as 1724 a masonry wall with a gateway remained standing.

The boundaries between different areas of authority, while real and having legal force, were in other senses unreal while they presented no hindrance to getting around the town. For the purposes of work or leisure people, for most of the time, must have crossed and recrossed notional boundaries with little thought. Nevertheless, the walls around the closes of great churches were real enough as were those around monastic precincts, often enclosing large areas of ground. What is more, the legal implications of some boundaries must have troubled burgesses from time to time. Beverley or Ripon – as towns of sanctuary – must have attracted a certain small criminal element, while those townsfolk who committed a wrong in one liberty might, with luck, evade punishment by crossing to another. Indeed, the reality of boundaries and liberties might be thrown into dramatic relief on occasion by violent disputes which arose between one liberty and another. One cause of continual conflict concerned the payment of tolls and trading rights. At Scarborough there were disputes between the burgesses and the Sheriff and garrison of the castle, as in the 1220s when the Sheriff took by force more than his due:

> When the butchers of Scarborough go through his bailiwick to slaughter cattle, the Sheriff's servants take the cattle away from them; part they kill, and part they retain by force, until they are ransomed. (YASRS 12: 122–3)

Nowhere, though, was such conflict more acrimonious than that between St Mary's Abbey and the City of York, a conflict based on the disputed borough and market rights of one liberty against the other. It reached its height perhaps in the mid-fourteenth century, when a siege of the abbey by York townspeople ensued accompanied by threats to crucify the abbot and his monks (VCH 1961: 68–9). Such incidents, if uncommon, were not all that rare, and must have made a striking impression on the popular imagination, serving to illustrate the vigour with which the privileges of liberties or precincts were to be defended.

CHAPTER FIVE

Sermons in Stones:
Form, Function and Symbolism in
Ecclesiastical Buildings

URBAN CHURCHES

MANY CENTURIES OF CHANGE and a secular society separate us from the religious ethos of the Middle Ages. If, however, we try to decouple the medieval church from notions of Christianity today and to reconstruct it in the light of the values of medieval England then we enter a world wholly unlike our own. The tolerance of other faiths characteristic of twentieth-century Christianity in England is one that could not have been supported at a time when to be a member of European society meant to be a Christian, and those who were not were marginalised. What is more, faith and religious life expressed themselves in varied ways, from the hermit living in seclusion and praying for the salvation of the world, to the merchant who used his wealth to endow a perpetual chantry where prayers for his soul might ease the way into heaven. The point is that to recognise the pervasiveness of medieval religion, the importance of its liturgy in shaping religious outlooks on the world, its extremes of asceticism and worldliness, dogma and popular cult, and with all its contradictions and points of intersection, is to put another perspective on the architecture of religion.

It is no coincidence, either, that the great medieval churches are to be found in formerly wealthy towns or that the cathedral and its bishop were the mark of a city. The great churches were both the product of and a powerful stimulus

to urbanisation, for, as the focal points of religious authority, administration, civic ceremony, even pilgrimage, they attracted people, business and money to towns. The cathedral or minster was the apotheosis of religion, glorified in a profusion of the arts from architecture and sculpture to painting and stained glass and music. While a wealthy patron might so elevate a rural church, nevertheless the greatest concentrations of religious art and architecture were to be found in the towns.

We do not have to look far to find such developments in Yorkshire. Several outstanding urban churches are located in the county, the greatest being the churches at Beverley, Ripon and York. This small group may differ in several ways, but they are unified by their architecture and their ecclesiastical functions. Although architecturally they display widely differing styles – their west fronts alone all being of different styles and periods to one another – yet the architecture also unites them, for all are of the same architectural form: cruciform designs with aisles and double-towered west fronts, the towers here being the terminations of the aisles. York and Ripon have towers above their crossings as well. At each church a central entrance between the towers on the west front creates great visual impact, but this is achieved in different ways. At Ripon the gabled centre and flanking towers appear as distinctly separate units, and their austerity of decoration together with the bold use of glass with little wall to window space seems strikingly modern; at York the towers with their image niches act like a rich frame for the great west window and its curvilinear tracery; at Beverley the emphasis is on verticality and elongation, but also on the unification of the front with image niches, panelling and a correspondence of detailing to create a towered entrance rather than an entrance with towers. Within their respective towns the decoration

and huge scale of these churches made such an impact that they rose above almost every other building. But this effect was not confined to the interior townscape, for outside, their high naves and towers – originally with spires at Ripon – were recognisable miles away as both religious and urban landmarks.

These three churches may be regarded as the finest cruciform churches of their type in the

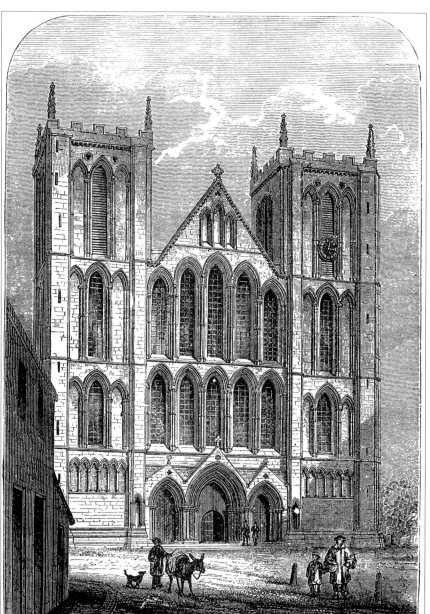

St Wilfred's, Ripon.

*York
Minster.*

*Image niches worked into the buttresses of the towers on
the west front of York Minister – 'In my Father's house
are many mansions' (John 14: 2).*

Beverley Minster.

county, but there are others. At Bridlington the Augustinian Priory church of St Mary seems to have been rebuilt to this same form largely in the fifteenth century, but leaving the perhaps thirteenth-century northwest tower in place, suggesting that this was also the form of the earlier church on the site. The Augustinian Priory at Guisborough contained a similar church which had been rebuilt in the late thirteenth–fourteenth century. At Old Malton the Gilbertine Priory church of St Mary was rebuilt in this way probably around the beginning of the thirteenth century. All of these churches were monastic churches and suffered during the Reformation, especially Guisborough. A further church also dedicated to St Mary and largely destroyed as a result of Civil War bombardment was the church at Scarborough.

The distribution of such churches within the county is interesting. While they occur at some of the largest urban centres – Scarborough or York – they can also be found at some of the smaller ones – Bridlington. Where they are not found, however, is in the rural areas of Yorkshire as village churches at the centres of large, even administratively important, parishes, and they are rare as the forms of rural monastic churches, Kirkham Priory being the exception, although this church lacks aisles and the western towers are curiously detached from the body of the church. The conclusion seems to be that as far as Yorkshire is concerned, the cruciform church with a double-towered western front and aisles was very much an urban phenomenon.

If the above can be regarded as the county's great churches, a number of other towns possessed both large and architecturally complex churches – Howden, Hull and Rotherham, for example. At St Peter's, Howden, a smaller-scale west front has been constructed containing the entrance to a cruciform church enlarged from the thirteenth to the fifteenth centuries by the bishops of Durham. The church had several striking features such as the chapter house and the east window and its gable was enriched with image niches and crocketing, but it is the crossing tower that makes maximum impact. Begun in perhaps the late fourteenth century it

was completed towards the end of the fifteenth when it had reached a height of 135 feet (41 metres), the highest church tower in Yorkshire and a powerful landmark in the largely flat landscape of Howdenshire.

Both Holy Trinity, Hull, and All Saints, Rotherham, are two of the largest parish churches in England, and like churches at other major towns in the county they tended to dominate their surroundings by their scale and architectural richness. Other churches in this category would include St George's at Doncaster or St Augustine's at Hedon, St Germanus, the abbey church, at Selby or All Saints at Wakefield. Again, it was not only in their urban locations where these churches loomed large, they were also landmarks – the Rotherham and Wakefield churches have the highest spires in Yorkshire. If the churches of some other important towns cannot be seen in this light, All Saints, Pontefract, or St Mary's, Tickhill, being two cases in point, then it is usually because some other important landmark building predominates – urban castles at the latter two places, for example.

The great churches and those in the major centres were also an expression of all that art could do to impress upon the laity the ineffable nature of the Almighty. The very form of many – in the shape of a cross – mirrors the Second Coming when 'shall appear the sign of the Son of man in heaven' (Matthew 24: 30). Interior space was of the utmost importance. The first thing that strikes the individual about the interior of, say, York Minster or Beverley Minster, is the height and the shaping and modelling of a great volume of space – the more striking when floors were not encumbered with pews or seats. This at one and the same time overawes and reduces man to his puny scale. As one moves around such interiors the whole iconography and symbolism of the detailing and its spatial organisation tend to reinforce this impression, from the seemingly infinite rhythms of the arcades, to rose windows symbolic of divine perfection and Christ the centre of the cosmos. This scale and complexity is relevant externally also, for as Christopher Wilson has observed:

Bridlington Priory from an early nineteenth-century engraving showing the badly mutilated church before later restoration. Remains of the thirteenth-century tower are to the left.

The remains of the priory church at Guisborough.
The bases of the piers to the nave arcade give some
idea of the scale of this church.

Externally, there was a still sharper contrast between the ideal quality of the house of God and the low, cramped, irregular and impermanent character of men's earthly dwellings. (1992: 10)

Lay authority was also represented within the church. With the exception to some extent of York Minster which was very much the clergy's church in York, all contained the tombs of powerful members of the laity. At Howden, for example, the Metham and Saltmarsh families are represented in effigy, their swords and mail proclaiming their knightly estate, and the same could be said of many other churches. One of the finest of all Yorkshire's medieval monuments, however, is the Percy Tomb in Beverley Minster. Dating from the early fourteenth century it is among the most lavish and confident pieces of medieval English sculpture and a pow-

St Peter's, Howden, a collegiate church belonging to the Bishops of Durham. After the dissolution of the college during the Reformation this large church suffered several centuries of neglect. The chancel roof collapsed and the chapter house, seen here on the left in this nineteenth-century print, lay in ruins also.

erful symbol of both lay and religious authority, linked as it once was to the shrine of St John of Beverley by the Percy Screen which carried the shrine. If these tombs represent aristocratic power, the lay managers of the town, the aldermen and mayors, tend to be represented in their parish churches, some parish churches in the large urban centres becoming more associated than others with an aldermanic group – All Saints, Pavement, at York, for example.

Indeed, churches like All Saints suggest a special relationship with such urban elites –

according to Raine (1955: 173) thirty-nine of the mayors of York were buried at this church. Significant, perhaps, is its position in the centre of a market place which had been at the heart of the Scandinavian town and which continued to be an important commercial centre of the later medieval city. It is only at York that we find such a concentration of churches, and one which may well indicate an early association of mercantile activity/municipal leadership with a particular church. There is evidence of this phenomenon at cities in other parts of the country – Winchester, for example (Keene 1985: 505–6) where the fraternity of the Kaledars were associated with St Mary's church in High Street, or Lincoln where excavation of St Mark's revealed a great deal of Anglo-Saxon funerary sculpture (Gilmour and Stocker 1986) whereas other church excavations produced little.[1]

Nowhere, however, is the symbolic power of great-church architecture in the expression of religious and lay authority more clearly visible than in the early history of St Mary's Abbey, York. To the northwest of York, just outside the walls, stood the church of St Olave built around 1050 by the Earl of Northumbria and dedicated to St Olaf, King of Norway. But the Norman count Alan Rufus founded a Benedictine abbey there, building a large Romanesque church dedicated to St Mary. Norman triumphed over Anglo-Scandinavian, and St Olave's with its Scandinavian and hence rebellious overtones became both literally and metaphorically overshadowed. Significantly, William II laid the foundation stone of the new church of St Mary in 1088.

The great church and large parish churches were not the only urban church types. What, indeed, characterises some medieval cities is a proliferation of small churches. York is a good example of this development with (depending whether one counts just within or without the walls) around forty churches. What is more, York's churches had mostly come into existence by or before the beginning of the twelfth century. This is perhaps significant, for as Morris (1989: Chapter 5) has argued this is before canonical control established a strict supervision of the

parish system. With few or no parish boundaries there were few reasons why churches should not be brought into being, and a variety of reasons why they should – private domestic chapels which developed into churches, neighbourhood churches, churches of guild foundation used as meeting places as much as places of worship, bridge, wall and gate chapels where protection for those on journeys might be asked or thanks for a safe journey might be given. If correct, this also has implications for urban origins, since one would expect to find larger proliferations of churches in towns which were well-established before the extension of canonical control to parishes in the twelfth century, and this would further suggest populations large enough to sustain large numbers of churches. The only place in Yorkshire that fits this bill is York, and it explains very well why other large centres of population – Beverley or Hull – did not possess the same large numbers of churches. While Beverley, for example, had a church of pre-Conquest origins and some urban characteristics, there is no evidence of a large population; Hull was a town developed from perhaps only the late twelfth century, initially by the monks of Meaux Abbey.

That said the smaller churches of York varied immensely in terms of size, architectural pretension and location. At one end of the spectrum is All Saints, Pavement, mentioned above, a church of pre-Conquest foundation sited in the Marketshire area of the city in an island position within the market place. By the sixteenth century it contained perhaps six chantries. Not only was it a favoured burial place of the mayors of York, but from time to time in the fifteenth century it was used for meetings of the council. Although altered a good deal in later centuries it retains the tower and superb stone lantern originally built in the late fifteenth century. At the other end of the spectrum is St Andrew's in St Andrewgate. Built in a relatively poor neighbourhood, St

Typical of many tomb effigies are those of the Metham and Saltmarsh families at Howden.

Not all effigies were of the aristocracy. This is the tomb slab of Thomas Jackson, 1529, merchant of Bedale, in St Gregory's. Jackson keeps company with the Fitzalans, Lords of Bedale, and other knightly effigies.

The Percy Tomb Canopy at Beverley Minister was exceptional, being one of the finest of medieval monuments. It is thought to have been worked for a female member of the Percy family.

Andrew's was probably typical of a number of churches relegated to side streets. Like All Saints, it too is of pre-Conquest foundation, but lacked a vicarage and was dependant for much of the fourteenth and fifteenth centuries on St Martin's, Coney Street. In 1586 it was united with St Saviour's parish. It has been constructed without aisles and had no tower or spire, but consisted of simply one small nave and chancel with probably a wooden bell turret.

In the thirteenth century there were further additions to the numbers of churches at the large towns in the form of friaries. The first friars began to arrive in England in the thirteenth century and by 1300 numbers of friaries had been established. Since the mission of the friars was to beg for alms and to preach the large towns provided them with their most concentrated market, and most friaries were, thus, urban religious houses. For the reasons given in Chapter 4 one might expect friaries to be humbly built, but many were not because of the largesse of wealthy patrons. Scarborough, for example, had three friaries, the churches of at least two being built of stone and in use by the inhabitants of Scarborough as well as the friars, although all three were said to be in extreme poverty at the time of their dissolution (VCH 1913: 276). The Franciscan Friary at York, however, was presumably more lavish, since it had been under the patronage of the crown from its foundation in about 1230. The house continued to enjoy royal favours and both Edward II and Edward III had resided there, preferring the friary to the accommodation offered by the castle. The parliament of 1322 was held in the friary church. Friaries suffered badly during the Reformation and little is known about their churches, although there is little reason to suppose that they were different in major ways from other churches judging from scanty remains in the county at Richmond. Their importance lies more in the fact that they provided yet another phalanx of churches.

No other town in Yorkshire could match York for its numbers of churches, whether parish churches or monastic churches, but, having said that, most towns possessed more than one and some possessed several. Only the populations of small towns like Bedale, Otley or Sherburn-in-Elmet found a single church sufficient to cater for their religious needs. However, the churches at small towns probably illustrate a further factor in church provision: the powerful individual. All these and other such places tended to be in the hands of a single seigneur who might well have had the power to lay down religious provision, limiting it to immediate needs. At large towns, however, a plurality of authority may have been a determining factor in the often prolific numbers of churches.

By the fourteenth century the larger regional centres usually had a parish church and one or more separate chapels, while some large towns might contain more than one parish. Ripon illustrates the point well. St Wilfred's was the principal church, but there was a further parish church of All Hallows. There were also a number of chapels or chantries – the Chantry of Our Lady near to St Wilfred's but separate from it, the Chapel called the 'Lady Churche in Stamergate', the chapels at the Hospital of St Anne and the Hospital of St John the Baptist, and on the edge of town was the chapel of the Hospital of Mary Magdalene. Further examples can be found around the county. At Malton the parish church was the Gilbertine Priory church at Old Malton, while New Malton was served by the Chapels of St Leonard and St Michael together with the Chantry of St John, the latter possibly a bridge chapel since it bore the obligation to repair the bridge and the highway near it. There was also a chapel in the castle. Wakefield possessed its parish church of All Saints in the market place; within a quarter of a mile were the Chantry of St Mary the Virgin on the bridge and the Chapel of Mary Magdalene; within a mile of the parish church at the town ends were the Chapel of St John and the Chantry of St Swithun. At Selby, whose townscape was dominated by the great monastic church of St Germanus, there was in addition the Chapel of St Genevieve in Gowthorp and probably a further chapel near the monastic church ('venellam quae ducit a via de Mikelgate usque ad parvam ecclesiam in Seleby' – YASRS 10: 137). Even some small towns – like Tadcaster

Although altered over the centuries, All Saints, Pavement, York, nevertheless preserves its tower of about 1500 with a lantern termination.

St Andrew's, York, was made redundant in the sixteenth century along with a number of other small churches, but has survived demolition to be partially rebuilt today. It nevertheless retains its earlier form.

The tower of the friary church at Richmond.

– might have more than one church. St Mary's was the parish church of Tadcaster, but there was also the Chantry of St John the Baptist. This was possibly a bridge chapel, but it was more likely to have been a chapel on the far side of the bridge from the church and across the River Wharfe because 'there is a great water betwen the sayd parysshe and the chauntery, so that when it cresit with waters, the people there cannot come to the sayd parysshe churche' (SURTEES 92: 225).

However, documents suggest that not all chapels and chantries were used solely for the purposes they had been founded, usually to provide perpetual devotion on behalf of the souls of their founders. While many were private chantries, some came to be used as overflow chapels, probably when large numbers of people were in town who would require religious services. At Ripon the chantry of Our Lady had been founded in 1314 near to St Wilfred's by the Archbishop of York, although according to Leyland it was a rebuilding of the 'old Abbay of Ripon' (Toulmin-Smith 1907: 80). While the primary purpose of its priest was to pray for the soul of the archbishop, he was also 'to mynystre sacrementes in tyme of nede', a phrase often used in the Reformation surveys of churches but usually applied to chantries *within* churches (SURTEES 92: 355). Here one wonders whether the chantry across from the church was to be pressed into use when large numbers of people were in town.

This sort of development could be found elsewhere. The provision of services for those passing through towns was an important function of some chantries. Thus the chantry of Our Lady in the church at Boroughbridge also catered 'for the ease of strangers reparynge through the same being one thoroughffare towne of the Kinges strete ledyng from London to Karliel and Barwyke' (SURTEES 92: 264). Similarly at Doncaster the chantry of St Nicholas within the parish church of St George was said to provide an additional altar 'as well for th'inhabitaunts of the sayd towne as other strangers passing thrugh the same' (SURTEES 91: 175).

Both of these towns were on the Great North Road, as the extract concerning Boroughbridge emphasises. There may well have been further such arrangements at other towns along the route – Northallerton, perhaps – but evidence is hard to come by. On some of the east–west routes, especially those connecting regional centres and important markets, similar provisions seem to have been in operation by the late Middle Ages, if not before. Skipton stands on the old highway to Kendal, and probably attracted a good deal of through traffic as well as being the site of regular cattle markets. At Skipton church the chantry of the Rood provided an additional early morning mass 'for the purpose

that as well the inhabitants of the said towne, Kendalmen and strangers may here the same' (SURTEES 92: 243). Markets, fairs, festivals, pilgrimage – the arterial routes across the country all brought crowds into towns, and chantry chapels seem to have been one means of coping with the religious demand.

A related aspect of the provision of chapels was their use for isolating the victims of plague while at the same time providing a place where the afflicted could hear mass and receive the sacrament. This was the function of the chapel in Stammergate, Ripon. The same was true of the chapel of St Mary Magdalene at Doncaster, possibly once the parish church but superseded by St George's. At Wakefield the chapels of St Mary Magdalene and St Swithun provided this refuge, and a clear statement of function survives relating to the latter:

> The necessitie is to say masse and dyvyne service in the same in tyme of plages for the seck people thither resortinge that the rest of the parochians may com to ther paroch church withowt danger of the infection of the seeke. (SURTEES 92: 315)

This was a development that could have taken place only after 1348.

Consideration should also be given to the origins of urban parish or principal churches. Excluding York, the origins of the churches of thirty-five towns can be classified with some certainty as being pre- or post-Conquest: twenty appear to have pre-Conquest origins; fifteen have post-Conquest origins. The majority of the post-Conquest churches were built in the eleventh and twelfth centuries. Just under half the urban churches were being founded, therefore, in the centuries when the places in which they were built were receiving confirmation of their urban status. At the same time the pre-Conquest churches were being rebuilt or extended. This mirrors urban growth in the county, but one should be careful not to push this conclusion too far since it is also a response to developing architectural styles and probably population growth which affected the whole of both urban and rural England. More interesting is the number of pre-Conquest churches, suggesting that over half the county's towns had a pre-urban nucleus probably well defined by a church, and lending further weight to the argument advanced in Chapter 3 that the urbanisation of the county had begun before the Conquest.

A remodelling of many of these churches occurred in the fifteenth century. This raises Postan's question, 'What do the Perpendicular churches prove?' (1973: 46), an issue recently re-examined by Morris (1989: Chapter 9). But this cannot be looked at in isolation for it raises one of the longest running debates in medieval urban history and one that continues to divide historians: was there, and when exactly was there, a late medieval urban decline? The stages in this debate have been well catalogued by Palliser (1988). It is sufficient to say here that some historians, perhaps the majority, have accepted that an urban decline or declines occurred in the period between the mid-fourteenth century and the sixteenth century; other historians, notably A. R. Bridbury (1975, 1981), have argued that such decline is a misinterpretation.

If we accept that a decline occurred in the fifteenth century, the architectural evidence of the Perpendicular churches would seem to contradict this. From St John the Baptist, Halifax, to St Mary's, Thirsk, from the west front of Beverley Minster to All Saints, Rotherham, fine Perpendicular urban churches can be found in most parts of Yorkshire and form the only group of churches which preserve a certain unity or purity of architectural style. This is in opposition to Postan's assertion that the Perpendicular churches show a lack of unity, many of them being started but not finished for years because of financial problems. Moreover, several Yorkshire urban churches of the fifteenth century are outstanding. Of the great churches the west front of Beverley Minster has been mentioned above, but some smaller churches, such as St Mary's, Thirsk, are no less impressive in their way, not to mention Holy Trinity, Hull, and All Saints, Rotherham.

In considering churches like these, one is bound to agree with Morris (1989) whose general conclusion on the subject is that Perpendicular churches tend to indicate the continuing – indeed strengthening – centrality of the parish church in the lives of parishioners. However, one is also seduced by Postan's warning that activities such as church-building should not be used in an oversimplified way as proof of periods of economic expansion. The problem with this is that it rebounds on Postan. His general point is that there is not necessarily a connection between architectural activity and the economy. The most prosperous periods, he argues, do not always give rise to a proliferation of fine buildings such as the Perpendicular churches. But he then suggests that a slump in church-building between 1425 and 1475 indicates recession. If one statement is false then the other one must be: he cannot have it both ways.

There is nevertheless some virtue in the argument if it is not pushed too far. Closer scrutiny of Yorkshire's urban churches, for example, points up the varied nature of the funding and motivation of church-builders and remodellers at this time. In other words there is no mono-causal explanation of their creation. Some forty-three medieval urban churches or chapels outside of York remain intact in the county. Of these, perhaps twenty-four have been substantially remodelled or rebuilt between about 1380 and 1530, but from a variety of causes.

One seemingly obvious cause of the rebuilding of some West Yorkshire churches is the shifting economic base and relocation of the clothing industry in the late Middle Ages from the old centres of York and Beverley in the east to expanding centres of production in the west. Bradford, Halifax, Leeds and Wakefield all gained enlarged and rebuilt churches during the course of the fifteenth century, and it is probably correct to say that this ensued from the prosperity brought about by industrial endeavour. It is equally clear that other factors were also at work. Take Halifax – here was one of the new urban centres of the clothing industry with perhaps the largest cloth hall in the west of the county to bear witness to this success, yet the enlargement of the church was a result as

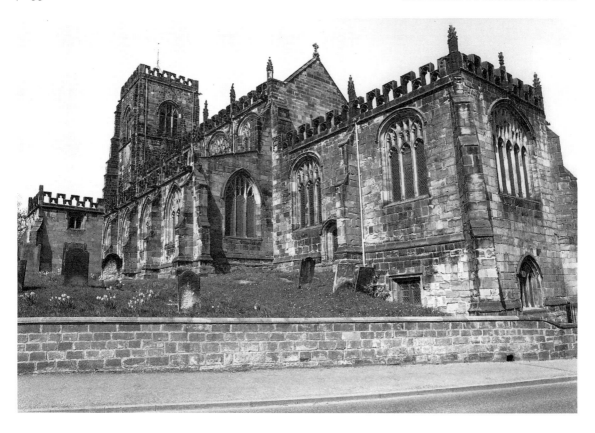

St Mary's Thirsk.

much of gentry and clerical bequests to its fabric as it was to those of clothiers and other tradesmen, although this influence was also important (Hanson 1917).

A contrasting example is Hedon which historians would agree was a declining town by the fifteenth century, and by the beginning of the sixteenth at least two of the town's chapels had been demolished as a result. Nevertheless, the principal chapel, St Augustine, acquired a new crossing tower, an enlarged vestry and a new east window; along with Patrington, it was one of the finest churches in Holderness. Between perhaps 1427 and 1437 the tower was under construction and was paid for both by a levy on the burgesses and by individual donations, some of them quite substantial (Boyle 1895: 121–2). In other parts of the county the impetus behind

such impressive Perpendicular churches as All Saints, Rotherham, or St Mary's, Thirsk, was the wealthy patron or the religious house – Rufford Abbey and Archbishop Thomas Rotherham at Rotherham, Robert Thresk at Thirsk.

Nor does the evidence of urban church-building and remodelling support either Postan's assertion that few churches were built between 1425 and 1475 or Dobson's (1977) contention that the century between 1450 and 1550 was one in which many churches were removed and the rate of building slowed. To begin with the evidence is far too tenuous to able to say with precision, and then what evidence does exist tends to suggest a far more complex picture of development than simply a decline: the position in Hedon with regard to churches demonstrates this. As far as the removal of churches in towns is concerned, this was perhaps more a consequence of too high a density of provision in the tenth and eleventh centuries in some towns rather than later economic decline. At York, for

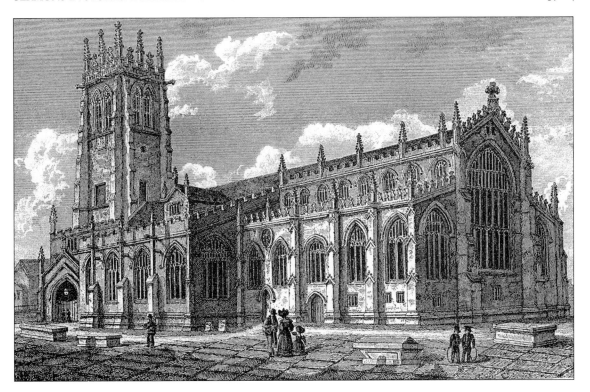

St John's, Halifax.

instance, the first losses occurred in the four-teenth rather than the fifteenth century.

Moreover, the rebuilding of urban churches at several of the county's towns continued throughout the fifteenth century and into the next, right up to the Reformation. Thus, while the rebuilding of Thirsk church may have been begun around 1430, there was a prolongued building campaign probably not at an end until the beginning of the sixteenth century. Similarly, the rebuilding of All Saints, Rotherham, was begun around 1409 with the tower, interior detailing being carried out in the mid-fifteenth century, but it was not completed until late in the century, the Chapel of Jesus being added by Thomas Rotherham around 1480. The same development can be seen at some of the expanding towns in the west of Yorkshire – the great tower of St John's, Halifax, was not completed until around 1482 and interior remodelling seems to have continued in the early years of the sixteenth century. While the body of the church at neighbouring Bradford was remodelled in probably the mid-fifteenth century, the

tower was not rebuilt until 1507–8. At York we have one of the latest of all late medieval urban church rebuildings in St Michael le Belfry, completed in 1537.

What then *do* the Perpendicular churches prove? Whether one accepts that there was an urban decline in the late Middle Ages, or whether one agrees with Bridbury that we should 'see the later Middle Ages in perspective, as a period of tremendous advance not only constitutionally but also in social and economic affairs' (1975: 108), one thing becomes clear: church building in Yorkshire towns during the fifteenth and early sixteenth centuries cannot be used in support of either position. If the urban churches of the county support any view then it is that of Susan Reynolds who has suggested that local factors must always be taken into account, making it 'essential to study each town against a background of the general demographic and economic trends' (1977: 146).

CHANTRIES AND CHAPELS

A further development taking place from perhaps the fourteenth century and continuing until the Reformation was the creation of perpetual chantry chapels within churches or as separate buildings, sometimes standing on bridges. There are several reasons for the growth in the numbers of chapels. Some were doctrinal, such as the growing acceptance of Purgatory as a place of waiting separate from Hell given definition at the Council of Lyon in 1274; chantries with their chantry priests saying masses for the soul of the departed might speed its release from Purgatory. Other reasons were perhaps connected more with a desire among some sections of the laity to gain a measure of control in church matters, an end which the endowment of chantries might effect. As Dobson (1992) has shown, around 140 chantries were founded in York churches by the end of the fifteenth century, probably a larger number than in any other provincial English city. The mayor and corporation were sometimes directly engaged in administering the finances of these chantries which had often been endowed by the York commercial elite. There were, however, chantries founded by or associated with craft and religious or fraternal guilds – still in York, St Crux church had its Butchers' Chapel (Raine 1955: 192) and at Holy Trinity (also known as Christ's Church), King's Court, the other church serving Shambles, butchers made requests to be buried in the Chapel of the Crucifixion (Raine 1955: 43). The same pattern can be found in other towns. At Wakefield the chapel of St Mary Magdalene was 'the fundacion of the well disposed parochians' (SURTEES 92: 314), at Pontefract the chantry of St Roch in the parish church was 'nominate by the maior and his brethren . . . to th'entente to be prayed for and ther ancetors' (SURTEES 92: 273), while at St Mary's, Hull, the altar of St Anne was endowed by Jeffrey Thuriscresse – not directly but by leaving property to be administered on the clergy's behalf by the mayor and commonalty. But if lay participation in church matters was one motive for the founding of chapels, it was not the only one and it did not mean that the

clergy lost control. Many chantries, indeed, continued to be founded by priests and other clerics – a late foundation, for example, is the Rokeby Chapel at Halifax parish church founded by Archbishop William Rokeby and built sometime between 1521 and 1533.

ARCHITECTURAL PERSPECTIVES

Considering the county's urban churches from an architectural perspective, one is struck by the wide variety of architectural expression from the eleventh century onwards. Equally as striking is the amount of rebuilding that has taken place at most churches – great or small – the result being that there are few pure examples of a particular architectural style and only some of the Perpendicular churches having any unity as a group. Building, rebuilding, enlargement and enrichment, the addition of aisles, clerestories and towers – all these are part of a process that seems to have continued until the beginning of the sixteenth century.

One might have expected the greater resources available to the builders of the great churches to have produced unified designs but this has not happened. Long and varied campaigns of building at York or Beverley, for example, have produced churches that can be read almost like a textbook on Gothic architectural styles. But having said that, stylistic changes of direction at some churches have been incorporated in harmonious ways with earlier work to produce buildings that present no glaring discontinuities. The decorated centre of the west front of York Minster is complemented by the Perpendicular towers that frame it while the towers on the west front of Beverley Minster have been combined with the earlier base from which they rise with a finesse seldom found at other great churches. Not all of the county's urban great churches, however, can be seen in this light. The parish church of Malton, the Priory Church of St Mary, had a large Perpendicular window brutally inserted as part of the rebuilding by Prior Roger Bolton around 1510 and remains completely at odds with the late

The Holdsworth chapel at St John the Baptist, Halifax, is an unusual double chantry chapel founded by John Holdsworth (d. 1497) but not built until 1521–36. Notice how the buttresses impale the gargoyles.

Romanesque and Transitional work that flanks it. A similar mismatch occurs at Bridlington.

The reasons for the rebuilding of so many urban churches in the county are varied and range from disasters such as fires or collapses to changes in ritual or the need for greater accommodation as urban populations rose. The patronage of prelates and seigneurs together with endowments of mercantile wealth ensured that the great urban churches received the attentions of the best masons as well as stylistic and constructional innovation that only the designers employed by such patrons could provide. If the best of the county's great churches are to be found in the large towns, it is precisely because they were a product of an urban culture that interlocked with national, or even international, cultural developments as well as local ones. For this reason one cannot wholly agree

with the arguments of some architectural historians, most recently Wilson (1994: 216), when they suggest that a process of 'deregionalisation' had begun in the fifteenth century, since this assumes the existence of identifiable regional styles at great-church level. While the work of local masons/designers is evident in several great urban churches it displays design that was nevertheless in touch with national trends – personal interpretations rather than regionalism.

An often quoted example of metropolitan influence on regional traditions is the work of

*St Michael le Belfry. Rebuilt between 1525 and 1537
on the eve of the Reformation, this fine York church
represents probably the last rebuilding of an urban
church in Yorkshire in a late Gothic style.*

William Colchester, a mason of Westminster
Abbey sent by Henry IV to work at York Minster
in 1407. His work there should be seen as not so
much the intrusion of a southern style (Harvey
1977: 167), but as innovation, the beginnings of
a new style which was to develop in different
ways in the hands of different designers in different parts of the country, although the arrival
in York of this new way of working together with
a mason from London may have been viewed
with suspicion and certainly with jealousy at the
time.

It might be argued that, on the contrary, the
great urban churches never represented any
strong regional tradition of architecture but were
the work of highly skilled masons and designers
whose numbers were small in any generation
and who were carrying out work on behalf of
patrons whose interests spanned England or
France. They themselves were located in a particular county or possibly moved around a
somewhat larger area giving personal definition
to styles we now classify as Early English,
Decorated or Perpendicular – categories which
are no more than the typologies constructed by
Rickman at the beginning of the nineteenth
century. What we see in the great urban churches,
therefore, is not regionalism, but the work of
individuals working in a particular part of the
country within a developing architectural aesthetic, of which some were at the forefront while

St Mary's Priory Church, Malton. Central window inserted about 1510. The loss of the north, left-hand, tower occurred post-Reformation.

others followed. Their work is no more a regional interpretation of Gothic than John Carr's work could be called a regional interpretation of Palladianism.

It is not only the great churches at places like York or Beverley where architectural excellence and individuality can be found. The churches at several of the large towns display little regionality in their appearance other than the use of local materials. Churches at Hedon, Hull, Rotherham, Wakefield and the ruined All Saints, Pontefract, if remodelled in the fifteenth century, all contain fine work of different periods, including at Pontefract a double-helix staircase in the tower – scarcely the work of a provincial mason set in his ways.

If regionalism can be found, then it is among the churches of the smaller towns, places which had more in common with villages. Ironically, it is at the period when architectural historians begin to argue in favour of the disappearance of regionalism that one of the larger regional groups is identifiable – the Pennine Perpendicular churches. These are characterised by their long and often low naves contrasting with a tall western tower, some having square-headed windows, a feature of late examples. St Peter's, Bradford, or Holy Trinity, Skipton, belong to this group, and a more complex working of the form is St John's at Halifax, already mentioned.

Many churches in the west of the county were rebuilt in this way during the fifteenth and early sixteenth centuries, and some can be found in more easterly parts of the old West Riding such as Tadcaster. They are much less in evidence in the southeast and east of the county. This can perhaps be accounted for through the working practices of two or three generations of masons adapting Perpendicular to the simpler demands of the small town and village, the large number of remodellings being a reflection of rising prosperity brought about by the textile industry, although with the reservations noted above. However, on account of this thorough rebuilding it is now difficult to say whether or not a similar regionality of style would have been observable in the churches of earlier periods. The result is a more or less standardised form that could be

elaborated as occasion demanded. Details and features could be copied or reworked, and probably the same families of masons were responsible for a number of churches. The western tower at St John's, Halifax, for example, may well have been the model for the tower at the neighbouring St Peter's, Bradford, for although the Bradford tower is squatter it has the same weak termination to the tops of its buttresses and similar double belfry openings.

In the north of the county different forces were perhaps at work. Some churches there have western towers that appear almost as if they could have been used for defence. The clearest example is the tower of St Gregory's, Bedale, the lower stages of which are strongly buttressed, while internally there is a heated room with a garderobe above a vaulted ground floor, the connecting staircase having once had a portcullis. Dating from the first half of the fourteenth century, the implication seems to be that it could be used as a refuge from bands of Scottish raiders, a real threat in this part of the county after Bannockburn. The tower of the church at Thirsk similarly looks as though it were intended as a defensive tower, although supposedly built in the fifteenth century as noted above. Nevertheless, while the tower shares exaggerated buttressing with the porch and has a pierced battlemented top, the generally austere construction is at odds with the delicacy of much of the other fifteenth-century work, and is perhaps earlier work with later fenestration and a new top.

If defence were the purpose of these towers – as it certainly seems to have been at Bedale – one might ask, 'Defence of whom or what?' It could surely not have been the defence of parishioners, since they could not have fitted into such small spaces. Moreover, from what documentary evidence there is, it would appear that parishioners sought sanctuary within the *body* of the church in times of violence. Thus, when the Scottish army marched into Ripon in 1318 they plundered the town, 'and from those who entered the mother church and defended it . . . they exacted one thousand marks instead of burning the town itself' (Maxwell 1913: 221).

All Saints, Pontefract. Civil War bombardment did the damage here, and since the centre of the town had relocated further west with a chapel in the market place, the now isolated church was never restored.

Holy Trinity, Skipton.

The tower of St Gregory's, Bedale – notice the stair turret to the right of the clock.

The tower of St Mary's, Thirsk. Possibly originally a defensive tower like that at Bedale.

Small defended rooms like that in the church tower of St Gregory's at Bedale were probably intended for the defence of the priest – and not only the priest but also relics, church plate or other valuables.

These churches might properly be said to show regional influences since they have been built within a tradition of workmanship or are a response to social and economic factors peculiar to some parts of the county. What they tend to point up is the difference between the major urban centres and the small towns. Practical factors would have to be taken into account in explaining why this should be – like village churches, they served smaller and less wealthy populations, for instance. However, some large churches were built at some of the small towns. Halifax and Leeds were new and growing centres of the clothing industry in the fifteenth century. While they remained small towns, they were nevertheless centres of large parishes and thus they required large churches. Yet although St John's, Halifax, and St Peter's, Leeds, are striking churches, they could hardly be considered dazzling examples of late Gothic styles. The explanation of this probably has something to do with factors more difficult to assess but which suggest that the clergy and congregations of small town churches were not a part of that mainstream urban culture which resulted in sophisticated architectural expression in the major centres. In this respect, the prelate, seigneur or religious house – people or administrations in touch with the culture of cities – might transform a small town or village church by their donation or endowment, and sometimes spectacularly so. The Augustinian Priory church of St Mary had this effect on Bridlington, while it was the Archbishop of York and other local connections with the city that produced perhaps the finest decorated parish church in England at Patrington before the Black Death brought building there to an end in 1349. Bereft of such influences, the churches of small towns were more a part of the vernacular traditions of the region.

OTHER ECCLESIASTICAL BUILDINGS

The church was also the principal provider of what we would today call social welfare. The care of the sick, for example, was one of the corporal works of mercy. Along with this the church ministered to the poor, the infirm and the dying, and had a duty to perform charitable works generally. In order to carry out such a mission, specialised buildings were required, usually in the shape of the hospital. However, the word hospital needs some clarification in view of the meanings that it has taken on in modern times, and there are several other aspects of the medieval hospital that would benefit from a more careful scrutiny.

Medieval hospitals were institutions quite distinct from modern notions of medical provision. To begin with we need to differentiate between religious hospitals and the medieval medical callings – the *medici* or physicians and surgeons and apothecaries, together with the humbler practitioners such as bone-setters. The treatment of the sick in hospital infirmaries was based on the easing of pain and the adjustment of the sick to their circumstances rather than on attempting a physical cure and thus interfering with the natural world and the will of God. Some of the sick, those suffering from horrible contagious diseases such as leprosy, might live in hospitals located on the edge or outside of the town and became marginalised. The problem here was not that medieval medicine could not cure such diseases – which it could not – but that the diseases themselves might have been the result of carnal excesses and should not be interfered with beyond the bounds of Christian charity. Another feature of some large hospitals was the presence of children – foundlings and orphans. As one historian has observed, both the abandonment of children and infanticide led to hospices in certain cities receiving 'the new mission of providing an alternative to infanticide', a serious crime since 'it barred access to heaven for all eternity to a child who died unbaptised' (Klapisch-Zuber 1990: 304). We can add to these concerns the sheltering of the poor and the duty of some hospitals to provide

The interior of St Gregory's, Bedale, is typical of many small urban churches, and in its intimate scale little different from large village churches.

hospitality for travellers, especially poor pilgrims. In other words, the proprietors of hospitals targeted the relief of specific forms of poverty. It is also true to say that by the fifteenth century, the lay foundation of hospitals had become a popular work of charity among the wealthy.

Taking the above into account, we can better distinguish between hospitals which were small institutions caring for a few sick or poor men or women and large, complex institutions with an array of specialised buildings. The largest in the county was St Leonard's Hospital at York, of which the chapel and part of the infirmary survives. Documents, however, list many buildings within the hospital precinct next to St Mary's Abbey – an infirmary, orphanage, domestic offices, master's house, hall, cloister and church with tower (VCH 1913: 336–43). The hospital expanded to house 206 poor and sick people, and there were also between forty and sixty

It is mostly at the regional urban centres with greater populations that larger church interiors are found as at All Saints, Wakefield.

children. They were tended by thirteen brothers, eight sisters, two schoolmasters and four priests, all supervised by a master. Only a small part of the hospital survived dissolution in 1540. Indeed, the Reformation dealt a severe blow to hospitals throughout the county and little remains – none entirely, since the ones that were allowed to remain were usually rebuilt in the eighteenth or nineteenth centuries. Yet the majority of towns possessed hospitals and the major urban centres might have had several, sometimes with specific missions – the Hospital of St Giles at Beverley, for example, made provision for the shelter of women.

Great churches were also found at urban monasteries. This is the interior of the priory church at Bridlington. The church was part-demolished at the Reformation and only the nave survives. This nevertheless gives an impression of the scale and fineness of the work. The nave was used as the town church; beyond (the demolished transepts, crossing and chancel) was used as the monastic church.

A town such as Beverley or Hull illustrates the provision of hospitals within a more complex urban environment where both large and small were to be found. At Hull, for instance, the largest hospital appears to have been the Hospital of St Michael situated next to the Carthusian monastery and later known as the Charterhouse Hospital. It stood in one and a half acres of grounds, the foundation of the immensely wealthy Michael de la Pole around 1394, and was to cater for thirteen poor men and thirteen poor women. But there were others – Gregg's Hospital, Riplingham's Hospital, Selby's Hospital, Trinity Hospital and Trinity House Hospital. The latter, founded in 1441 by the Guild of Holy Trinity, arose from Hull's position as a port, since its mission was to provide for thirteen people who had fallen into poverty through misadventure on the sea.

A detailed study of the above hospitals together with hospitals in other towns would show that many were intended for the occupation of thirteen poor people (a reflection of Christ and the Apostles). Many, perhaps the majority, were founded by rich laity usually with some instructions for the inmates to pray for the souls of the founders and their families. Numbers of these smaller hospitals, usually little more than almshouses, were known as *maisons dieu*. They existed in quite large numbers, especially in the major urban centres – York had over twenty. They might range from timber or stone buildings

The cellar of the infirmary at St Leonard's Hospital, York, where the high quality of the masons' work survives. This reflects the hospital's position among the largest and wealthiest hospitals in the country.

incorporating a chapel to rows of two or three cottages built or converted from a larger dwelling to house poor widows or old men. In St Andrewgate, York, for example, there was the *maison dieu* founded by Cecilia Plater in perhaps the fourteenth century. This was a women's *maison dieu* to which Leonard Shaw of York in 1532 left three shillings for 'the pore women in the beade house of St Andrewgate . . . and to the reparacion of the chapell there 4s-4d' (Raine 1955: 57). This was perhaps a moderately sized establishment having its own chapel. So was Craven's Maison Dieu near Layerthorpe Bridge, York, where a stone house had been converted by John Craven, a mayor of York, to accommodate thirteen poor persons. From his estate they were to be paid '3d a week to each of twelve poor persons and 4d a week to the thirteenth who says prayers evening and morning' (Raine 1955: 99).

It would be a mistake, however, to imagine that all hospitals or *maisons dieu* were well run and well maintained. The visitations of bishops and others show widespread malpractice, the cheating of the poor and rundown buildings. Not all were even fully occupied and some seem to have fallen out of use before the Reformation. At Northallerton, for example, the Bishop of Durham had founded the Hospital of St James to the south of the town in the twelfth century to cater for thirteen sick and thirteen poor. Yet by the mid-fourteenth century it had fallen into decay and by 1379 had only three infirm persons lodged there (VCH 1913: 315–17). The same could be said of many leper hospitals as the incidence of leprosy began to decline in the late Middle Ages.

Leper hospitals were usually located outside the town, and for this reason they will be dealt with more fully in Chapter 9. But this does raise the question of location. In the large urban centres it is easier to comment on where hospitals were not located – it would be a rarity to find them around the market place. That being said, however, they occupied almost any other position from prominent streets through the town to sites next to monastic precincts, churches, bridges, bars or on the edge of or outside of town – at Pontefract the Hospital of St Nicholas

stood on the castle ditch. In other words, there seems to have been no attempt to hide away the poor and sick in poor quarters of the town or behind the frontage buildings of main streets. Where hospitals were located outside of town this would appear to have been for the purposes of isolation or lack of suitable space within the town.

If hospitals were once widespread, being built at many towns and in some numbers at large towns, they have now largely disappeared for the reasons given above. This means that it is difficult to make much comment on them from the point of view of either their plan or architectural detail, and related matters also are difficult to speculate about – was there, for instance, a significant difference between the urban hospitals and rurally located hospitals? What remains tells us little, although it is probably true to say that the *maison dieu* built as a row of cottages or converted from other types of property was perhaps more of an urban phenomenon. It is certainly true to say that in Yorkshire there were greater numbers of hospitals in towns. This can be accounted for in a variety of ways – larger populations at the major urban centres, hence larger numbers of poor or sick; a concentration of mercantile wealth and property that might be used to endow and supply hospitals; the attraction of numbers of poor travellers to towns and the greater need for hospitality; the greater likelihood of epidemic diseases among concentrated yet mobile urban populations.

In terms of their plan we know both from archaeological excavation and documents that a minimum requirement was a range to shelter the inmates and that in more elaborate examples infirmaries, chapels and wardens' or masters' houses were included, the complex sometimes being enclosed by a wall or ditch. Occasionally evidence of a gatehouse or similar building emerges as at the Hospital of St Mary Magdalene at Bawtry where a gatehouse is listed among several other buildings which included the master's house, stables, barn and dovecot besides the usual chapel and infirmary buildings (Peck 1813: 21). At St James's Hospital near Northallerton there was a 'Great House' together

This building in Kirkgate, Knaresborough, is the rare survival of a small-town hospital or maison dieu, although converted to shops in the nineteenth century.

Only at the rear do we see something of its earlier
origins.

with other buildings and by the gate a hospice where poor beggars too infirm to be turned away might be given shelter for the night (VCH 1913: 315–17). This hospital, like many others, also had its own cemetery. Architecturally, these buildings might range from stone-built complexes with some decorative detail as the remains at St Leonard's Hospital, York, indicate, to simple timber-framed rows.

Finally, although I have stressed the dearth of standing remains as far as hospitals are concerned, fortunately at Ripon the chapel of St Anne's Hospital survives and a record was made of the complete building before its part demolition in 1869. It appears to have consisted of a low stone-built range of a single storey. This contained a small chapel at the western end and a main hall running from it. Presumably the hall was laid out like a dormitory with either beds or cubicles. It would appear to have been founded in the early fifteenth century to provide shelter for four men and four women and was supervised by a chaplain. Unusually it was not endowed but relied on requests for alms. It also contained two common beds that could be used by 'every lone travelling man that hath noe spending and there he may be cared one day and one night in fulfilling of the seaven workes of mercy' (VCH 1913: 329)

It is worth including a note on schools at this point. Although they were not religious buildings, it is relevant to consider them here since the church was the guardian and disseminator of knowledge. Education was a further way in which the church strengthened and maintained its authority. Whether children were educated privately by a tutor in the aristocratic household or at a public grammar school, the church usually supplied the teaching and regulated what was taught. Schools could be found in all the major urban centres of Yorkshire and in small towns as well, but few have survived in their original state. At York, grammar schools stood on the southwest side of the minster and within St Leonard's Hospital. We know from documentary records that there were others – at Boroughbridge, Pickering and Richmond, for example (SURTEES 91: vii–x). Schools might be freestanding structures or they might simply be places within a church where a priest could give instruction, or they might be attached to a religious building. At Thirsk one of the duties of the priest of the Service of the Altar of Our Lady within the parish church was 'bringynge up and techyng of chyldren' and 'to teche a grammar scole within the sayd town' (SURTEES 91: 92; 92:

St Anne's Hospital, Ripon, from a nineteenth-century drawing.

SOUTH ELEVATION OF HOSPITAL AND CHAPEL

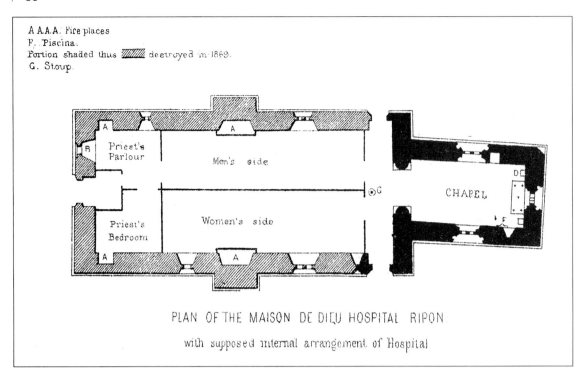

A A.A.A. Fire places
F. Piscina.
Portion shaded thus ▨▨▨ destroyed in 1869.
G. Stoup.

PLAN OF THE MAISON DE DIEU HOSPITAL RIPON
with supposed internal arrangement of Hospital

Plan of the hospital made in the nineteenth century.
The part in light tone was the hall demolished in 1869,
and may have been partitioned in the way suggested.
Note the through passage between hall and chapel.

3). The best survival of a grammar school occurs at Howden. Dating from about 1500 the school has been incorporated into the fabric of the church at the southwest end.

CONCLUSION

Urban churches and other religious buildings reflect several elements of medieval town life, from the prosperity of a town or its prelate to perhaps its importance as a centre of religious administration. Accordingly they tend also to reflect the clerical order itself in the numbers and hierarchy of buildings, from the archiepiscopal seat to the humble parish priest or chaplain in a poor living. At some towns a further element was present: pilgrimage. Beverley, Ripon and York were the most important in this respect, since St John of Beverley, St Wilfred of Ripon

and St William of York were saints that attracted pilgrims from throughout England and their churches possessed shrines which were in themselves works of art. Some lesser known local saints were also venerated as well as saints unrecognised by the church but who became the focus of cults. At Howden there were two local saints – St Osara or Osana, a somewhat obscure Anglo-Saxon saint, and St John of Howden who was never officially canonised.

In addition to this there were numbers of holy relics. Here was another reason, if not exactly for pilgrimage then at least for visiting the churches of some towns: the lure of relics whether divine or of local saints or other cult figures. They ranged from the three splinters of the Holy Cross at Bridlington Priory to Thomas Duke of Lancaster's girdle and hat – said to ease the pains of childbirth and headaches respectively – at St John's Priory, Pontefract (YASRS 48: 18). Even though the devotional importance of pilgrimage may have waned in the late Middle Ages, events might still throw up a local cult which for a time attracted fervent worshippers as in fifteenth-century York after

The grammar school at Howden.

the execution of Archbishop Scrope for his part in the rebellion against Henry IV. Soon after Scrope's decapitated body was placed in the minster miracles were alleged to have happened, and although never canonised, he was venerated as a saint locally for most of the fifteenth century. We should not underestimate the importance of pilgrimage: at times it brought people, money and trade into the towns as well as gifts and bequests to churches and shrines.

Crowds of people passing through or lodging at the large towns on religious business must have made them a different experience compared to most towns today. To find their equivalents – although on a vastly greater scale – we would have to look at Lourdes or Rome. Also the clusters and diversity of religious buildings within towns is something that we have almost completely lost. The greatest numbers in the county were built at York. Apart from the minster and around forty churches there were four monasteries, four friaries, and more than twenty hospitals and *maisons dieu*, not to mention the archbishop's palace, the dwellings of clergy, an ecclesiastical courthouse and church schools. Yet even within some small towns there is an echo of this. Knaresborough, for instance, had its parish church and, after the death of the local hermit Robert Flower in 1218, a Trinitarian priory; by

1252 Flower came to be venerated as a saint, attracting pilgrims to his cave and chapel by the River Nidd. There was also at least one *maison dieu*.

At many towns were what have proved to be the most ephemeral of religious monuments – wayside shrines, stone crosses and the boundary markers of ecclesiastical jurisdictions. On several bridges into towns, if there was not a bridge chapel, there was often a shrine of some sort, such as that mentioned in the will of Richard Langfellay of Otley who left money for the repair of the bridge and 'a substanceall crosse to be sette theropon with a litle ymage of oure ladie' (Jervoise 1931: 97). Similarly, on the approach to Howden there was a shrine to the Virgin known as Our Lady of Belcrosse.

Religious structures large or small made a great impact on the urban environment through the range of buildings and their varied detail, roof-lines and even the materials from which they were built. They animated the townscape of small towns and produced a rich texture of building in the major urban-ecclesiastical centres. Their interiors echoed with singing, and their bells summoned people to mass or to market, or marked the passing of the day and the passing of life itself.

NOTE

1. I am grateful to Richard Morris of the Council for British Archaeology for pointing this out.

CHAPTER SIX

Seigneurial Residences

URBAN CASTLES

MONARCHS AND ALSO MANY seigneurs built castles or, at least, fortified houses. In towns, as elsewhere, they represented visible might and were a fortification against invasion and civil unrest. They also provided administrative premises and a residence. Some archaeologists (Drage 1987; Schofield and Vince 1994) have argued that castles in towns should be considered as belonging to one of two groups: castles which formed a pre-urban nucleus around which a town later formed, and castles which were inserted into already established towns. This is an important distinction in as far as it acknowledges that urban origins can in some instances be the result of castle-building, although as Drage has commented, it would be inappropriate to continue to use the phrase *urban castle* to describe castles at towns that had failed or had never really become established. Nevertheless, it is important to recognise the urbanising influence of castles. Many castles began life as Norman motte and bailey types with timber buildings and palisades, but were mostly replaced with stone in later years, some not until much later – after 1245 at York for example – while some ancillary buildings within the bailey might remain built of timber. Castles also differed greatly in size, strength of fortification and architectural elaboration.

Two contrasting castles which illustrate all of these points are Pontefract and Richmond. Richmond is an early castle which has retained much of its Norman origins. Unusually planned with its keep to the front of the inner bailey wall like a massive gatehouse, it was begun by Alan of Brittany, Earl of Richmond, in the late eleventh century, probably to safeguard routes to the north and to the west since it is positioned near to the present-day A1 and Scotch Corner. Much of the castle, including the enceinte, seems to have been largely of stone from the beginning, a reflection of the importance of Richmond Castle, perhaps as Alan's principal English residence. The tower keep, however, dates from between 1146 and 1171 and was added by Conan, Duke of Brittany, one of Alan's successors. This was a small castle with little architectural pretension, built on what appears to have been a virgin site overlooking the River Swale, hence its new Norman French name le Riche Mont. If there was a small English settlement not far away, the new town of Richmond, nevertheless began to develop around the castle and was given encouragement by the Earls of Richmond.

Pontefract Castle was built by Ilbert de Lascy soon after the Conquest. The positioning of the castle next to, or even within, the English town of Tanshelf seems to have had the double purpose of acting as a check on local opposition and maintaining a strategic presence near to roads north and an important crossing of the River Aire. Over the years the castle was to pass from aristocratic to royal ownership, from Norman stronghold to a castle of immense proportions and architectural complexity. At the same time the new town of Pontefract appears to have developed out of the old town of Tanshelf, a process directly influenced by the presence of the castle and the willingness of seigneurs to grant borough status.

Castles were not simply the focal point of

A motte without a castle – Skipsea Castle. It was the stronghold of Drogo de la Beuvriere, built before the end of the eleventh century, but destroyed or part destroyed in the early thirteenth century. It had led to the development of the small town of Skipsea Brough, which seems to have withered away to a village or hamlet.

Richmond castle: the keep seen from within the bailey. This is a tower keep built in the position we would expect to find a gatehouse. It probably dates from between 1146 and 1171.

Pontefract Castle: the castle was destroyed after the Civil War, but this seventeenth-century engraving gives a good idea of this large and architecturally impressive castle lavishly rebuilt and extended in the late fourteenth and early fifteenth centuries.

might and defence. They often provided an administrative base within a region for monarchs and seigneurs thus becoming the seat of manorial or even urban administration, or they might be the centre of administration within an honour. Courts were frequently held in castles, felons held in their prisons and taxes or other payments secured in their treasuries.

York Castle typifies this combination of defence and civil administration within an urban setting. Two mounds with wooden fortifications had been built at York by William of Normandy in 1068–9 as defences on either side of the Ouse; the castle on the east bank was also protected by a moat. The timber buildings remained for a long time, but during the thirteenth century they were remodelled in stone by which date further buildings had been added to the easterly castle

within a walled bailey with a gatehouse (see Figure 6.1). The buildings within the bailey comprised a chapel, residential/administrative buildings, stables and prisons. The motte and bailey across the river to the west was not developed in the same way, and eventually came under the jurisdiction of the Archbishop of York.

By the fifteenth century, however, the crown possessed more castles than it could maintain with ease, while at some seigneurial castles the requirements of residence were beginning to take precedence over the need for defence. Even in the fourteenth century some monarchs when in residence at York preferred the Franciscan Friary to the castle, suggesting that although the castle possessed residential quarters they lacked the accommodation preferred. By the sixteenth century castles had generally fallen out of favour as residences. At Skipton, for example, a domestic range with a great hall had been located on a craggy ridge above the Eller Beck and had been enclosed by an enceinte with drum towers probably by the thirteenth century. This provided a strong and highly defensible castle. By the late fifteenth century, however, enlargements of the

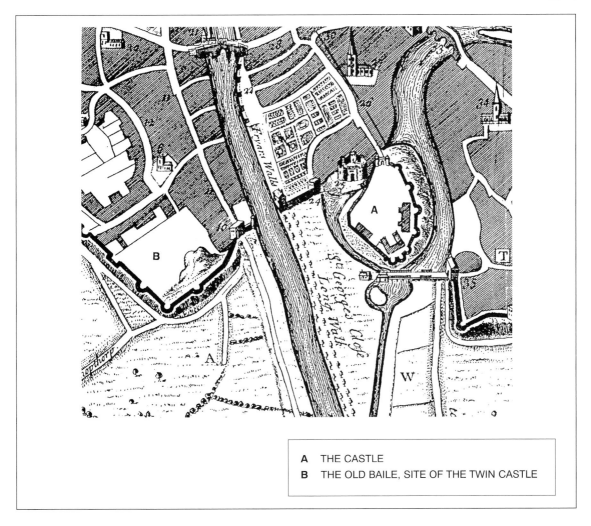

A   THE CASTLE
B   THE OLD BAILE, SITE OF THE TWIN CASTLE

domestic accommodation were taking place inside the inner bailey; then in 1536 a new residential wing was added. As Williams has commented:

> Although Skipton Castle was still to face its greatest trial, the Civil War siege of 1642–45, it is clear that by the end of the Middle Ages its owners no longer saw it as a stronghold but rather as a home in which they could invest money and put down roots. (1981: 15)

This process of upgrading the accommodation of castles continued well into the sixteenth century – Helmsley Castle is a further clear example.

Figure 6.1 York's castles from Drake 1736

Williams (1981) also records that in 1422 Skipton Castle lay in need of repair, a situation common to many urban castles in the later Middle Ages. There are several reasons for this, but two are of importance – the rising cost of maintaining castles, especially royal castles, since by the fifteenth century the crown had acquired a large number, and the declining need for defence, especially in towns. Drage (1987) has commented that with some exceptions (York, for example) urban castles or fortified residences were little needed for the internal

Clifford's Tower, York, is a quadrilobate keep on a motte. The entrance to the tower was renewed in the seventeenth century, although it contains the remnants of an earlier chapel.

A short run of the bailey walls also survives. All date from after 1245.

defence of towns. Although some may have been kept up for status purposes or as seigneurial seats, many were simply allowed to decay, sporadic and sometimes inadequate repairs being carried out. Pickering Castle was described in 1297 as ruined and of no profit (YASRS 31: 72). Despite repairs in the following century it continued to be described as in need of repair and Leyland's description of it in the first part of the sixteenth century is perhaps a fair portrayal of the effects of pragmatic expenditure and neglect:

> The castelle stondith in an end of the town not far from the paroch chirch on the brow of a hille, under which the broke rennith. In the first court of it be a 4 toures, of the which one is caullid Rosamunde's Toure. In the ynner court be also a 4 toures, wherof the kepe is one. The castelle waulles and the toures be metely welle, the logginges in the ynner court that be of timber be in ruine . . . The castelle waulles now remaining seme to be of no very old building. (Toulmin- Smith 1907: 63)

Scarborough Castle is similarly a story of decay and repair. A survey of 1260 recorded that several buildings including the great hall had defective roofs, others were in danger of collapse, the defences were in a state of decay, the bridges weak and rotten and 'there is an entire deficiency of cross-bows, quarrels, and all manner of arms necessary for its defence' (YASRS 12: 72–3). One might seek to explain this as the exaggerations of wardens and surveyors in an attempt to impress upon royal officials the urgency of expenditure on repairs. What we should also be mindful of is the size of castles: most were far bigger than large houses and some churches, had long runs of walls with towers and were often located in exposed situations. It is hardly surprising given this amount of building to maintain that a survey would find fault. The fact is that castles required constant maintenance. However, the collapse of a number of buildings and parts of the walls of Scarborough Castle in 1278 was certainly not an exaggeration. It suggests that, despite a healthy degree of scepticism, we should nevertheless take some reports of the decay of castles at face value.

One must not view all castles, however, as in a complete state of dereliction by the fifteenth century. Scarborough was repaired, and Leyland could describe it as 'an exceding goodly larg and strong castelle' (Toulmin-Smith 1907: 60). At Pontefract a campaign of rebuilding and extension had begun in the late fourteenth century and continued into the fifteenth. Although several parts of the castle were in a state of disrepair according to a survey of 1564 (PRO DL 44/114) the body of assessors went on in their report to conclude that:

> The said castelle ys mete and conveniente to be amendyd and repayred from tyme to tyme, for that yt is a howse mete for a prince, the like ys not to be seene in the north partes of the realme.

It is also clear from architectural evidence that even some early castles, while built for defensive purposes, had builders with an eye to residence and comfort as well. This was probably a factor in the unusual development of a gatehouse tower keep at Richmond: the great hall of the castle was located to the rear of the bailey on a naturally defended river cliff overlooking the Swale. While this first hall/keep was defensible, its location also gave fine views of the countryside. It is significant that when the tower keep was built in the following century the older keep and great hall, Scolland's Hall as it became known, was retained.

Although we tend to think of castles as primarily defensive buildings, defensive works might be put to other uses. At Scarborough part of the rents due to the castle in the thirteenth century were for allowing fishermen to spread out their nets to dry along the mound of the castle and its earthworks (YASRS 12: 163–4), an odd twist that should remind us never to take things for granted.

OTHER SEIGNEURIAL RESIDENCES

Castles were not the only type of seigneurial urban residence; there were also tower houses and quadrangular-plan houses, sometimes on moated sites. Most seem to date from the fourteenth and fifteenth centuries, and it is difficult to explain their appearance in towns at these dates unless documentary records from earlier periods have survived. Urban tower houses do not seem to have been built for reasons of internal defence, that is defence of seigneurs against urban civil unrest. However, some fourteenth-century tower houses, especially those in the north of the county, may have been a response to Scottish raiding after Bannockburn in 1314. One or two, however, were earlier, such as the de Stuteville castle/tower at Kirkbymoorside the origins of which were in the twelfth century. Some were later and built probably for display with only occasional residence in mind, such as the 'castle' – or more accurately the hunting lodge – of the Nevills, Earls of Westmorland, again at Kirkbymoorside. This probably replaced the early castle, although on a different site, and seems to have been more of a quadrangular plan house with turrets at each corner. Both houses/castles have now virtually disappeared, but in 1570 the Nevill house was described as 'but symple for an erle, but a good house for a gentleman of worshipp' (VCH 1914: 511).

The so-called Scolland's Hall of Richmond Castle seen from the Swale. This was the original great hall of the castle, and its positioning both for defensive purposes and to take advantage of the view was probably a conscious decision on the part of the builders.

Besides tower houses six quadrangular-plan houses – urban palaces – were built by the archbishops of York and the bishops of Durham. These were at Beverley, Howden, Northallerton, Otley, Ripon and York, and there was probably another at Sherburn-in-Elmet, although whether it was of quadrangular plan has yet to be established. Little of any of them has survived above ground, except for the palace of the Bishop of Durham at Howden. From archaeological investigation, early drawings and documents (Butler and Powls 1994: 15–22) it is possible to piece together something of the Howden palace. It

was a large rectangular building enclosing a courtyard, built partly of stone but also of timber and brick, suggesting development over a number of years. From surveys and other documents it is seems likely that there was a palace on the site from at least the twelfth century, and that the last major building phase was probably the late fourteenth-century great hall, perhaps rebuilt by Bishop Walter Skirlaw. Within the ranges around the quadrangle were the great hall, lodgings, kitchen, service rooms and stables. This had been a grand house and was visited on at least two occasions by English monarchs – Edward II and Henry V – as well as other members of the royal family.

Harewood Castle – a tower house built by William de Aldborough around 1366, and now the best surviving remains of an urban fortified house in Yorkshire, although its character may have derived as much from a display of status as defence. It has lost its outer defences.

What becomes evident from the study of documents relating to these houses is that in the late Middle Ages, the archbishops of York in particular had far more palaces – there were further rural palaces at Cawood and Bishopthorpe, for example – than they could or were

willing to maintain. Their routines were also changing – more time spent at Westminster, less on progresses around their Yorkshire estates. As with some castles, several of these palaces seem to have fallen into decay. Of the palace at Beverley, Leyland commented in the sixteenth century: 'The prebendaries houses stande round about S. John's chirche yard. Wherof the Bishop of York hath one motid, but al yn ruine' (Toulmin-Smith 1907: 46).

A further type of seigneurial residence which should be included are the houses of abbots or priors. They should not be discounted, for as we have seen, monasteries controlled liberties within places like York and also whole towns such as Bridlington, Guisborough, Selby or Whitby. Few such houses have survived on urban sites, and those that do are mostly from the later Middle Ages when abbots and priors were building grander houses. Standing remains and below-ground archaeology, suggest that such houses may have differed little in their planning, broadly speaking, from some quadrangular-plan houses. A good surviving example is the abbot's house at St Mary's Abbey, York. Originally a quadrangular-plan design of the

The east range of the abbot's house, St Mary's Abbey (King's Manor). Although greatly remodelled in the sixteenth and seventeenth centuries, parts of the earlier house survive on this eastern side, such as the large chimney. The diagonal buttress (right) marks the extent of the original house.

late fifteenth century, it was remodelled in the sixteenth and seventeenth centuries as an open courtyard with ranges around three sides to form premises for the Council of the North, becoming known as the King's Manor.

Although there were some exceptions, the majority of Yorkshire's medieval towns contained a seigneurial residence of one type or another. At York alone we would have to reckon three or four, corresponding to the different liberties. The castle and the archbishop's palace were two major seigneurial residences, but there was also the abbot's house at St Mary's Abbey and Davy Hall, apparently a quadrangular house within a tiny royal liberty. There were in addition the urban houses of some of the county's aristocratic families. Raine (1955: 108−9) notes the houses of the Nevilles and the Percies in Walmgate, the latter being apparently of quadrangular form with the principal range running parallel to Walmgate. Apart from York, out of forty towns in the county, twenty-six possessed such residences for certain; five may have – Bradford, Leeds, Pocklington, Tadcaster and Stokesley; nine probably did not at any stage of their development up to the Reformation – Bawtry, Boroughbridge, Brough-on-Humber, Halifax, Hedon, Ravenser-odd, Rotherham, Snaith, Yarm.

Urban seigneurial residences along with religious buildings were usually among the largest buildings in towns. A castle could dominate by its physical presence alone and was symbolically and literally a manifestation of seigneurial authority. But such authority did not rest solely and crudely in the exercise of physical force. When monarchs, prelates or other seigneurs were in residence they might have a profound economic influence on a town. The great man, his guests, his retainers, his guests' retainers – all had to be fed and services had to be provided from shoeing horses to laundering linen, and from legal services, if the castle were a centre of administration, to demands for luxury goods, if the king and his court sojourned in one of the major urban centres. Although royal and seigneurial residences might be provisioned from far afield, many goods and services might also be obtained from townspeople. If castles have long been thought of as one of the origins of towns and a stimulus to urbanisation, more consideration ought to be given to the life of the castle or the grand urban residence as one of the maintaining forces of towns.

CHAPTER SEVEN

The Structuring of Authority

WHILE THE GREAT CHURCHES and castles represented seigneurial authority in towns, there were further buildings which were more directly concerned with the exercise of law and the control of the urban environment. Most castles together with churches whose prelates had jurisdiction over a town or liberty contained gaols and courthouses within their precincts. Few ecclesiastical gaols or courthouses have survived, and while every castle open to the public nowadays promotes its 'dungeon', the gaols and courthouses – important parts of the array of structures within the bailey – have often been demolished or replaced.

A good case in point is York castle. Gaols for both men and women were constructed within the bailey of the castle. There were also courts of justice. But owing to several campaigns of building at the castle these were all replaced, notably in the eighteenth century when the courthouses and gaols were completely re-planned and the older buildings replaced. York castle represented royal jurisdiction, but as we have seen, there were other liberties in York, and further courthouses and gaols, demonstrating just how complicated the structure of authority could be. St Peter's Liberty had the Chapter's court and gaol in Minster Yard. The archbishop also had a gaol, possibly for clerical offenders, within the palace. It may also be that he kept a further gaol in the Old Baile within the tower called the Bitch Daughter. Other gaols were kept by St Mary's Abbey and at Davy Hall, the latter a unique Forest Gaol for trespassers in the royal Forest of Galtres. Then there was the civic gaol, given the sardonic name of Kidcotes and probably located on Ouse Bridge next to St William's chapel.

At Ripon the collegiate church had a courthouse and gaol, something of which survives. Although rebuilt and altered, it would appear to have consisted of a long range of two storeys with a first-floor hall reached by an external staircase. Where courthouses have survived in other parts of the country, they tend to this pattern, and rebuilt courthouses in the county's towns usually continue what was probably a medieval precedent: that is the first-floor hall arrangement. But a note of caution should be sounded against assuming that all first-floor hall ranges near to churches or castles were courthouses, or that all castles or seigneurial residences contained purpose-built courthouses. At Knaresborough castle a range of the above description has long been assumed to have been a courthouse, but as Atkinson (1938) has shown through careful scholarship, courts at Knaresborough were held on the first floor of the keep in an apartment called the King's Hall. The range within the bailey seems to have been the receiver's lodgings until converted to a courthouse in perhaps the first part of the seventeenth century.

Courthouses must have been a feature of some urban religious houses which exercised control over towns. Bridlington, Selby and Whitby or St Mary's Abbey, York, are the obvious choices here. However, no buildings identifiable as courthouses survive in monastic plans, although it seems likely that they would have been built within the outer precinct of a monastery, and probably near to the main entrance or gatehouse. The gatehouse itself, might well have performed this function. At St Mary's Abbey there is reason to believe that a courthouse was built as a timber range adjacent to the gatehouse, which

Despite a good deal of rebuilding, the basic form of this stone-built courthouse of the collegiate canons of Ripon survives.

itself became a courthouse for the liberty after the dissolution of the monastery. One positive identification of a gatehouse used in this way is at Bridlington Priory (illustrated p. 45) where a survey of 1537 refers to it as containing the 'three Weks Courte . . . the hie Chamber where the Courte ys kepte' and 'a Prison for offenders wtin the Towne called the Kydcott' (Earnshaw 1976: 4). 'Kid cote' seems to have been a common name for a gaol.

The church and lay seigneurs were not the only ones to impose their authority within towns. A third institution was to be found in municipal government. It is not possible to lay down hard and fast rules about the organisation of municipal government since it varied from town to town and depended on whether a borough was incorporated or was a free or mesne borough with certain limited privileges awarded by a seigneur. Generally speaking, however, the composition of town councils tended to be a body of common councillors and a select group of aldermen usually drawn from a town's elite families; if there was a mayor, then he too would be chosen from among the aldermen. Where this structure of government occurred at the small towns' demands on space and civic buildings were modest. But at the large towns councils required a grander show, both as a visible presence within a large population and as the need arose for office space to cope with a greater volume of business.

At York and other large towns, councils built halls, although few have survived, partly because some sites were in continuous use, the halls being rebuilt as town halls in the eighteenth and nineteenth centuries. Judging from documents and fragmentary survivals the best of these halls were at Beverley, Hull and York: the Guild or Common Halls at Hull and York, while Beverley had its Hansa House. York is the most complicated example, because the city possessed two council chambers, one at Ouse Bridge which has been demolished and one at the far end of Coney Street, Guild Hall, which has survived. It was part destroyed in a German air raid of 1942 which gutted the interior, but today it has been restored. Although dating from 1460 it

replaced an earlier building on the site (Raine 1955: 134–44), and was erected probably to the designs of the York mason Robert Couper. The Guild Hall is built of stone and presents a broad, low-pitched gable in its principal elevation combining in a single span nave and aisle roofs which were open to the rafters. The timber roof was carried on octagonal posts running the length of the building. The hall was originally enclosed and approached through a castellated gatehouse standing next to the chapel of the Guild of St Christopher, a merchants' religious guild. Thus civic authority was given architectural expression both by the use of prestige materials, its size and quality of finish, and also by association with castellated and religious forms of architecture – the gatehouse and chapel.

The exact forms of other guild or town halls are either unknown or difficult to recover. At Beverley only a stone doorcase and some internal panelling from the Hansa House of around 1500–2 have survived, although this is of good enough quality to suggest more than basic accommodation. At Doncaster the town hall was stone built and stood near to the church of St George. According to Leyland (Toulmin-Smith 1907: 238) it had perhaps been rebuilt with stone from Doncaster Castle, or may even have been converted from castle buildings. At Hedon, the Town Hall or Toll Booth originally stood in the old market place, and was of three storeys, incorporating a gaol in the basement. At Hull also the Guild Hall stood by the market place with the town gaol adjoining. The possession of a gaol was an important part of municipal authority where a council exercised a wide control, and courts might be held within the town hall itself. While the Guild Hall at Hull was rebuilt in later centuries, the gaol was not, and eighteenth-century illustrations depict a strong brick tower with angle buttresses and small windows with lancets on the topmost storey.

Documentary records suggest that the small seigneurial boroughs also possessed civic buildings, but not on the scale of places like Beverley or York. The problem here is that *only* documentary records are available for the study of these buildings, since every one in the county has

Common Hall or Guild Hall, York. Only some parts of the original fabric survive; the rest of the building has been carefully restored to its original form.

either been demolished or rebuilt. What does seem clear is that the civic buildings in smaller boroughs were small and usually multi-functional. At several boroughs civic buildings stood in or near the market place – Bedale, Malton, Richmond, Skipton, Wakefield, Yarm, for example – and were often referred to as the market house or toll booth. This was because their primary functions were connected with the regulation of the market and collection of tolls. But they also seem to have been the places where the municipal body might sit and courts might be held. Having said that, even in some

small towns two separate buildings might be erected to house these functions

In the market place at Wakefield, for example, there was a toll booth with a gaol beneath, the Kidcote as at York and Bridlington. The court of pie powder probably sat here also to settle market disputes.[1] Then in 1516 a moot hall was added reflecting Wakefield's growing importance (Goodchild 1991). At Skipton it seems likely that the borough court sat in the building remodelled as the town hall in the eighteenth century and sited at the south end of High Street. At Knaresborough a plan of the seventeenth century depicts a toll booth at the corner of the market place. This was built in the sixteenth century together with the courthouse of the borough court and a lock-up to the rear, and was a replacement of earlier arrangements. This remained the site of civic administration and

The doorcase of the Hansa House at Beverley.

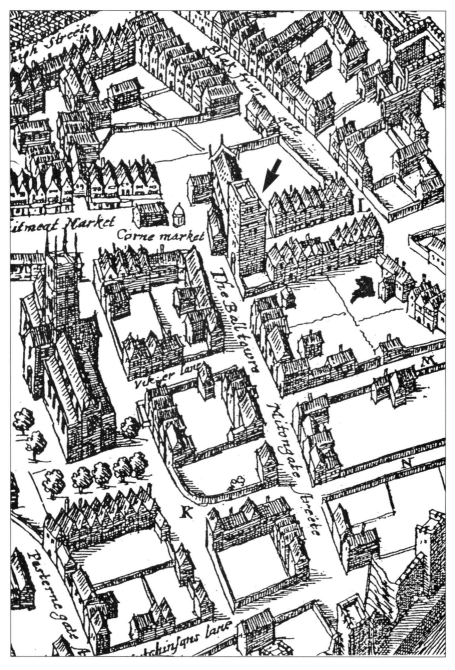

The gaol of Hull stands opposite the market place in this detail from Hollar's bird's-eye perspective of the town. Alongside is the Guild Hall, shown as a long, tall range. This was perhaps the medieval structure.

was again rebuilt as the town hall in the nineteenth century. At Bedale a nineteenth-century painting shows a two-storey market building of sixteenth-century appearance in the market place by the market cross, possibly an older site. The interesting thing about all of these buildings is that although rebuilt in later centuries they nevertheless seem to have retained what can be established as medieval architectural form from survivals at other towns. In other words, they tended to be of two storeys with the principal room on the first floor often reached by an external staircase. The ground floor served a variety of functions, from butter market to lock-up.

Whether these sorts of arrangements could have been found at all small towns is difficult to say. It seems likely that at some tightly controlled seigneurial boroughs the business of the manor and the business of the borough were conducted in the manorial courts. This would appear to have been the case at Bradford, for example, where a number of the early manor court rolls have survived. The buying, selling or renting of burgages, the letting of stalls in the market place and the regulation of the market and trades within the town were all dealt with in the manor court along with business relating to the manor itself. We also know from documents of the sixteenth century and later that the hall of pleas and town lock-up stood at the corner of Ivegate and Kirkgate, two of three streets that converged on the market place. This building overlooked the market place itself, and the corner on which it stood was known as Pie Corner until at least the eighteenth century, suggesting perhaps not food but a market court – pie powder. Bradford would have to come at the bottom of anyone's list of medieval towns in terms of size and urban complexity, for as discussed in Chapter 3, along with a number of the county's other small towns, it was as much an agricultural settlement as a town. Yet although manor and town business would appear to have been transacted in the one place, there was probably a purpose-built court capable of dealing with all business. Furthermore, it was located in the most public of places within the town, probably for both ease of access and public display of authority.

A further type of building associated with the control of the town and its business should be included here: the halls of religious and trade guilds. It is difficult to know where exactly to include these institutions which were especially common in the later Middle Ages, for although historians have made distinctions between religious guilds, and merchant and craft guilds, there were many grey areas of overlap between these types. We may accept that religious guilds were what the name appears to imply: lay

associations devoted to worship and good works as well as the supply of religious and charitable aid to members at their deaths. We can also draw a distinction between these and other guilds which were more concerned with pursuing the interests of trade, the enforcement of standards of quality or probity and arbitration in disputes. But at the same time many craft guilds had a religious outlook and were concerned with the spiritual as well as the material welfare of their members, while some religious guilds seem to have attracted mostly the wealthier sorts of burgesses, so that it is difficult at times to disengage guild activities from the activities of town government or trade, especially mercantile trade. What is more, a similar blurring of distinctions occurs between the functions of some guildhalls and churches. Many guildhalls contained a chapel, and vice versa some churches were associated with some guilds, to the extent that members might assemble there for worship and on guild business.

The essential point is that as social institutions guilds represented a complex of lay authority in towns at a point where religion and interest group intersected with municipal government. Some guilds might constitute a controlling influence within a municipal authority; others operated as associations formed to regulate a trade or craft. Some religious guilds probably provided one means by which burgesses, especially newcomers, might ascend the social and political hierarchy by making the right sorts of contacts and moving in the right sorts of circles.

Religious guilds could have been found in most towns and villages throughout late medieval England, but it was in the towns and cities where they were at their most prolific, and it was here too that the craft and mercantile guilds were formed. They could be found from Whitby to Bawtry, from Hull to Richmond. We also know that in several towns both religious and trade guilds built their own halls – at Guisborough, Hedon, Richmond and Scarborough, for example. However, there are only documentary references to these, since none of the buildings now exist. The only place which retains some of its guildhalls is York. Here what were probably the finest in the county have survived. They illustrate not only the kinds of halls guilds built, but also the interleafing of trade and religious guilds.

Nowhere is this better demonstrated than by the building known nowadays as Merchant Adventurers' Hall. The Guild of Our Lord Jesus Christ and the Blessed Virgin Mary, a religious guild, was formed in 1357, and construction of its hall, chapel and hospital was begun in the same year. But the membership of the guild came to be dominated by mercers, and by around 1420 some of the functions of the religious guild were absorbed into the Mercers' Guild. Despite some extension in the sixteenth

and seventeenth centuries the hall remains much as it was originally built: two ranges, gabled and timber-framed, running parallel to one another above a brick-built undercroft with a stone-built chapel projecting from its south-eastern end. The undercroft housed the hospital which remained in use as such after the guild had been taken over by the mercers; the great hall of the guild was on the upper floor.

Here the distinction between religious and trade guild is far from clear-cut and is reflected in the continuing use of the building partly for religious purposes. Similarly the Common or Guild Hall, one of the seats of civic administration in the city, is difficult to disentangle from the Guild of St Christopher, a religious guild, which by the fifteenth century had rights to use Common Hall on certain days of the year. The guild also had a chapel dedicated to Saint

The Mercers' (Merchant Adventurers') Hall 1357–61. The sash windows and the chimney are later additions.

Christopher in the Minster where the aldermanic group of York Council sometimes met – 'Beyng togadder in counsaill behynd Saint Christopher' (Raine 1955: 134).

Some guilds were, ostensibly, either trade/craft guilds or religious guilds of which there were many in York. The Guild of St Martin was an association of complex origins whose guild-hall, St Anthony's Hall, has largely survived. Dating from perhaps the mid-fifteenth century, this was a large hall comprising three gabled ranges which made up a central great hall with aisles. Originally the hall and aisles would have been completely constructed of timber over a stone undercroft. Although the outer walls of the great hall were rebuilt in brick in the seventeenth century, internally much of the original framing survives. Like the Mercers' Hall the undercroft was used as a hospital and chapel.

Several religious guilds constructed multi-functional buildings: hospital, chapel and hall was a typical combination. The Corpus Christi Guild of York was a wealthy and influential guild, but one which lacked a hall. In 1428 the guild erected one together with other buildings next to St Thomas's Hospital, and in 1478 took over the hospital agreeing to maintain it as such. But it did more than this, for the hospital was rebuilt in the same year. It is perhaps significant that Corpus Christi could afford to construct a hall and hospital of stone, and in a form similar to the Common Hall – a long, shallow gable,

St Anthony's Hall, York, mid-fifteenth century. The brick is a seventeenth-century replacement of timber-framed walls to a central great hall with aisles.

end-on to the street, the space inside probably divided into an aisled hall.

Other guildhalls have been lost, in particular those of the craft guilds of York. The butchers, haberdashers and shoemakers, for example, all had halls, but we know little about them. However, a plan of York which appeared in Drake (1736) gives an indication that the Butchers' Hall may have been similar to the Mercers' Hall,

St Thomas's Hospital depicted on Whittock's view of York of about 1858. By this date a chapel to the left of the building had already been demolished and replaced by a row of shops.

consisting of two gabled parallel ranges. But not all of the city's guildhalls were like this. Merchant Tailors' Hall, which survives, seems to have been constructed around 1400 as a long hall range with a cross wing added later, although it was altered greatly in the eighteenth century when much of the outer walling was replaced with brick.

What all such guildhalls tend to reflect is the coming to prominence of guilds in the mid-fourteenth to fifteenth centuries as groups which regulated and controlled, whether that was at municipal or craft level, while the religious guilds could perhaps be seen as representing a widening area of control over and participation

in religion by laity. But whether the guildhall or any of the other types of building discussed in this chapter, all such edifices either made a forceful architectural display or were located in key positions within the town. We may look at churches, castles, town halls and guildhalls and view them separately in terms of design and architectural development. Yet we should be mindful that they were also the physical embodiment of the structure of authority. This was especially significant as far as the principal building types were concerned: churches, abbeys or castles gave distinctive profiles to the urban skyline, investing it with both a real and symbolic dominance as we have seen. But within the town, guildhalls, courthouses and toll booths gave an internal texture and a visible reminder of the presence of hierarchical structures of control.

NOTE

1. Pie powder was a court intended to give speedy justice for market offences (e.g. short measure, poor quality) on market days, hence its name from the French *pied poudre* or dusty foot. The implication is that justice was meted out before there was time to brush the dust off your boots, or that justice was provided for those who had travelled into town to sell their wares and had dusty feet, or that you had dusty feet because the court may have been held out of doors – take your pick.

CHAPTER EIGHT

Spaces for Trade

THE BUILDINGS DISCUSSED so far were developed in response to the means by which control was maintained over society through religion, the law and seigneurial and civic administration. Some of these buildings – churches and castles – were common to both towns and countryside even though some may have developed into characteristically urban forms, as we have seen. Others, town halls for example, were specialised urban buildings. Control in the large towns was exercised by an urban establishment composed of prelates, aristocratic families and burgesses. If at times these groups came into conflict, their urban fortunes were, nevertheless, bound together by mutual economic ties. While burgesses, even the wealthier ones, might be considered the socially inferior group largely because they lacked noble birth and engaged in trade, it was this very characteristic that enabled them to exert a further measure of control – the control of urban commercial and economic space. Since wealthy merchants and burgesses usually formed the upper echelons of municipal government in the large towns, it is no surprise that a priority was the maintenance of monopolistic trade practices and the regulation of urban space to that end. This is why models that construct the medieval town as a chaotic jumble of streets lack precision, since the ordering of medieval towns into spaces for trade and structuring them in terms of both layout and the regulatory practices and buildings required was a prime concern of those engaged in trade and commerce.

That being said, there was an obvious difference between tightly controlled mesne boroughs or non-burghal towns, and boroughs in which

merchants/burgesses had a much larger measure of authority. While some seigneurial boroughs like Bradford or towns like Selby which was under the thumb of its abbot might appear to have been dominated by one master, nevertheless it was in no one's interests to ignore the needs of trade, and so the ordering and regulation of space to suit trade and commerce occurred in mesne boroughs and non-burghal towns in ways similar to towns where the municipal body had greater freedom.

Of central importance in all towns, sometimes literally so, was the market place. It was usually designated by the erection of at least one market cross. The origin of the market cross is obscure, but it probably signified divine protection and freedom from violence while the market was held, and a place where honest bargains might be struck. No entire medieval market crosses survive in the county's towns, either through weathering, replacement or the attentions of religious fanatics, but all seem to have been built to a common, simple pattern: a shaft surmounted by a cross, the whole being set on steps. Crosses, however, did not just mark the place of trade. In the days before mass communications the central and elevated nature of the cross situated amid the crowd provided a useful platform from which to deliver news or important pieces of national or civic information. It was in market places, for example, that friars minors were ordered to preach in favour of the crusades in 1291 by Archbishop John Le Romeyn (SURTEES 123: 113). Some crosses developed into small enclosed spaces of timber or stone providing shade from the sun for the sale of perishable products such as butter. Again none of the county's medieval butter crosses have survived. Not all enclosed crosses were used for the sale of butter, however. At Beverley the cross was the point of sale for poultry, while butter was sold in a building on the west side of High (now Saturday) Market called Butter Dings.[1]

From even a cursory survey of medieval markets it soon becomes clear that specialisation was taking place at early dates. The provision of specialised premises – however basic – for perishable foods is one example. A closer look reveals that much larger-scale differentiation of functions and subdivisions of market places were common. Markets were the point of sale for grains and other foodstuffs, for craft products, raw materials such as hides or wool, and livestock. One basic differentiation was that made was between livestock and the rest. Thus at Pontefract the north end of the New Market was the Neat (cattle) Market, the New Market being left free for other trade. New Market had developed by 1220 (YASRS 25: 140), although it was not chartered until around 1255. What happened to the old market place in Micklegate is uncertain, although it became known as Horse Fair in later centuries, thus suggesting a change of function. Even a small town like Snaith had its craft and produce market (in High Street) separated from the livestock market (Beast Fair) around a corner at the farther end of town.

In other towns, markets for livestock might be held well to the edge of or outside the town. At Richmond the produce and craft market was held centrally around Trinity Chapel, but the Neat Market stood on the northwest edge of the town. At York there were numbers of small sites throughout the city, but the chief grounds for cattle markets were at Horsefair, just outside the city walls at Gillygate to the north, and from 1416 at Toft Green, just inside Micklegate Bar to the west.

In some towns, perhaps because of better documentation, specialisation and subdivision of the market place is more readily observable. At Wakefield the large triangular market place was divided into a number of specialist areas. The cattle market was to the north, the Swine or

Hog Market to the northeast, while butchers' shambles were located among them. Livestock and related trades were thus confined to the more northerly areas of the market. Then, near to the entrance of Northgate into the market place, was Fish Shambles where the fishmongers plied their trade (Goodchild 1991). The craft and general provision market was more centrally located near the parish church. Specialisations at other towns are evident from documentary references or street names that may persist even today – to return to Pontefract, we find Leather Market, for example (SURTEES 92: 276).

The striking thing about Wakefield's market place is its size which, although in-filled by modern development, can still be traced. Large open spaces are characteristic of several important regional markets – Doncaster and Sheffield in the south of the county, Wakefield and Pontefract in the west, Hull in the east, Richmond and Yarm in the north. At some of the major urban centres, it was perhaps numbers of market places as much as their size which was important, some being designated for different days of the week. At York there was the market along Pavement and also Thursday Market near to St Sampson's Church; then there were two fish markets – freshwater fish on Ouse Bridge and sea fish on Foss Bridge – and there were also the cattle markets already mentioned. Beverley had its cattle market, Lower Market and Higher Market, the latter being of considerable size.

Within the market place municipal buildings such as toll houses or market houses were sited which, as we have seen, might have gaols attached or might be used as borough courthouses or for sittings of market courts. One might also expect to find other buildings related to trade and commerce sited within or near the market place, buildings connected with the buying, selling and regulation of goods. Chief among these in the towns and cities of Europe, especially Flanders, were the cloth and wool halls at markets within textile producing regions. It seems remarkable, therefore, that in England textile regions lacked specialised facilities of the scale found on the Continent. It seems particularly remiss in Yorkshire where a large trade in wool and cloth was carried on both internally and with Europe. Beverley, Ripon and York, for example, while being the centres of wool and textile marketing, nevertheless do not appear to have had cloth halls. Cloth markets and fairs appear to have been held in the open. On the other hand, a great deal of the cloth produced in medieval England was sent to London which did have a cloth hall, Blackwell Hall, more of a great complex developed to deal with the wares of different districts of the country. Here cloths could be sold to London merchants for resale in home or export markets.

It might be argued that because much of the wool clip was exported, especially by monastic houses, only some warehousing and little in the way of wool halls would have been required. But what about the sale of wool and cloth *within* the county? If the civic ordinances of more towns had survived then they might have shed more light on the pattern of textile marketing in medieval Yorkshire. As it is, we can only conjecture from a few sporadic sources. At York, for instance, both wool and cloth appear to have been sold in the open in Thursday Market, while some dealers in cloth sold quantities from the inns in which they were lodging. However, from the fifteenth century orders of the council state that both linen and woollen cloth should be sold in Common Hall, where there was also a leather market (VCH 1961: 484–5). At Beverley, from 1345, cloth was to be sold at the High Market in the Dings, a market/municipal building converted from a palace which the Archbishop of York had made over to the town in 1282. In other words some guildhalls, the seats of municipal government, also seem to have fulfilled a mercantile function at some period of their existence.

This was not, however, a textile marketing practice common to all the county's towns. From at least the sixteenth century Richmond, for example, had a Wool House in the market place where wool was to be weighed, bought and sold. But most surprising of all is to find that the merchants of Halifax, a place which had only grown into a town by perhaps the fifteenth century, developed far more sophisticated markets and buildings for the sale of cloth than

any other town in the county including York. First there was the area known as Wool Shops not far from the parish church. This was the principal wool market. Although it is difficult to know precisely what this meant, Wool Shops perhaps consisted of merchants' shops and warehouses. However, the medieval usage of the word shop was elastic enough to refer more simply to a booth. There was in addition to this market a cloth hall which had been in existence since at least the beginning of the sixteenth century. Significantly it was called Blackwell Hall, named after the London cloth hall. The building was replaced long ago and without visual record. Fortunately a brief description of it occurs in a document of 1588 (Garside 1921), and from this and one or two other references we know a little about its appearance. It consisted of probably two parallel ranges the whole of which was estimated by an Elizabethan surveyor to measure ninety feet long by thirty-six wide (Garside 1921). This would have created a substantial cloth hall within the centre of the town – a measure of the way in which the rural industry of the west gathered around the towns of Bradford, Halifax, Leeds and Wakefield was beginning to eclipse the traditional centres of Beverley and York in the east.

The discussion so far has revolved around market places and their buildings. Quays or staiths at ports were further important spaces for trade. Whether we are talking about inland, estuarine or coastal ports, the county had a well-connected water transport system during the Middle Ages along the Derwent, Don, Idle, Ouse, Tees and Ure, as well as along the Humber and to the North Sea and east coast. The principal coastal ports were Scarborough and Whitby. The trade of Bridlington is more difficult to gauge, although it was probably never great. The monks of Bridlington Priory held the port rights by a charter of King Stephen made between 1138 and 1154 (Farrer 1915: 442), but it may have functioned as little more than a domestic port serving the priory. However, by the fifteenth and sixteenth centuries it was obviously more active and accounts returned after the dissolution of the priory show that colliers and French ships were putting in at the port and cargoes included barley, salt and fish (YASRS 80: 42–3). Inland ports varied in size from the important King's Staith and Queen's Staith at York to the little port of Bawtry on the River Idle in the far south of the county. But it was the ports of Hedon, Hull and the vanished Ravenserodd that dominated trade on the great estuary of the Humber, giving access to the North Sea.

All needed quays. Hull was the most unusual here, since the port was ranged along the River Hull at its confluence with the Humber. Merchants' houses were built along the Hull each with its own private staith, although there was in addition a common quay. This private access to staiths directly engaged in foreign trade was unique in England and was disliked by the crown, since it afforded opportunities for the evasion of duties. Hedon was also unusual and poses a problem difficult to resolve. The Haven, Hedon's port, was a creek of the Humber

which provided the main quay to the south of the town.

But Hedon was flanked by further waterways to the east and west which were also connected to the Haven. The problem lies in how far these can be considered quays for the berthing of ships, and how far drains or part of the town's defences. There seems little reason to disagree with Hayfield and Slater (1984) who suggest that the waterways may well have served all three purposes. If this is true, then the western Haven at Hedon, a man-made feature, was a rare example of a medieval dock.

Some sources, Leyland for example, give the impression that quays at several ports were in a poor state of repair by the beginning of the

The Haven to the south of Hedon has been filled in, but the stretch of rough grass marks the site of a once important medieval waterway and port.

sixteenth century. As with some other indicators this appears to be good corroborative evidence of urban decay, but it is probably not. Rather it suggests two things peculiar to ports, especially coastal ports: first the constant struggle against tides and weather, and second the widespread use of timber as a building material for quays, timber piles and revetments being common. At Doncaster, for example, recent archaeological investigation suggests that parts of the hulls of seagoing vessels had been reused as a revetment to the quay at North Bridge and that these existed alongside areas of stone-built quay and slipway (Lilley 1994). And there was a further reason for the rebuilding that can be observed taking place. At successful ports more and more quayage was required and this was obtained by successive reclamations, thus extending the waterfront. At Hull, for example, this happened even on the private quays or staiths. At Blayd's Staith on the Hull there is evidence that the timber revetment to the staith was moved further into the Hull in the fourteenth century (Evans 1990a: 7).

One building commonly found at ports was the warehouse, and it was perhaps the warehouse as much as the quay itself that gave urban waterfronts much of their character. This is at odds with Girouard's contention that in the Middle Ages 'separate warehouses scarcely existed', and that the familiar type of warehouse was 'imported from the Netherlands in the seventeenth century' (1990: 40). This is not supported by what remains, both architecturally and in the form of documentary records. These sources suggest that there were public and private warehouses, together with a third category which supplied warehousing for religious or seigneurial institutions.

There appear to have been few public warehouses, probably since the tolls chargeable would not have justified the expense of construction or maintenance, although such buildings as wool houses or weigh houses were considered necessary in order to weigh and warehouse wool on which duty was payable. The Hull Wool House was built around 1389, or may have replaced an earlier structure, and through subsequent

extension had become a quadrangular form perhaps by the fifteenth century, if not before. It was a multi-functional building: the range to the Hull had a centrally placed four-storey tower which contained the Custom House on the first floor, the High Street range opposite consisted of an open arcade to provide shelter on entering, while the two flanking ranges that closed off the courtyard provided warehousing for foreigners and further rooms that might be leased. There was also a weigh-beam and common crane. This quadrangular arrangement of warehousing lasted probably until 1620 when it was rebuilt (VCH 1969: 434).

Most warehouses were private and were replaced as trade grew and larger warehouses were needed. However, the warehouses of religious and other institutions seem to have survived a little better. At Selby, for example, where a good deal of the Ouse traffic put in, warehouses had been built along the northeast bank of the river, at a landing known from at least the fifteenth century as Abbot's Staith. This was the abbey's quay and timber yard where the abbot had built these warehouses, long ranges probably of two storeys in height with taking-in doors on the first floor. Much of this survives, perhaps because magnesian limestone was used in their construction and they continued to serve the purpose for which they were intended.

Although the first floor has been rebuilt in brick in later centuries, this perhaps did not replace a timber-framed first floor but is more likely to be a heightening to create a further floor.

Long ranges of two or three storeys were probably a typical warehouse form. A structure like this, called a 'storehouse' as warehouses were alternatively known, was used for the warehousing of supplies for Pontefract Castle at a landing place on the River Aire at nearby Knottingley, and was illustrated in a plan of Knottingley of 1594 (Knottingley Civic Society 1979). Although a crude drawing it depicts a possibly stone-built warehouse of three storeys with taking-in doors on the top floor and five windows on each of the floors. The warehouse was said to have been built on the orders of

The gables of warehouses at Abbot's Staith, Selby.
The brick courses are probably a heightening of the
original structure which dates from possibly the
fifteenth century.

Henry VIII in 1527. Interestingly it has a chimney, indicating – if the drawing can be relied upon – either offices or accommodation at its left-hand end.

This is the pattern that was probably in use for the design of some waterfront warehouses until perhaps the late seventeenth century, and related designs can be found at several other ports on the east coast. At Hull a greatly altered warehouse of the seventeenth century has survived at 52 High Street, although there are indications that it was the extension of earlier work (RCHME 1994: NBR 92322). It consists of a long, low brick range with detailing of the six-teenth–nineteenth centuries. At Newcastle Doves Warehouse on the Tyne comprises a quadrangular arrangement of mostly three-storeyed brick, stone and timber-framed warehouses dating from the sixteenth century and later, but with traces of earlier work (RCHME Report 1986), while at King's Lynn, although encased in later remodellings, a large section of medieval waterfront has survived complete with several such warehouses (Pantin 1963a; Clark 1979).

Markets and quays were concerned with more than just the sale of goods. The movement of goods and their regulation by measurement came under the increasing mercantile control of spaces for trade. At the ports especially, there is a human dimension to this in the minute ordering of labour, for there were porters of various kinds with specifically designated tasks: there were salt and grain meters engaged in measuring these commodities, catchmen toing and froing in small boats unloading cargoes, and even barrel-rollers had their place marked out in the scheme of things. It is scarcely surprising that standard sets of weights and measures were kept in the toll booths of every town, or that toll booths and weigh houses were situated in market places or on quays, since this was the way in which the municipal economy operated: by the taking of tolls on a variety of goods and services, and by the control of labour engaged in these activities. Tolls were exacted not only for the obvious services and privileges such as the right to trade in a market or berth at the town quay, but also for passage through the town walls or the use of the town or common crane. Cranes were, indeed, an important feature of the quayside, and common cranes are recorded at Hull and York. Cranage was charged on a variety of goods from lead to linen, wine to woad. Moreover, a divine authority might be claimed for all of this, for as one well-known text ran: 'thou hast ordered all things by measure and number and weight' (Wisdom of Solomon 11: 20).

This ordering and measurement was extended by the urban elite to encompass not only goods and services but time itself. A certain time-discipline had probably always been a part of the urban routine. While town and village dwellers both experienced the summons to religious services, it was in the town that daily life was punctuated by further summonses – the opening and closing of town gates at morning and evening and the curfews associated with this, or the summoning of councillors to meetings of the municipal body. At Ripon, for example, we know that the Wakeman, a town official of probably Anglo-Saxon origins, was to sound curfew by blowing a horn from the four corners of the cross in the market place and then to watch the town overnight (Ripon Civic Society 1972: 14). But time-disciplines operated in markets also. Usually this was by the ringing of a bell to signal the opening and closing of trade – trading outside these limits was often a punishable offence. At York the markets held in Pavement were opened and closed by the bell of All Saints or Ouse Bridge Chapel. The Butter Dings in the market place at Beverley had a bell tower for the same purpose, Hull also had a market bell, while bells signalled the opening and closing of the market at Selby. The hours of work generally were regulated by bells. Masons working in York, for instance, began or ended their work by the bells of the Minster. In this way a quite definite urban routine and time regime developed, separate from rural time and work on the land which was regulated more by the seasons and the weather. Furthermore, the urban time regime was to tighten. Around 1370, a new ordinance was introduced at York which stated that the masons should work 'tille itte be hegh none smytyn by ye clocke' (Salzman 1952: 61).

A significant advance occurred with the development of the mechanical clock from perhaps the late thirteenth century. Now the interests of the urban elite were to be served by a more precise control over the measurement of time. In European cities it was not long before clocks were being built into public buildings – Paris 1300, London between 1326 and 1335, Bologna 1356, for example. Just when mechanical clocks became a common feature of provincial English towns is a trickier question to answer. They seem to have been a rarity in Yorkshire towns except at the major urban centres, and even then it is difficult to decide just when they *first* appeared. At York, for example, the clock was in the tower of St William's Chapel on Ouse Bridge by 1370, and it regulated the ringing of the city bell. Other clocks include the one at Hedon where the town accounts of 1389–90 mention payments for the repair of a clock. Repair is the important word, for it suggests that the clock had already been going for some time, perhaps putting it nearer in date to the first appearances of clocks in continental cities. It may have been the same clock that John and William Clokmaker were repairing in the tower of St Augustine's, the great chapel which overlooked the market place. The date is uncertain, but according to the church warden's accounts and the records of the building of the tower it looks as if a remodelled clock was being fitted into the new tower built between 1427 and 1437 (Boyle 1895: cxxii–iii). Hull had at least two clocks: one in Holy Trinity church, repaired 1426,

and one in St Mary's (Gillet and MacMahon 1989: 91). Earlier than this was the clock at St Wilfred's, Ripon, which was in position in one of the bell-towers in 1379 (SURTEES 81: 101). These clocks may well not have had chapter rings initially, but may have been mechanical devices by which the hours were struck and time more precisely measured; they are mentioned mostly in connection with church bells and belfries.

The common link between the above mechanical clocks, then, is their siting in a church tower. While Le Goff (1977: 29–42) has argued for the strengthening of time-discipline by means of the mechanical clock and suggested that a division might usefully be made between the church's time and merchants' time, he is in some respects wide of the mark in implying that the church began to lose control of time in the later Middle Ages. The church might indeed reckon by scriptural time or the dates of feast and saints days for the purposes of doctrine or ceremony, but it is naive to suggest that churchmen had no consciousness or understanding of time measured by clocks. People worked in a plurality of timescales according to what was appropriate to the context. Time was a gift from God to be used wisely, and the merchant in seeking a more precise measurement of time sought to do just that. Far from losing control of time, the positioning of clocks in church towers was more than just a practical measure: it was a symbolic expression of the divine origin of measurement and gave religious approbation to the better ordering of towns and town life.

NOTES

1. The word *dings* occurs at several of the county's towns. The English Place Name Society suggests a connection with Old Scandinavian meaning 'dung', but unless used humorously, Butter Dings seems a strange combination. It may be connected with the obsolete dialect word *ding* meaning low-lying. At Hull, for instance, the Dings appear to have been shops partly below the level of the street in the market place, and Raine (1955: 60) states that *ding* was used in York to mean a cellar. However, an alternative explanation is that the word is connected with Old Danish/Old English *thing* meaning an assembly or council. This would make more sense in Beverley where the ecclesiastical premises made over to the council was also known as Thinghall.

CHAPTER NINE

Urban Houses

ANYONE WHO STUDIES the medieval town will sooner or later come across the term *burgage*. Indeed, some historians have proposed that the existence of burgage plots is one of the marks of a town along with borough charters and so on (see Chapter 1). While such arguments should not be dismissed, we should nevertheless take care that we do not ascribe to a legal term a physical reality in the form of either a piece of land or the buildings on it. The use of the term *burgage* needs to be clarified from the start.

A burgess was someone who had a right to a burgage, that is a holding of land usually in the shape of a long plot which carried with it certain tenurial privileges: essentially, the freedom from agricultural services due to seigneurs. Strictly speaking the word is a legal term. A burgage might, however, imply that the holding contained a house as well as land, and the whole might be loosely called a burgage. Thus, where the term occurs in legal documents such as the deeds of sale, the house itself might be referred to as a burgage. Nevertheless, this is a legal usage implying that burgage tenure applied to the house. In other words, a burgage is no more a physical reality than are other legal terms referring to property such as tenement. This has implications: we should not think that the division of land into plots with buildings was somehow physically different in boroughs and non-burghal towns; they differed only in their legal rights of tenure. Although an obvious point, what we are dealing with in the medieval town is town or urban houses, and what we should be trying to determine is their common characteristics and how they differed from or were similar to rural houses.

TYPES OF HOUSE

Chapter 6 has already dealt with some types of urban residence – the urban castle or fortified house and the quadrangular-plan palaces of bishops. Some minor landed families and merchants also seem to have built the latter type of house, the outstanding example in the county being the de la Pole house at Hull. This no longer exists, but was exceptional in being illustrated in the sixteenth and seventeenth centuries. The maps of Hull by Hollar or Speed, for example, show the house standing at the north end of the town, and while they can hardly be relied on as accurate architectural drawings they are nevertheless consistent in depicting two features: a quadrangular form of house with a tall gatehouse or tower. A drawing probably of the 1540s by the Tudor engineer John Rogers (Shelby 1967: plate 13) tends to confirm this although it is uncertain whether this is a depiction of the house as it then stood, or as it might look after some remodelling. A survey of 1538 (Shelby 1967: 164) states that the tower was of three storeys and built of brick. There was a hall, great chamber and chapel as well as a large number of other chambers and service rooms – the sort of planning that one would expect to find in the houses of prelates and seigneurs. Indeed, it seems probable that this had been the house of the King's Keeper of Hull acquired by the de la Poles after 1330 when it seems to have become known as Hull Garthe or Courthall, although Speed in 1610 names it King's Place probably because it had been taken back into royal ownership in the sixteenth century when Henry VIII had toyed with the idea of making it his residence.

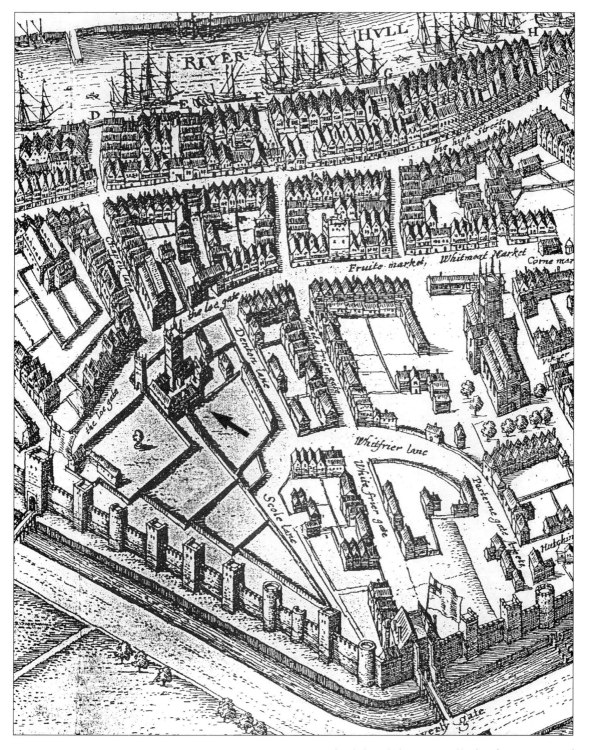

The de la Pole house at Hull taken from a section of Hollar's plan.

What the survey of 1538 also reveals is a development which was typical of even the best commercial and mercantile families – parts of the house given over to business. Surprisingly, perhaps, the entrance to Hull Garthe was 'a gatehows buylded with timber and covered with tile wherin is two chambers and the entrye buylded on bothe sides with warehouses of tymbre werk covered with tile'. They measured one hundred by twenty feet.

Unfortunately this house and others like it within the county have not survived, yet documentary records indicate that they were once more common. In Hull there were two or three houses with towers, while in Skipton there was Winterwell Hall which stood in Swadford Street. The house was in existence by at least the

---

St William's College, York. Although there has been a good deal of alteration and restoration over the centuries the house preserves the basic construction of stone ranges with timber first floors built around four sides of a quadrangle, with the entrance in the centre of the long side fronting the street.

mid-fifteenth century when it belonged to Bolton Priory, and a description of it in 1522 – when it was owned by a lawyer – lists 'the tower, the grete parlor and chamber ov' it, the study chamber and parlour or study under it' among other rooms (Whitaker 1805: 439).

Some quadrangular-plan and moated houses were situated just outside towns. At Beverley, for instance, four such houses were located just beyond the built-up area and belonged probably to merchant/landowning families such as the Coppandale family's house near Pighill Lane or the Bedford's house near Scrubwood Lane; there were two others at Woodhall and near Pottergate (RCHME 1982). Similarly, at Hedon the Twyers, a lesser landed family occupied what was probably a quadrangular-plan house on the edge of the town to the north. All of these houses, however, are known only from maps and archaeological investigation. There were further quadrangular-plan houses to be found within towns, some of them intended for collegiate occupation such as St William's College, York, the dwelling of the minster chantry priests. This house had been begun about 1465, and

continued as a residence even after the dissolution of the college in 1546 when it was converted
to a single dwelling, probably for Sir Michael
Stanhope.

While the towers of the houses of some
magnates could probably be used for defence, it
is more likely that they were built as a mark
of prestige, having seigneurial associations.
Similarly, from what is known of their construction, stone or brick was used for the towers and
perhaps for halls, while other parts of the houses
were built of timber or part-timber and stone.
All-masonry construction was more usual in the
central and later Middle Ages for churches and
castles, and thus its use for towers and halls once
again reinforced the impression of authority and
prestige.

Aside from the houses of the magnates, most
town houses were not simply houses but shops,
inns or commercial premises of various sorts.
Trade areas such as shops usually fronted the
street; domestic residential accommodation was
located to the rear and/or above the shop itself.
Pantin (1963b) proposed two basic plan-forms
in his work on English medieval town houses:
first a house with a hall range parallel to the
street (see Figure 9.1 (A)); second a house with
a hall range at right angles to the street, but
possibly with trade premises fronting the street
(see Figure 9.1 (B)). Both of these plan-forms can
be found among surviving houses at York. Bowes
Morrell House in Walmgate (early fifteenth
century) has a hall parallel to the street and a
cross-wing. Numbers 49–51, Goodramgate (fifteenth–sixteenth century) consisted originally of
a range parallel to Goodramgate, probably commercial premises, with a hall at right angles to it
at the rear.

From the fifteenth century it seems to have
become more common to build some smaller

Figure 9.1 Position of hall in town houses

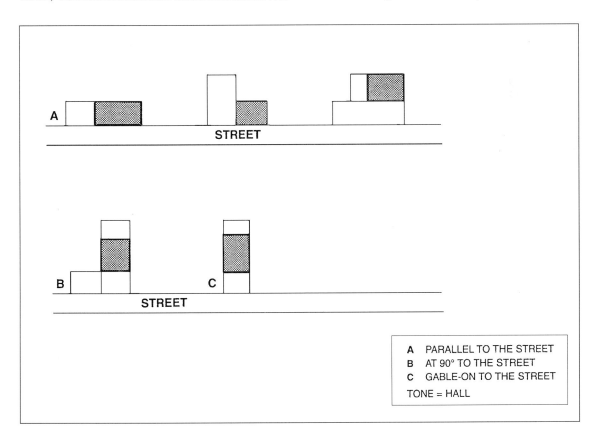

A   PARALLEL TO THE STREET
B   AT 90° TO THE STREET
C   GABLE-ON TO THE STREET
TONE = HALL

Bowes Morrell House, Walmgate, York. The short hall lies parallel to the street with a cross-wing to the left. Later development has taken place to the rear.

*Houses and shops in Goodramgate, York, have
commercial ranges parallel to the street front . . .*

. . . but a hall range at right angles to it at the rear.

houses with narrow gables set end-on to the street with between one and three rooms in a line behind (see Figure 9.1 (C)). This type of house might be one or two storeys, but seems always to have had its gable jettied and facing the street front. Typical examples occur along Shambles and Low Petergate where they can be found built in groups of two or three – speculation, perhaps, or possibly some form of concerted building activity? The gabled front elevation seems to have been a shop and the rooms to the rear seem to have supplied domestic accommodation.

Houses of similar plan-forms to these York houses can be found in other towns. In New-biggin, Richmond, the Unicorn Inn was formerly a house or shop of the early sixteenth century with a hall aligned parallel to the street; a house known as the Ark at Tadcaster similarly had a hall range parallel to the street. Both houses had cross-wings. In this same category was the house known as the Wakeman's house at Ripon, but only the cross-wing now survives, its adjacent hall range being demolished in the nineteenth century. Hall ranges at right angles to front ranges can be found in New Market, Pontefract, and at what was formerly the Three Cranes inn, High Street, Rotherham.

While the major urban centres appear to share many similarities in the development of town houses, there were some differences between these and the smaller towns, and between York and all the others. One difference is that houses with narrow frontages gable-on to the street are less common in all other towns than they are in York, to the point of being non-existent in some. It may be that greater numbers survive in York simply because there had been greater numbers of them, York being one of the largest cities in medieval England. There are also some grounds for thinking that the form was once more common in other towns. One survives in Ladygate, Beverley, and at 116 High Street, Yarm where only the rear timber range remains (Cleveland and Teeside Local History Society 1989: 4). There are probably more at Scarborough. Here a number of tall, slim, gabled houses near to the harbour in the old town,

although dating from the sixteenth to the eighteenth centuries, probably represent the replacement of timber houses with stone yet retaining the earlier form.

Further differences between housing in large towns and small towns is reflected in plan-form. Hall ranges set at right angles to the street seem to be far more common in the large towns, whereas in small towns plan-forms more usually associated with rural housing are common. The latter would include the hall and cross-wing plan with large halls, and linear-plan houses where three rooms are arranged in line along the street rather than at right angles to it. These types of house also create a different impression, probably because they are lower, are generally of two storeys rather than three and have a regional appearance – a vague term for a quality difficult to describe. The house called the Ark at Tadcaster previously mentioned is a good example. While located in a small town not far from the market place, it is not significantly different from the sorts of hall and cross-wing houses that wealthy farmers of the fifteenth and sixteenth centuries were building in villages or farm hamlets. Similarly, the house known as the Rectory House overlooking the market place at Helmsley is of two storeys and a hall and cross-wing form, and like the Ark would not have looked out of place in the country. Although of early modern date, it shows the persistence of this form in small towns.

There also seem to have been more houses built for agricultural purposes in small towns. Probably more of them were also single storey – not cottages but longhouses, built both on the perimeters and near to the centres of towns, a practice which continued in the smaller North Yorkshire towns until well into the seventeenth century, as one recent RCHME study has shown (1987: Chapter 6). Such differences hint at perhaps some fundamental differences between the large and small towns – between small towns more closely linked to agricultural traditions and containing greater numbers of people with agricultural occupations, towns moreover where competition for commercial space was less acute than in the bustling major urban centres,

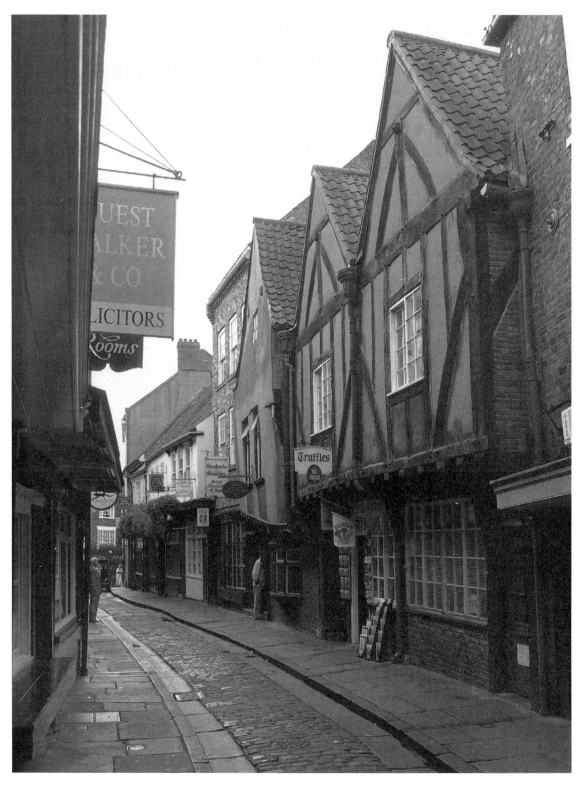

Timber-framed shops in Shambles, York, with jettied gabled elevations facing onto Shambles.

A late medieval house/shop at Pontefract with a front range parallel to New Market, and a hall range to the rear now largely rebuilt. The building has been successively remodelled, but the jettying of the front is immediately recognisable.

The same plan-form in High Street, Rotherham, but with a gabled frontage dating from perhaps the late fifteenth century. This is what remains of the Three Cranes.

The so-called Richard III's House at Scarborough dates probably from the sixteenth century, but may be the replacement of an earlier structure of similar form.

The Ark, Tadcaster. The hall is central; only the far wing has survived and a further wing should join the hall at the left of the picture.

although due note must be taken of fluctuating urban economic fortunes.

These were not the only types of house to be found within medieval towns. In fact Pantin (1963b) deliberately excluded both large and small houses from his study in order to concentrate on what he saw as rural house types built on urban sites. This chapter began with large houses, the sort of towered, quadrangular plans built by wealthy merchants and lawyers or other magnates, and has been concentrating on Pantin's core group of urban houses placed either parallel or end-on to the street. These latter were the houses of merchants, shopkeepers, craftsmen and probably professional families.

What have so far been excluded are the houses of those lower down the social ladder, the poor craftsmen, hucksters or labourers, for instance.

The houses of these people are difficult to study as far as some towns are concerned, since although their dwellings are occasionally mentioned in medieval documents, very few of them have survived, probably because they were not of an enduring build in the first place and because they were not worth maintaining other than for the rents they might bring in; they might, therefore, easily be redeveloped as a more profitable investment. Poor craftworkers must have occupied houses at the bottom end of any scale of housing – perhaps one-up, one-downs. Few dwellings of this sort can be found, although a house or cottage that stands on the corner of King's Court, York, may well be a survivor of the type. Although it has undergone a good deal of alteration, the basic form seems to

The Rectory, Helmsley, is an early modern example of late medieval rural forms of house continuing to be built in small towns.

have been a two-roomed, two-storeyed house, the first floor being jettied.

Many labourers, apprentices or servants, moreover, would not have had a house or cottage of their own, but would have lived on their masters' premises, at least for the period of their training, if not longer.

Fortunately there is a huge exception to the lack of standing remains in most towns, and that is York, where lower orders of housing survive along with a certain amount of documentation. A feature of the development of York streets in the central Middle Ages was the building of rows of cottages. In a scholarly article Short (1980) has shown that these were often the result of speculations by the church to provide income for chantries and for other uses. Availability of land in prime trading areas of the city was low, so that strips of churchyard adjacent to some lesser streets or land held by

religious houses might be used on which to build shallow, longish rows of cottages suitable for those of humble standing. The earliest of these – and the earliest documented terrace in England – is located along the edge of Holy Trinity churchyard in Goodramgate. This is Lady Row, dating from 1316, a jettied timber-framed terrace of eight cottages, although they originally appear to have extended further along Goodramgate by another three dwellings. Each had one ground-floor and one first-floor room. The first tenants are unknown, but Short, using the 1381 Poll Tax return for York, has suggested that the parish in which Lady Row is located contained many labourers and journeymen.

House in King's Court, York.

Several such rows were built and some survive although they have been altered over the centuries and do not present so clear a picture as Lady Row. Others are known from documentary sources but have been demolished such as a row by St Martin le Grand in Coney Street, also mentioned by Short (1980). A later row, Church or All Saints Cottages, can be found in North Street by the side of All Saints church. These are again built as a row under a continuous roof, but stand at right angles to the street, the house fronting North Street having a short hall in addition to the single-roomed ground-floor accommodation of the rest, suggesting that the tenant would have been of higher social standing. Short suggests that they date from around 1410. Further rows can be found in Newgate and Micklegate, but these are of three-storeyed construction, suggesting they were perhaps intended for people of somewhat higher social standing. Rows like this almost certainly existed in other Yorkshire towns and the short hospital row in Kirkgate, Knaresborough (see Chapter 5, pp. 83–4) tends to confirm this. However, further evidence of this type of urban cottage development is difficult to find.

DESIGN AND CONSTRUCTION

Although there were exceptions, the majority of houses in towns were built of timber. While this is correct as a generalisation, there are some finer points to be considered. The all-timber house has now become something of a rarity in urban locations with the exception of York. It is more common to find houses built with timber upper floors above a ground floor built of stone or brick. Part-timber and stone houses of this sort can be found, or are known to have been built, in all the major urban centres, especially York where perhaps the largest group of medieval timber-framed houses in the country survives. In some towns, documentary records seem to imply that municipal bodies might enforce this type of construction. At Richmond, for instance, the commonalty assigned to William de Hotone a piece of land in the bailey requiring him to build a burgage house 'de muris lapidibus et maeremio quercorum' – with stone walls and oak timbers (YASRS 39: 141–2).

The problem is that over the centuries alterations have taken place, and since the majority of survivals in towns have been converted to shops or offices, such alteration has been severe, making it difficult to recover the original appearance of the stone ground floor. Here, nineteenth-century illustrations are useful, especially those produced by serious-minded antiquaries and architectural historians such as John Henry Parker. In his *Concise Glossary of Architecture* of 1846 he illustrates what appears to have been a fourteenth-century part-timber and stone house in Newgate, York.

Although already a good deal altered by 1846, changes had taken place mostly to the first floor. On the stone-built ground floor it is still possible to identify some fair detailing – a pointed-arch doorcase with moulded jambs, soffit and drip moulding at the apex of which appears to have been a mask. There is also a shouldered-arch two-light window to the right-hand side and a small window (later converted to a doorway) to the left with a drip moulding and decorative stops. The remains of the building, today almost unrecognisable, show that the ground floor was constructed of the magnesian limestone ashlar so commonly encountered in the Tadcaster/York area. In other words this house can be thought of as showing some sophistication of design, and had probably been expensive to build. How frequent this sort of quality was and how widespread is now difficult to judge because of demolition, alterations and a lack of reliable illustrations, but it may well have been more common. What is more, when the design qualities can be considered more fully they present a very different view of medieval urban housing than the towering, tottering quaintness that settlement and heavy alterations have caused over a period of six hundred years.

But if timber and part-timber and stone houses seem to have predominated, there is also evidence of houses built entirely of stone. Stone houses, it has been argued by generations of architectural historians, are rare in medieval English towns – or anywhere else – because of

Lady Row, York, dating from around 1316 is one of the earliest surviving urban terraces of cottages.

expense. Stone was therefore employed only by those who could afford it – the church, royalty, aristocracy – and became a prestige building material as a result. There is some truth in this line of argument, and it is noticeable from what survives and from illustrations of what does not that castles and other defensive buildings together with churches and the buildings of religious communities and corporations were the chief structures to be built of stone. Even the houses of some prelates, for example the Bishop of Durham's palace at Howden, or merchants and magnates, for example the de la Pole residence at Hull – had some parts built of stone while other parts were built of timber.

But was this the whole story, and was expense the sole determining factor as many seem to suggest? The prelates and magnates mentioned above undoubtedly possessed the wealth to build in stone if they had so desired. More significantly, we have perhaps too readily ignored sources which show that the town houses of some wealthy people *were* built of stone, many before the fourteenth century. At a small number of towns and cities throughout England there are standing remains and sometimes substantial parts of stone houses, such as Moyses Hall, Bury St Edmunds, the Three Old Arches and 38–42 Watergate Street, Chester, houses in the Strait and Steep Hill, Lincoln, and the house called Canute's Palace in Southampton. Little on this scale has survived in Yorkshire, although in Stonegate, York, set well back from the street, there is the remains of a stone house of the twelfth century containing a two-light window

Church Cottages, North Street, York, are built along the side of All Saints church, and date from the early fifteenth century.

Newgate, York, c. 1380.

House in Newgate, York, illustrated by Parker in 1846.

on the first floor and indications that this was once a first-floor hall (RCHME 1981: 225), as indeed many of the other surviving stone houses seem to have been.

The stone house at York, however, is not the only above-ground stone house to have survived in the county. The house known as the Old Vicarage at Tadcaster, although sadly mutilated in later centuries, represents the substantial remains of a fifteenth–sixteenth-century house built of magnesian limestone. It seems to have consisted of a hall range connected to a solar wing, and may represent the replacement of an earlier house (RCHME 1994: NBR 37575). The house was not located on one of the main

This is all that remains of a twelfth-century stone house off Stonegate, York. Notice the two-light window at first-floor level where the hall was probably located.

streets but set back from the town centre in its own garden. The use of stone for a domestic building within a garden setting in a small town points to a prestigious use of both materials and space.

There are documentary references to further stone houses. More once existed in York: between 1204 and 1220 William Fairfax granted to the prior of Durham a stone house in Coney Street, while Kirkham Abbey owned further stone houses in Walmgate and Bretgate (Farrer 1914: 200, 244–5). John Selby, one of a wealthy family of York merchants and one of the king's moneyers, had a stone house called Munsorel in Micklegate (VCH 1961: 51). The towered houses at Hull mentioned above would have been built in part if not wholly of stone, and one is referred to in the Hull Corporation records as the 'tower' or 'Stonehouse' (VCH 1969: 77). At Scarborough the revenues of St Mary's church had been granted to the abbot of Citeaux who had appointed a proctor to supervise the Cistercian estates in England. The proctor had established himself in Scarborough by 1202, not as some-times thought in a monastery there but in a house on Tollergate which excavation has shown to have been a stone house (Farmer 1979: 20). In 1220 William Fitz Everard granted to St John's Priory at Pontefract the rent from a stone house he owned in the town (YASRS 25: 140). John le Gras, one of the canons of Beverley, endowed the new bridge and its chapel in Hull with property in Beverley before he died in 1279. Among this property were 'two stone houses in Keldgate' (YASRS 111: 11).

It is possible, therefore, to piece together evidence of stone houses in the major urban centres. But although these appear to have been widespread, they would also, on the same evidence, appear never to have been built in any great numbers and to date mostly from the twelfth to fourteenth centuries.

The reasons for this must surely have more to do with shifts in taste, aesthetics and social perceptions rather than mono-causal explanations which seek to establish a purely economic determinant. Changes of taste in medieval English architecture have been examined by art

and architectural historians only at the highest of levels – the great cathedrals, abbeys and other churches, together with some castles – and largely in terms of the categories imposed on the study by Thomas Rickman. Houses have rarely been deemed worthy of such attention, and research has been in the hands of archaeologists and the historians of vernacular architecture whose priorities have, understandably, been more concerned with the recovery of plan, the study of function and construction, and the relation of this to a chronology. Explanations of the use of stone in the construction of houses have, thus, tended to be somewhat two-dimensional relying heavily on economic causes. While the economics of the situation must have been important, new ways of using materials and the perceptions about social status these conveyed may have been equally important but have never really been evaluated, since they are neither an archaeological imperative nor a fit with the prevailing aesthetic constructs of art historians.

A further, widespread change in the appearance of houses should also be considered in this light. While the use of gables, jettying and multi-storeyed construction can be found in the buildings of medieval towns throughout several centuries, their use becomes much more frequent in the late Middle Ages and usually in combination. Judging from surviving houses at York, many that were built before 1400 consisted of jettied two- storey ranges. But during the fifteenth century it seems to have become increasingly common to build houses with gabled elevations to the street and to carry them up to three storeys, always using jettied construction in gabled elevations. They might be built as individual houses or they might be built in groups of three or four. Also, some existing two-storeyed buildings might be converted to this appearance. This does not mean that two-storeyed houses parallel to the street and without gables ceased to be built, rather that they were built in probably smaller numbers. For example, Mulberry Hall, Stonegate, York, was built as a two-storey jettied range in probably the mid-fifteenth century, but the structure was heightened by the addition of jettied gabled

Mulberry Hall, Stonegate, York – sixteenth-century gables added to a fifteenth-century range.

upper rooms to the front of the range in the following century.

Houses of this type can be found in other Yorkshire towns, although nowhere have they survived in such numbers as they have at York. Drawings and nineteenth-century photographs clearly show them along High Street in Hull, Kirkgate in Ripon and Crown Street in Halifax, this last by the late fifteenth–sixteenth centuries a growing urban centre. They survive behind layers of rendering and generations of alterations at Lambert's Yard in Leeds, High Street in Rotherham and Silver Street in Wakefield. Further illustration in town plans such as those by Speed of around 1610 suggest that by the sixteenth and seventeenth centuries houses with multi-storeyed gabled elevations occupied the streets of most towns. But there are problems, here. Speed and other cartographers may have been using a graphic convention; and what is more, even if accurate, further rebuildings in similar styles would have undoubtedly taken place in the century or so before Speed and his contemporaries got to work. Nevertheless, if it were a convention then it was one based on current trends as we can see from the numbers

of houses which survive, and if further rebuildings had taken place then they were of a type very similar to late medieval types and in a direct line of development from the fifteenth century. Hollar's plan of Hull drawn in 1640 is probably a more accurate representation of the town than Speed's, being a carefully delineated bird's-eye perspective in which individual buildings are recognisable. This shows large numbers of multi-storey gabled buildings built densely along the main streets. The picture was probably similar in many of the large towns, and it is probably one which had emerged largely, though not wholly, by 1550.

It is also important to recognise that such developments occurred mostly in the towns during the fifteenth century. Rural society below aristocratic and gentle estate do not appear to have built these types of houses. Yeomen farmers, franklins and those of similar rank tended in the fifteenth and sixteenth centuries to build two-storey houses of hall and cross-wing form

*Three-storey jettied and gabled houses in Coney Street,
York, built as a group.*

Low Petergate, York.

Crown Street, Halifax, from a drawing made before the redevelopment of this street in the nineteenth century. On the right is a clear depiction of sixteenth(?)-century houses of jettied and gabled form. On the left, similar houses are just recognisable after later remodellings.

or houses with rooms in a line, that is linear-plan houses. If the latter have some similarities with urban houses, unlike them they were usually of only two and frequently of a single storey, as far as we can judge. Houses of three storeys at these dates and among these social groups appear to have been rare, and it was not until about the beginning of the seventeenth century in Yorkshire that gables began to appear as a marked and conscious display feature in the elevations of rural houses of wealthy yeomen. Only among the higher social groups do we find the use of multi-storey and gabled elevations before 1600

– for example, Barrington Court, Somerset, after 1514, and Little Moreton Hall, Cheshire, around 1559.

Allowing for exceptions like these, multi-storey houses with gabled elevations were predominantly an urban form. However, they were not restricted to Yorkshire, nor even England, but seem to have been part of a larger architectural development that can be found throughout northern Europe and parts of France. It is a phenomenon difficult to account for. The reasons usually given are that by the fifteenth century space in towns was at a premium and, therefore, expansion of properties was effected by building upwards, adding further storeys; timber-framed construction facilitated the addition of these extra units. This sort of argument has been advanced by historians, architectural historians and archaeologists (Braudel 1981; Brunskill 1997; Schofield and Vince 1994). While it should be taken heed of, it is also as well to be aware of its main failing, for it rests on the assumption that towns were continually expanding. It thus oversimplifies matters, tending to ignore the question of late medieval urban decline, a debate within which it should be contextualised.[1]

If historians' arguments concerning economic decline and the decay of towns in the late fifteenth and early sixteenth centuries are accepted then the assumptions of some archaeologists and architectural historians that pressure on space drove people to build upwards is a contradiction. In depressed economic circumstances there could have been little cause for a building boom, and even so, there should have been numbers of vacant or derelict properties to be taken over and redeveloped. However, even if one weighs in on the other side of the argument – that an urban economic decline has been exaggerated – there is still evidence to suggest that there were properties standing empty, but probably as a result of population depletion rather than economic decline. The re-edifying statutes of Henry VIII do seem to establish that there were indeed numbers of derelict properties in the major urban centres, but they can be used to confirm *both* arguments.

Yet whichever perspective one brings to bear, the fact is that houses were indeed rebuilt or expanded upwards. However, the resulting form was so widespread that it cannot be viewed simply as the response to local conditions, and even national demographic and economic factors cannot provide whole answers to the problems raised by an architectural development that crossed European boundaries. In other words the solution to the emergence and development of this type of house should be sought in a multi-causal explanation, a complex interplay of factors in which spatial and economic pressures should be carefully scrutinised, but in which more account ought to be taken of a shift in building fashion and the ways in which space *within* urban properties was used.

FUNCTION: HOME AND WORK

So far little distinction has been made between houses in terms of how they functioned. Urban houses might function in several ways – as residences, as commercial or mercantile houses, as craft shops, as retail shops, as inns. Perhaps the least common of these was the house used simply as a place of residence, since the occupiers of most urban houses carried on a trade from their homes. Only perhaps aristocratic families with a town house or labourers used their houses for residence only, in the sense that they did not also have some specialised part of it given over to trade, such as a shop, craft shop or warehouse.

The largest group of houses – those with a specialist function – are also the most difficult to research in some ways because medieval shop fronts and craft shops to the rears of houses have usually been destroyed in later remodellings even where the original house exists. A general sort of impression can be gained from medieval illustrative sources which suggest that some shop fronts had fold-out tables or shutters on which to display wares, as well as having protective awnings or pentices above to protect goods from the weather. These would appear to have been short roofs supported on brackets and running the width of a shop front either as individual roofs or as longer roofs shared by two or three shops. We also know from documentary records that shop signs were commonly set over the street on beams. This was sometimes a requirement of the civic authority with regard to certain premises, especially inns and taverns, as at York where an ordinance of 1477 stated that:

> no man ne woman within this said Citie, suburbs and precincts of the same holde non osterie commune [common inn] without that thai have a sygne ower thare dore. (YASRS 98: 21)

But all such commercial frontages and their display elements have largely disappeared now.

As far as the rears of houses are concerned it is mostly through archaeological investigation that we know anything about the sites of outbuildings. At Yarm, for example, a furnace and metal-working site have been discovered to the rear of 101 High Street (Evans and Heslop 1985), while at Doncaster work has uncovered three structures with evidence of metal-working situated near North Bridge (Lilley 1994). The rears of houses were probably the places where some of the blade-makers of towns like Sheffield had their smithies, several of which we learn about from wills such as that of William Hyne, 1498, which mentions his 'Smethyhous' on Water Lane (Hall 1913: 109). The survival of above-ground structures is, however, something much more rare.

Warehousing is a subject that has already been discussed in connection with quays, but warehouses also seem to have been built either within or attached to houses. As with craft shops, a good deal of private warehousing has probably been removed from domestic sites, although it is possible that some lies disguised in later remodellings. However, there are one or two survivals. At Swales Yard, Pontefract, a long part-timber and stone range of two storeys projects from the rear of a house that looks onto the former Neat Market. It is jettied to both sides and seems to have been the result of two periods of building from probably the fifteenth to the sixteenth centuries, the final range being 30.5 metres in length (Pontefract n.d.). Although its exact use cannot be ascertained, it was not residential accommodation and probably supplied either warehousing or workshops. It is strikingly similar in its size, simplicity of build and appearance to the part-timber and brick warehouse at King's Lynn which Hanseatic merchants built probably in the late fifteenth century (Pantin 1963a; Clark 1979). It may also have been similar to the two warehouses of the de la Poles built at the entrance to Hull Garthe, mentioned above.

Documents provide further evidence of shops and workshops. When he died in 1512 William Twhaites, a founder, had a house in York with a shop and a 'workhusse' in which there were tools, quantities of metal and a store of bells and candlesticks. A fellow founder of York who died in 1516 had besides his York shop a 'wirkyng chamber' and 'meltyng howse' (SURTEES 79: XXVII, LXVI). And when Richard King of

Sheffield died he willed his smithy to his daughter Alice together with his 'best stithie [anvil], bellowes, hammers and tonges with all thinges belonging to the same harthe' (BIHR vol. 13, fol. 434).

Looking at documentary sources such as probate inventories (of which very few survive) one is also struck by mention of specialist rooms not connected with the primary trade of the testator, confirming Swanson's (1989) view that some craftsmen practised more than one trade. John Cadeby of Beverley, for example, who was a mason, nevertheless had a malthouse standing next to his house when he died sometime between 1430 and 1450. This together with a 'gylehouse' – gyle was a flavouring and preservative of ale – suggests he may have been brewing on more than a domestic scale or perhaps selling the materials needed for brewing (SURTEES 45: XXV). Innkeeping was a trade which lent itself to just such a dual occupation. John Stubbs was a barber of York who also ran an inn. His probate inventory gives one of the few insights into the specialised buildings surrounding the county's inns. It contained two halls and six bedchambers, there was also a brewhouse and ancillary buildings such as a gyle house, there were stables and there was also a barber's shop where Stubbs no doubt shaved his guests.[2] In all of these examples the workshops and brewhouses were almost certainly located to the rear.

Just exactly how craft and sales shops were arranged to accommodate trade, however, still leaves a number of questions to be answered. It is assumed, for instance, and probably correctly, that the apartment(s) to the front of the house and fronting the street formed a shop. But what is often difficult to decide because of several centuries of change is whether the shop communicated directly with the house, or indeed, where there was a relatively long street frontage, whether there was more than one shop. This sort of arrangement – where several shop units might be built as a speculation – was perhaps more common than we realise. There are documentary records of such multiple occupancy as we shall see below, and there is also some

The warehouse to the rear of a house in Swales Yard,
Pontefract.

architectural survival. At 28–32 Coppergate, York, recent investigation (RHCME 1988: NBR 13279) has revealed the remains of a double timber range parallel to the street. That to the rear may have been domestic accommodation or, because of its size, possibly in institutional use or an inn; that to the front was separate shop units with accommodation over.

But there were yet other ways of accommodating trade. What sometimes gives cause for comment is the great spaciousness of some medieval market places, especially in linear-plan towns. This can be explained by the need to provide room for a large number of stalls, which is certainly a correct interpretation. But there is a further structure to be taken into account here: the booth. It seems likely that where there was room, short terraces of flimsily built timber structures of a single storey were built in front of some houses located around the market place. These were booths (Old Icelandic/Old Scandinavian *botha*, *bothus* – a hut or temporary dwelling) and provided covered sales spaces that could probably be locked. Thus, if some houses in linear-plan towns seem to stand well back from the street it was probably to allow room for booths to be built in front. Booths were intermediate between the stall and a house/shop, and some were perhaps used like lock-up shop units. Others may well have been the means by which shops were projected from the fronts of properties, allowing workshop room or full domestic use of the house behind. The medieval Latin terms *stallum* or *selda* do not present much of a problem and are usually rightly translated as a stall, meaning a table or trestle which could be set out in the market place, although these were perhaps not always taken down and removed. However, the Latin *taberna* is probably too often translated as 'tavern' rather than 'booth', its other meaning. Structures of this sort do not last and leave no trace in archaeological deposits since they probably had no more in the way of foundations than has a garden shed.

However, several documentary sources suggest that they existed, although, for the reasons given above, translation of the Latin can be a tricky business. The Bradford Manor Court Rolls provide several clear references to booths in the market place there, the term usually written in Anglicised French – *le bothe*, for example. The Grenehode family of Wakefield provide a further useful example. In 1322 Richard Grenehode conveyed to his son his stall in Wakefield market and his *tavern* according to one translation of the deed (YASRS 120: 179). This was almost certainly a booth and not a tavern – the same booth which had been referred to in English in 1316 and which stood between 'the booth of Peter the baker and the booth of German son of Philip' (YASRS 120: 178).

This last piece of documentation raises a further development, for we learn that the booth had or was built over the entrance to a cellar. The building of cellars or undercrofts beneath houses with access from the street in front, and possibly with access from within the house, became another way of extending the usable space of the house for trade purposes. Although this was noted and written about in the nineteenth century – Parker (1853) for instance – the pioneering research was carried out by Faulkner (1966) who described numbers of stone-built and often vaulted cellars in medieval town houses with access to the cellar from the street. Since there was no intercommunication between some houses and cellars, Faulkner concluded that these were probably shops or warehouses occupied by different tradesmen from those occupying the house or shop above. He was also able to demonstrate that this was a widespread phenomenon, recording examples at Chester, Exeter, Oxford, Southampton and Winchelsea.

Despite the RCHME's exhaustive survey of York, no traces of medieval cellars used in this way have come to light in what remains of the medieval city. This contrasts with other towns in the county. We have just seen documentary reference to a cellar in the market place at Wakefield, and there were others. The Dings in Hull seems to have been an area of semi-subterranean shops bordering the market place. At Malton a cellar below the Cross Keys in Wheelgate is thought to have been the site of a hospital of Malton Priory who owned land there

(Graham 1901: 37, 213; VCH 1914: 529). An alternative explanation is that it was once a cellar used for the purposes of trade. At Pontefract a cellar has survived below the Malt Shovel Inn in the present-day Beast Fair, while a little further along the road, the house fronting the Swales Yard warehouse mentioned above also had a cellar with external access to the street. The more elaborate of these two cellars is that below the Malt Shovel which has rib vaulting and carved bosses.

With due note taken of the usage of the Latin *taberna*, the use of cellars for taverns nevertheless seems to have been a common one, although they were not exclusively used in this way. Also, multiple occupancy of properties in which cellars were important units seems to have continued into the early modern period. A run of deeds relating to properties along Kirkgate and Ivegate in Bradford illustrates this well. Properties there are described as messuages and burgages, comprising houses, shops and cellars which were often in different occupancies. One property consisted of 'two tavernes or sellars under the house, one shopp . . . now in the occupation of Joseph Turner One Taverne or sellar under the same . . . One other sellar in the occupation of John Sikes'. The term 'tavern' here was being used in the sense of a place where alcohol was sold, since other documents in the series refer to wine taverns. The house and shops had in the past been occupied by a linen draper and a cordwainer, and were to be let to a glazier and a butcher. The premises adjoined the Toll Booth on Kirkgate and were known as Pycorner. Around the corner in Ivegate was Hoult House consisting of a shop occupied by a butcher and a cellar occupied by the butcher's son.[3]

When it comes to looking at the domestic accommodation offered by medieval town houses, the problems encountered above for these more specialised areas recur: alterations often centuries old in themselves have usually removed all traces of the original medieval planning. It is more profitable to comment on rooms and room functions which can be identified from sources such as wills and probate

inventories. The latter, however, are few and unreliable – they may or may not be accurate records or list all the rooms of a house, the function and furnishings of rooms do not necessarily tally, and probate inventories do not encompass the whole range of urban houses and their occupiers. They must, therefore, be used with caution. They do allow us to identify common rooms, bearing in mind that this is across a small sample of inventories (perhaps no more than twenty to thirty relating to urban properties). By the fifteenth century it seems that many of the larger houses possessed parlours and chambers. The former were probably on the ground floor, the latter on upper floors. John Colan, a York goldsmith who died in 1490, had several chambers together with a 'great chamber' (SURTEES 53: XXVI). It is tempting to see this as a room given over to grand entertainment in the way that a great chamber was in the sixteenth century, but there is little to suggest this was so. On the evidence of the inventory Colan seems to have been using the chamber as a bedroom with possibly a combined use as a warehouse for cloth. On the slim evidence presented by inventories, it was perhaps not unusual for chambers to be used in this way in the houses of tradesmen great and small: that is as a combination of warehousing and an apartment for sleeping. The inventory of John Danby of Northallerton who died in 1444 suggests he might have been a coverlet weaver. In his chamber was cloth and wool and ten coverlets, but there were also chests and a feather bed with its furnishings (SURTEES 2: LXIII).

It is also clear that most houses possessed kitchens, but whether these were within the house or, more likely, outside the house is not specified. Some rooms with specialised functions also appear. John Underwood's inventory of around 1515 records that his house had a 'studio libri' or library, a necessary room in the house of a York lawyer (SURTEES 79: LVII).

One room omitted so far which most inventories list and which is sometimes mentioned in wills and other documents is the hall. The function of the hall within the medieval house generally is one open to debate: did it remain a

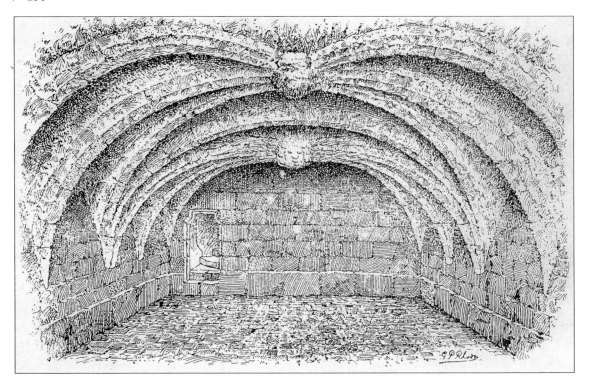

Cellar below the Malt Shovel Inn, Pontefract.

communal living area where the seigneur dined with his household as it is thought to have functioned in the early Middle Ages? Or was this function changing by the central Middle Ages as the seigneur and his immediate entourage withdrew themselves to more private arrangements in the solar or great chamber, leaving the hall to lesser members of the household? If this did occur, another question which arises is how changing use affected the functioning of wealthy non-seigneurial rural houses. For the urban house the question is not so much this as establishing whether such functions existed at all, or whether there was a certain amount of trade or commercial use of the hall. Was the hall, for instance, used to display wares in some houses? Or was it used to conduct business of a more commercial nature? Or could it have been used as a formal reception area for customers or merchants of repute? The furnishings of halls revealed by the inventories is inconclusive: they

are furnished very much as any medieval hall might have been with benches, chairs, tables, sideboards, wall hangings and cushions, but this does not preclude other activities. However, it does seem as though the relationship between hall, parlour and chamber above the parlour in some urban houses was similar to that of rural houses. The so-called Wealden House in Goodramgate, York, for example, had just such an arrangement of rooms with a central open hall and what appears to have been a parlour with a chamber above at the eastern end (see Figure 9.2).

On the other hand it is clear from both documentary sources and standing remains that this was not the only way of accommodating the hall, and that rooms might be arranged to suit trading needs. In York the RCHME (1981) have recorded four buildings with first-floor halls of fourteenth–fifteenth century date – well outside the date range usually associated with this form for rural houses. Of these four buildings, at least one was an inn, and this may have some relevance. We have already seen that specialised

arrangements existed at inns – that run by John
Stubbs of York had two halls. Some surviving
buildings show that the hall might be accommodated in unusual positions – to the rears of
parallel ranges as at 28–32 Coppergate, York
(RHCME 1988: NBR 13279), or they might be of
unusual proportions such as the rather narrow
hall of Bowes-Morrell House, Walmgate, York, or
that of the end house of Church Cottages, North
Street, York. Although similarities appear to have
existed between the position and functioning
of the hall in rural and some urban houses,
there also seem to have been a number of
dissimilarities. These are great enough to suggest a separate development of urban and rural
forms of house, influenced by spatial, cultural
and economic differences.

LOCATION

A traditional interpretation of residential land
use within the medieval town is one which

*Hoult House, Bradford, from a nineteenth-century
engraving. The tall building on the corner, left, is the
Toll Booth; the white building adjoining it is Hoult
House. Although these properties were rebuilt in the
seventeenth to the nineteenth centuries, they preserve
something of their former functions – note the people
entering the cellar of Hoult House from the street.*

places wealthy merchants and burgesses in a
central position around the market areas and
relegates the urban poor largely to the margins
and suburbs. A classic statement of this position
occurs in Sjöberg:

> The preindustrial city's central area is notable
> also as the chief residence of the elite. Here
> are the luxurious dwellings . . . the disadvan-
> taged members of the city fan outward toward
> the periphery, with the very poorest and the
> outcastes living in the suburbs, the fartherest
> removed from the center. (1960: 97–8)

It is a view that several geographers and historians have lent their weight to including Braudel (1981: 503–4). However, it is very much a generalised view, and one which has been questioned. Vance (1971), for example, proposed a multinucleic pattern of urban land use based on clusterings of trades and crafts. Yet although subjected to criticism and debate, no one has entirely rejected the model which stresses the wealth and importance of central urban areas and the poverty of suburbs. It is also one which holds good for English medieval towns and

cities, since to some extent it can be substantiated by documentary records, as the work of Goldberg (1992: 163–4) and others suggests. But before we go any further one question arises: how do we define a suburb – an area outside town walls or defences? a newly built addition to a town? a road leading into a town? In this section the word 'suburb' refers to areas of residential development occurring outside the main circuit of the town as defined by walls or ditches or bars, and often occurring along roads leading into towns. Industrial suburbs will be dealt with in the following chapter.

Taxation returns of different sorts which refer to Yorkshire's major towns were often drawn up by wards or parishes some of which are identifiable with suburbs, thus suggesting which areas

Figure 9.2 49–51 Goodramgate, York – sketch plan and section

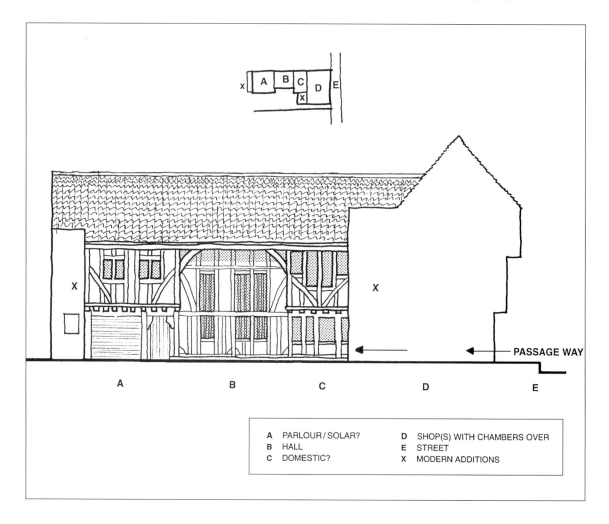

A	PARLOUR / SOLAR?	D	SHOP(S) WITH CHAMBERS OVER
B	HALL	E	STREET
C	DOMESTIC?	X	MODERN ADDITIONS

The end house of Church Cottages, North Street, York. The hall is to the right, and despite looking as if it has been truncated, it has not been.

paid most tax and which least. York had a number of suburbs, although the patchy survival of some of the city's taxation returns make comment difficult. However, the figures compiled by Bartlett (1953) do tend to suggest that it was the inner parishes of the city that were the wealthiest, while parishes to the southwest fringes of the city and suburbs like Bootham to the northeast were the poorest in the later fourteenth century. Bootham also seems to have been a place where cutlers had congregated, suggesting forging, grinding, noise and smoke (and, incidentally, illustrating Vance's argument for the multi-nucleic development of complex urban forms). We also catch a glimpse of the Bootham suburb in the late thirteenth century. It was situated on the road out of the town close to St Mary's Abbey and appears to have given so much cause for concern that in 1298 Edward I had ordered the pavements to be repaired and ruinous houses and pigsties to be pulled down (Calendar of Close Rolls 1296–1302: 218).

Suburbs had grown up around Beverley by the fourteenth century: to the north outside North Bar and Norwood, and, to a much lesser degree, to the west outside Keldgate. Taxation returns show that the inner wards of the city were the most prosperous, while the suburb of North Bar Without was the least so (VCH 1989: 53–5). Ripon too was divided into wards – known as constabularies – Market Stead, Skelgate, Stonebridge Gate and Westgate. As Mauchline (1972) has pointed out, the Poll Tax return of 1379 for the central ward of Market Stead lists a large number of people living there, many of them paying higher taxes and far more of them possessing servants when compared with the Stonebridge Gate ward, an area which corresponded with the eastern suburb. The same return for Hull shows that it was High Street, then known as Hull Street, which was the most densely populated and wealthiest part of the town. This street was lined with merchants' houses backing onto the Hull. It was followed by Marketgate, the market place, while poorer parts of the town were towards the western perimeters.

There are other ways of assessing the residential land use of towns. Doncaster has been the subject of a good deal of recent archaeological investigation. Slater (1989) has established that there were three suburbs: at Marsh Gate to the north, Hall Gate to the south and St Sepulchre Gate to the east. The latter, outside the town defences and on a main route into the town, seems to have consisted of cottages with irregularly enclosed plots. Marsh Gate near to the River Don seems to have been subject to flooding, and Slater suggests that it was an area of poorer housing as a result, although held in burgage tenure. Some towns – special cases, perhaps – had far-flung suburbs or satellite settlements, dependent on and under the jurisdiction of town authorities but located some way off because of the nature of their subsistence. Bridlington Priory, for example, possessed at least twelve cottages together about a mile distant from the town on the seashore which appear to have been the homes of fishermen, and there were other buildings connected with the port (YASRS 80: 5, 43–8).

If at some towns poor suburbs and marginalised areas dwindled away after the mid-fourteenth century, at some others they persisted. At Pontefract, for example, the road now known as South Bailygate which runs to the east of the town seems to have been a poor suburb during the Middle Ages and to have remained so in the sixteenth and into the seventeenth century, when it was depicted in a view of the castle. The painting shows a number of badly built cottages mostly of a single storey with dilapidated thatch and collapsing palisades to their gardens (Pontefract Museum). At Richmond, too, Cornforth Hill, the Green and Bargate formed a suburb descending from the centre of town to the southwest. In the granting of a new charter in 1441 the area was described as a place which 'artificers, victuallers [and] workmen' had been accustomed to inhabit, an area which remained so until even the nineteenth century according to Fieldhouse and Jennings (1978: 14, 271), although rebuilt with cottages and small houses over the centuries, some of them as poor housing.

Richmond, however, highlights another side of suburbs. The work of Keene (1975) and others has re-examined the view of suburbs as poor areas growing along the approach roads to towns, suggesting this to be an oversimplification. Keene has shown that residential suburbs were not simply the haunt of the poor, but that there were also wealthy suburbs. Similarly, the houses of urban magnates did not necessarily occupy central sites near to markets; some magnates preferred to build houses just outside town. So, at Richmond Frenchgate, a long street leading from the town to the east, formed a further suburb, and so did the eponymous Newbiggin – the 'new building' – that had taken place just outside the town to the west. Leyland considered Frenchgate 'almost as bygge as bothe the other suburbes' (Toulmin-Smith 1909: 24–5). If wealth were concentrated around the market place, it also spread to the Frenchgate and Newbiggin suburbs as well. At the latter a house with a stone hall of late medieval date has recently been discovered (RCHME 1988: NBR 86569). York also had its wealthy suburbs, such as along Micklegate and Walmgate where the aristocratic Percy family once had a stone house.

The point about the aspects of suburbs discussed so far is that they tend to represent wealth and poverty spatially. There must have been recognisable differences between one part of town and another. High-class and low-class, and well-heeled and deprived parts of town were characteristics present in medieval towns, and not just the social problems of later ages.

But matters were more complicated still. The dwellings of the poor were not uniformly restricted to the edges of towns: some resided within valued trading areas. At York, while the centre of the city was dominated by the houses of craftsmen, traders and merchants, the development of church yards with housing sometimes meant that small terraces of poor cottages were inserted into these areas – Lady Row, Goodramgate, for instance, or the row of cottages now demolished which were built along St Martin's churchyard in Coney Street (Short 1980) and which have been mentioned above. We can add

to this numbers of *maisons dieu* in York and the large towns and even in some of the smaller ones, so we find that quite a number of the urban poor lived at the heart of the town or city.

Keene (1975) raised a further important question. Since we know only a little about the origins and growth of towns in early medieval England, could it be possible that what we regard as suburbs might at some towns have been parts of the original settlement, the centre of focus having shifted over the centuries? This seems highly likely in one or two Yorkshire towns. Ripon's suburban growth has been detailed above. But Mauchline (1972) has suggested that the eastern suburb of Stonebridge Gate may well represent part of an original urban settlement pattern following a roughly north–south route along Stonebridge Gate and through the town leading to the minster and a crossing of the Skell at the south end of town. As the town developed in the twelfth and thirteenth centuries trade became centred on a new market place to the west, and the eastern arm of the town along Stonebridge Gate became a suburb eventually, with a leper hospital built at its most northerly end (see Figure 9.3). At Thirsk a decisive factor may have been the siting of a castle to the west of the old borough soon after the Conquest, followed by the relocation of the market place outside the castle. The new western settlement became the vill of New Thirsk, while the eastern settlement remained the borough of Old Thirsk where land continued to be held in burgage tenure. However, the 'Oldemerkat sted' in the east, as opposed to the new market in the west (VCH 1923: 59), had become a cattle market, and the main street of the borough Micklegate (now Long Street) was little more than a suburb being removed from the centre of trade in New Thirsk (see Figure 9.4). There is, incidentally, perhaps no better example than this of the dangers of regarding borough status as the determining mark of a town, since many of the commercial functions of the borough/town of Old Thirsk were transferred to the vill of New Thirsk which lacked borough status.

A further development concerns the houses

of the wealthy. At several Yorkshire towns there is evidence for the building of prestigious houses just outside the town by both commercial magnates and gentlemen. Again at Richmond a stone tower-house was built at Hudswell west of the Green by William de Hudswell probably in the fourteenth century. Similar developments can be found at Beverley where several quadrangular-plan houses had been located on the outskirts of the town, especially to the northeast around Pighill Lane. Here the Coppandale family, merchants and aldermen of Beverley, had a house in the fifteenth century, as did the Bedford family, a merchant family of Hull with interests in Beverley. At Hull the majority of merchants' houses lined Hull (High) Street, but the greatest merchant family – the de la Poles – had acquired the house of the King's Keeper as their residence which was set apart from the main areas of trade at the north end of the town where there was more open space.

CONCLUSION

English urban medieval housing has often been described in terms of a town full of traditional timber-framed houses; those belonging to the wealthier burgesses occupied the central streets, while the poor were pushed towards the outer limits, to inferior housing in ramshackle suburbs. It is not a view that should be dismissed. But this discussion of the forms, construction and locations of houses in Yorkshire towns has pointed up a number of problems, suggesting that some modification is needed. To begin with we have seen from the preceeding paragraphs that the large towns and York contained a mixture of people, the wealthy and the poor living cheek-by-jowl in some parts of the town, and also that merchants and those professional men of sufficient means had begun to move to houses in suburbs or on the outskirts of town at least by the fifteenth century, some high-class suburbs developing well before then probably in the late twelfth to fourteenth centuries.

Construction is another area which should be approached with greater scepticism. If the houses built for both rich and poor townsfolk were predominantly constructed of timber, there were, nevertheless, numbers of houses constructed of stone. As both documentary research and fieldwork progresses further stone houses are coming to light. What is more, many of these are referred to in thirteenth century documents, while standing remains show them to be of twelfth- or thirteenth-century origins, although one or two are later. All-stone houses of the fourteenth century do seem to have been a rarity, and the common structural materials appear to have been timber or part-timber and stone. The truly wealthy, however, seem to have continued using stone or brick, but in different ways: to emphasise important parts of their houses such as gatehouses and halls, while inferior parts might be built of timber. This would seem to represent a subtle attunement to the symbolic significance of building materials, but it may well be the explanation. However, the point should not be pushed too far: as late as perhaps 1544 Leyland could describe Beverley as 'welle buildid of wood', while the 'hole Toune of Danecaster is buildid of Wodde'; but, having said that, he also noted that the houses 'be slatid' (Toulmin-Smith 1907: 47, 238).

A further problem arises in relation to the type and functioning of houses. When Pantin (1963b) carried out his ground-breaking work on medieval town-house plans it was to analyse them in terms of rural houses, for he made the assumption that superior types of rural house were the model for all others. For him the problem lay in accounting for 'adapting what was probably in origin a country-house type to urban conditions'. While this may have been true of many of the quadrangular-plan houses of the elite, this sort of argument does not hold good for all urban house-types, and the possibility of an analogous or a mixed development in towns did not enter his calculations. Any deviation from an assumed definition of rural

Figure 9.3 Ripon, Thos Jefferys 1775

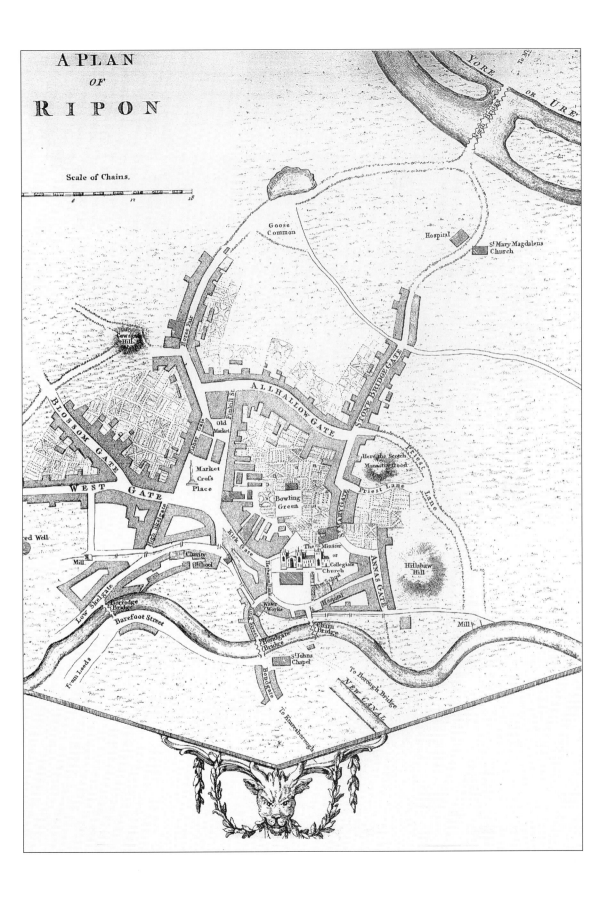

A PLAN

OF

RIPON

Scale of Chains.

6   12   18

YORE OR URE

Goose Common

Hospital

St Mary Magdalens Church

Horse Fair

News Hill

ALLHALLOW GATE

STONE BRIDGE GATE

Priest Lane

BLOSSOM GATE

Finckill St

Plaxet Gate

Old Market

Here the Scotch Monastery stood

Priest Lane

WEST GATE

Market Crofs Place

Bowling Green

Hillshaw Hill

red Well

High Skelgate

Rick Gate

ANNAS GATE

Mill

Charity School

The Minster or Collegiate Church

School

Low Skelgate

Horridge Bridge

Harthamlane

Hospital

Water Works

Mill

Barefoot Street

Blondgate Bridge

Chain Bridge

From Laeds

St Johns Chapel

Bondgate

To Borough Bridge

To Knaresborough

NEW CANAL

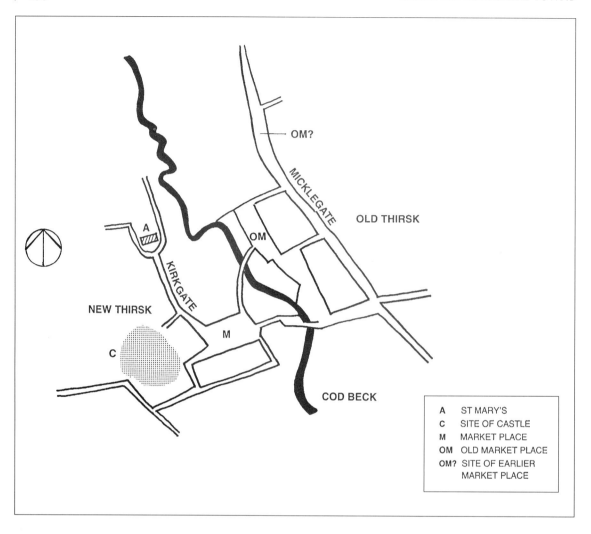

Figure 9.4 New and Old Thirsk

house-type was disposed of by categorising it as an adaptation. While Pantin constructed two useful categories – ranges parallel or at right angles to the street – he nevertheless refused to discuss them *as* urban house-types, and as a result the distinction between houses which seem similar to rural houses and those which seem to have been specifically developed to meet urban demands was lost, or at best blurred. Thus hall and cross-wing and linear-plan forms of house can be found in both town and country. Where such forms exist in some small towns there is often little difference from the village, and such urban/rural forms of house may have functioned and been occupied in much the same ways. But there were houses in the larger towns which, for the reasons given above, were different in several respects. Houses of three storeys with shops, workshops and perhaps cellars or warehouses, some of them in multiple occupation and perhaps built with this sort of functioning in mind – these were a reflection of the varied life of towns and a distinct way of dividing and apportioning space both within the town site and within the house. They evolved separately and should be seen as urban houses.

NOTES

1. The best summary of this debate to date is Palliser (1988).
2. BIHR, Dean and Chapter Original Wills and Inventories: John Stubbs 1451, and quoted in Swanson (1989: Chapter 2).
3. West Yorkshire Archive Service, Bradford, Deed Box Collection – 3/case 14; 5/case 44; 15D74/1/7; W. E. Preston Papers box 2/5/7.

CHAPTER TEN

Public Health and
the Urban Environment

THE PUBLIC HEALTH OF towns is a subject that has attracted an immense volume of research as far as the nineteenth-century town and city is concerned. Comparatively speaking, less effort has been devoted to early modern and eighteenth-century towns, and little has been written about medieval towns. Where public health in medieval towns is commented upon, it is usually to portray the unwholesomeness of the urban environment, an interpretation frequently put forward and rarely questioned. Typically, a document such as Edward III's letter to the mayor and bailiffs of York in 1332 is quoted in confirmation of the foulness of towns:

> The King, detesting the abominable smell abounding in the said city, more than any other city in the realm from dung and manure and other filth and dirt wherein the streets and lanes are filled and obstructed, and wishing to provide for the protection of the health of the inhabitants and of those coming to the present parliament, orders them to cause all the streets and lanes of the city to be cleansed from such filth. (Calendar of Close Rolls 1330–3: 610)

Although it is important to acknowledge that documents such as this may be used to highlight the unhealthy nature of the medieval urban environment, the recital of such grossness with little further comment does not get us very far. More importantly it is wrong to assume that it is our more sophisticated twentieth-century sensibilities which are offended, and that those

of brutish medieval townsfolk were not, having become inured to the practices of dumping manure and rubbish in the streets. For here is the nub of the problem: an interpretation implicit in which lies the idea that through scientific and technological advances we have made a steady progress away from such conditions, until, in the twentieth century, our understanding of public health is near perfection. More than any previous age we are aware of the dangers of neglecting such matters and have the capacity to do something about it. A classic expression of this view can be found in Cooper (1913). It is wrong to think in this way, however, for what documents record about the condition of medieval towns besides the filth is a profound concern for public health on the parts of the church, seigneurs and municipal bodies. At times the measures they took were effective; at other times they were not. Either way they understood the hazards posed to health. A better course of research, rather than to recoil in mock horror at the vile conditions endured by medieval townspeople, is to discover what remedies *they* sought to make their towns healthier places.

ENVIRONMENTAL HEALTH

The subject of environmental health is particularly relevant to towns. As Addyman (1989) has demonstrated in a pioneering article on the subject, some of the characteristics that gave towns their different identities – concentration of population, intensive settlement, a variety of trades and industries within the town itself – might also contribute to the ill-health of their inhabitants, more so than in a village. While processes such as sewage disposal or the provision of a pure water supply might be the concern of both village and town, it was the scale and intensification of urban population and housing that created the bigger problem. It also allowed epidemic diseases to be transmitted more easily.

It is clear that steps were being taken by municipal bodies to regulate the health of the urban environment, although this can be more easily studied in the large towns where concentrations of people were greater and where municipal bodies seem keen to have acted in the public interest. On the other hand this may simply be a documentary representation skewed towards the large towns, since the records of these towns survive in greater numbers. Nevertheless, many town ordinances were specifically concerned with environmental health. There were four principal areas of control and provision which were in practice connected: refuse disposal and the cleanliness of the town, sewage disposal, pollution control, and securing a pure water supply. A fifth area of control, although less commonly expressed, was over the standard of food sold.

As far as the disposal of refuse is concerned, municipal administrations were bound by an Act of 1388 to compel people to keep the streets clean and cease from dumping dung and rubbish in them. If orders for the removal of dung and rubbish become more frequent in municipal records after 1388 it is probably because of the Act (Pickering 1762: 306–7). But some administrations had begun taking action before this date. The corporation of York, for example, was ordering butchers and fishmongers not to throw offal into the rivers and making provision for regular cleansing of the streets and the removal of dung in the 1370s (SURTEES 120: 17–18). By the beginning of the sixteenth century the corporation had instituted a more effective campaign of refuse disposal: 'ther shalbe a dung cart in every ward' which was to convey dung outside the city where it could be 'layd so that husbands of the contrie may come ther to and have it away' (YASRS 103: 165). Hull, too, had a

similar system by the fifteenth century. There, a refuse cart made its rounds of the town three times a week and the refuse collected was placed in a dump near the Humber called the Mamhole. The ebb and flow of the river eventually carried the refuse out to sea (HCR BB 3A: 86, 130).

But at York it was not only the corporation which had jurisdiction. The monarch was also concerned about the state of health in the city, though perhaps from more selfish motives, since royal ordinances were more likely to be forthcoming before a parliament or royal visit. One such royal letter appears above. The glimpse we get of the suburb of Bootham quoted earlier (Chapter 9, p. 154) comes from another such letter aimed at cleaning up the district, because 'the air is corrupted and infected by the pigsties' (Calendar of Close Rolls 1296–1302: 218).

At Selby, the abbey was the seat of authority and the abbot's court regulated the town environment. Throughout the fifteenth century and up to its dissolution in the sixteenth, a series of orders were made concerning public health. Some were general, forbidding the pollution of water courses by throwing dung or carrion into them. Others were directed at the activities of specific groups. Butchers and their disposal of offal were a common cause of complaint and action – 'yt the bothchers kype well and honestly thayr bowlels and blode' (SURTEES 85: 32). Individual issues of food quality can also be found among these proceedings:

> Item that Richard Dysshford had in his shop fyssh by xiiij daes to it stanke in so mykell it was caried to Ouse, yerefore, if he do any more for to forfett vjs viijd. (SURTEES 85: 28)

The danger to health was taken seriously, and the penalties imposed were not light.

The prohibition of obnoxious trades and practices was a constant battle, with butchers, fishmongers and tanners the most suspect groups because of the health problems that their disposal of offal might cause. Thus at Beverley the butchers were forbidden to 'caste any maner of offal as blode, hornes, bonnes, gutts in the strete', tanners must not 'wash hides or other tainted thing in the ditch on the south side of Wolfkeld or elsewhere near a well' and everyone was under pain to ensure that 'no ashes, straw or other thing fouling or stopping the flow of water should be put in Walkerbek or Milnebek', while muck put on 'le Beckbank should be moved before two high tides' (Leach 1900: 22, 43, 129). The records of Hull Corporation similarly deal with butchers throwing offal into the market place or tanners steeping hides in the town dikes.

Most corporations were also keen to cleanse and maintain pavements so that movement around the town was made easier and pleasanter. The difficulties of paving the town streets was bad enough, since in many places householders were responsible for the section of causeway in front of their doors. Enforcing such by-laws was difficult, and matters were made worse by the rough use that most medieval streets received. The Beverley borough records illustrate the problems well noting that the municipality ordered in 1367 that carts and waggons shod with iron were to be prohibited from entering the town (Leach 1900: 21). In spite of such difficulties most of the major centres appear to have had a good part of their towns paved or surfaced in some way and documentary records or archaeological excavation have established this for Beverley, Hull, Richmond, Malton, Scarborough, Selby and York.

Along with paved streets went gutters or sewers, often running down the centre of the street. Again municipal and other authorities would appear to be constantly issuing orders to keep these clear of rubbish, and at times flushing and scouring the streets. This was so at York, for example, while the municipality of Hull in 1413 allowed Richard Hornse, a merchant, to build houses in a lane in the town on condition that he built and maintained a sewer in the middle of the lane, led it to a common sewer and kept both flushed (Hull Corporation Records D 223). The inhabitants of Selby, a town that had been paved at least along its main streets by the thirteenth or early fourteenth

century, seem to have been regularly ordered to cleanse the streets and gutters, as in 1483 when everyone should 'clens his gutters againe the payment for uschuyng [issuing] of the water', while in 1519 'all wattersewers' had to be 'dykid and scoried be Withsonday' (SURTEES 85: 29, 31).

The firm line (or so it would appear) that was taken on public health by the abbot of Selby Abbey is perhaps idiosyncratic of religious houses, for both monasteries and friaries might be said to have made positive contributions to what might be thought of as sanitary engineering. Where possible rural monasteries were sited next to rivers. Typical monastic planning would include arrangements to divert water from the river and through the precinct returning it to the river at a point downstream after passing through a system of conduits. The water passing through the monastery could be directed to the uses of cooking, washing, laundering and flushing, water for cooking and drinking being kept apart from water for other purposes. It is probably no coincidence that the majority of the county's urban monasteries were situated in towns on rivers and their waterfront sites were usually well developed. Friaries followed this pattern also, but as somewhat later developments, less favourable sites were available in some towns. York provides the most complicated development with three friaries and three monasteries (four if Clementhorpe nunnery is included) within or adjacent to the city walls. Of these, two of the monasteries and three of the friaries were located on the Ouse and the Foss – hence the complaints of the friars minors in 1371 about butchers throwing offal into the Ouse just above their house (SURTEES 120: 15).

The friars of York, however, were lucky in obtaining a riverside location for their houses. At several other towns they were unable to do so. At Richmond the friary was situated not on the river, but to the north of it, just beyond the town wall. But even in this position water appears to have been brought into the house by means of a conduit, as Leyland observed: 'There is a conduct of water at the Grey Freres els there is none in Richmont' (Toulmin-Smith 1909:

24–5). Similarly Bridlington Priory seems to have made arrangements to convey water from a spring to the priory (Lancaster 1912: 18). The Franciscan Friars of Scarborough planned to construct an underground conduit from a spring on Falsgrave Moor and to lay pipes under the town's streets, a scheme which had been the subject of some dispute, but was resolved by licence of Edward II in 1319 (VCH 1913: 274–6).

The water supply of many towns was provided by rivers, streams springs or wells near to or within the town. Wells, both private and public, were a particularly important source, and it was partly for this reason that municipal bodies forbade the dumping of rubbish or the processing of hides in streams, since these practices might lead to the contamination of the water supply. Private wells were sunk to the rears of houses where possible, and these have sometimes been uncovered in archaeological investigation of town sites. Addyman (1989), for instance, has suggested that it was becoming a common practice at York to line wells with barrels with the bottoms knocked out, while in other places rubble, stone blocks and, by the later Middle Ages, bricks were being used for well linings.

But there were some towns which possessed few naturally occurring wells and no streams or other suitable water supplies. In these towns methods similar to those of the monastic houses had to be employed. At Hull, wells in Bishop Lane and Fleshmarket were insufficient to supply the town which had proved a long-standing problem. During the fourteenth century schemes had been mooted to supply Hull with water from elsewhere via a dike, but it was not until 1402 that a dike was constructed running from a spring at Anlaby. In 1447 a conduit consisting of a lead pipe was proposed and by 1449 it had been laid together with a number of pipes under the streets of Hull. Operation of the system commenced amid great ceremony, a barrel of wine being sent through the pipe to mark the completion of the work (VCH 1969: 74–5). However, it was lifted in 1461 and the lead sold to pay for Hull's civic debts, occasioning a return to water supplied in the open dike. How efficient the piped water scheme had been is uncertain, but it had certainly been a cause of civic pride and one to which several of the leading families of Hull had contributed:

> Feb 16th 1448–9, Robert Holme burgess of the town of Kingston-upon-Hull . . . [bequeaths] To complete in lead the new conduit between Hull and Analby, if it be done before the feast of St Martin in the winter after my death 100 l. (SURTEES 45: 182)

In the matter of sewage disposal a usual way of dealing with the sewage was for individual householders to construct cess pits at the rears of their houses. This was a widespread practice which archaeological investigation has revealed at both major urban centres and small towns – Skipton, for example (Williams 1981: 13–15). At the houses of seigneurs and wealthy burgesses there were probably internal lavatories discharging into cess pits rather than a midden house located to the rear of the house with facilities above the pit. We know the former arrangements could be found in abundance at Hull Garthe, the de la Pole house at Hull, for according to the survey of 1538 (Shelby 1967: 164) the tower had three rooms with a 'Jak' to every one of them', and ten upper chambers had 'chymneis & Jakys to them'.

As we have also seen, by the fifteenth and sixteenth centuries the removal of dung was being carried out by some municipal authorities. In addition to this public lavatories had been provided on Ouse Bridge at York, presumably discharging into the Ouse, and there were also public lavatories provided on the common staithes in Hull. Again at York archaeological observation in the last century distinguished a 'system' of ditches or open sewers which ran around the city to discharge into the Ouse or the Foss (Cooper 1913: 279–80). But some religious houses had carried matters a stage further in the construction of subterranean sewers to discharge into rivers. The best preserved subterranean sewer is at York cut for St Mary's Abbey. This was lined with limestone blocks built into a

pointed-arch profile and ran from the abbey to the Ouse. It can be regarded as the urban equivalent of the sort of planning and sanitary engineering that can still be seen at rural monasteries.

However, lest we get carried away with the idea that sanitary provision in large towns of the Middle Ages was widespread, we should realise that although sanitary engineering techniques were well understood and could be put into practice, this affected mostly a minority of wealthy families or clerics. As Palliser (1982: 95) has pointed out, urinating in the street for want of lavatories may have been common in medieval York.

FIRE AND FLOOD

While seigneurs and municipal bodies might try to improve public and environmental health, there were some circumstances over which they had little or no control. Medieval towns were particularly prone to natural disasters such as fire or flood, perhaps more so than most towns in England today. Towns and villages situated in the flat, marshy lands of Holderness to the east and along the Humber were liable to frequent, sometimes serious, flooding – we have seen how Ravenserodd was completely destroyed by floods, although this was an altogether unusual town. Flooding in the Hull/Humber region became frequent as the sea level rose gradually during the thirteenth century and there were serious floods in both the mid-thirteenth and mid-fourteenth centuries. In March 1355, for example, the Humber burst its banks flooding Myton and Hull, which probably led to the construction of what was basically a storm sewer to carry flood waters away. Further measures included the raising of some causeways so that communications could be maintained and so that there might be access to fresh water supplies in the dikes (Gillet and MacMahon 1989: 24, 33–4). Flooding of the Hull and other water courses

Part of the sewer constructed for St Mary's Abbey.
(York Archaeological Trust)

accounted for the flood defences known as the New Dike being cut to the southeast of Beverley near Figham around 1284, and a flood bank was erected on Swine Moor in 1433 (VCH 1989: 33–6).

But the Humber region was not the only one liable to flooding. Still in the east of the county, Saltmarshe (1920) has shown how the Derwent and the Ouse in the vicinity of Howden were the subject of flood defences in the form of ditches and embankments. Drax had also suffered flooding of the Ouse around 1405, which may have been a factor in the disappearance of the town. Archaeological investigation suggests that flooding of the Don had occurred at Doncaster. Depositions of river silt in the area of staiths near to North Bridge suggests that these had been abandoned by perhaps 1300 because of regular flooding (Lilley 1994). However, the inhabitants of other towns might be thought to have contributed to the problem of flooding by extending quays into rivers thus causing channel-narrowing. This happened on the Ouse at York, and the results have been with us ever since.

Flooding seriously disrupted life in the medieval town – there was little in the way of flood-relief aid as we know it today and no insurance. Sections of towns might have to be abandoned as at Doncaster or, very rarely, towns might be destroyed. Bridges might be damaged, houses made uninhabitable and trade brought to a standstill. Although flood defences were built, it also seems likely that the ways in which trade was promoted – such as through the enlargement of quays by building into rivers – aggravated the problem.

Yet, on the whole, towns survived floods, and were to survive the other disaster that visited itself on many medieval towns, fire. Put this way it sounds as if fire had a life of its own. It did not, but was caused by accidents, lightning or acts of violence. Nevertheless, once fire had taken hold, it must have seemed as if it were alive and in possession of an evil will. Its wrath was quick and unstoppable. The most obvious cause of the alarming rate at which a fire might spread in the medieval town would seem to have been the combustible materials from which many houses were built. Timber frames with their interstices filled with plaster or earth daubed on thin laths seems like the ideal kindling. This certainly did not help, but it was not the principal cause of the rapid spread of fire. The real culprit was thatch. Thatch easily caught light, and once ablaze small bundles of burning thatch could be taken up by any wind and blown onto neighbouring roofs like so many incendiaries.

All towns must have had fires, but the small ones were probably contained. It is fire disasters, where whole sections of towns were burning, that characterise medieval and early modern towns. Not until the eighteenth century did the incidence of fire become less of a threat to the urban environment (Jones et al. 1984), and fire disasters struck Yorkshire towns throughout the Middle Ages – from York in 1137 when a large part of the city burned with damage to the Minster, St Mary's Abbey and St Leonard's Hospital, to Hedon sometime before 1544 when Leyland commented that it had grown decayed by 'choking of the haven and fier defacing much of the town' (Toulmin-Smith 1907: 62).

One related disaster that afflicted some medieval towns was violence, civil unrest or even war, all of which might have devastating consequences for the urban environment. Life for the inhabitants of Yorkshire, especially those living in the north of the county, became more hazardous after the Battle of Bannockburn in 1314 when raids and more organised campaigns by the Scots laid waste to several towns in the north of England generally. The spring of 1318, for example, was particularly bad as the Scottish army invaded England as far south as Ponte-fract, 'burning the town of Northallerton and Boroughbridge and sundry other towns on their march'. They exacted 1,000 marks from the burgesses of Ripon, and then 'went off to Knaresborough, destroying that town with fire'; thence to Skipton 'which they plundered first and then burnt' (Maxwell 1913: 221).

However fires were started, problems were compounded by the means available to medieval townspeople for fighting them. These consisted largely of buckets, long hooks to pull down burning thatch and chains to help pull down buildings to act as a firebreak. The municipal accounts of Beverley, for instance, mention a hook and chain for use in case of fire (BCMSS 1541: 175). Gillet and MacMahon (1989) have suggested that Hull's lack of serious fires can be attributed partly to its easy access to abundant supplies of water. This cannot be so, since several towns were located on rivers and suffered fire damage – Hedon, for example. The problem was not so much one of water supply as how to direct water at burning buildings when nothing better than buckets was available. Nevertheless, water was one means of firefighting.

Prevention was a better way of dealing with the problem. Thus at York the minster authorities were careful to keep a zone free of buildings around the minster in order to act as a break, while other civic authorities in the city scrutinised the effect new building might have on access in bringing relief to burning buildings. This, and the horror of fire, is well illustrated by an inquisition of 1249 as to whether the enlargement of a chaplain's house to take in a part of the lane called Patrick Pool would be safe or 'whether, in case of fire breaking out (which God forbid), water for extinguishing it could as expeditiously be brought from elsewhere as by that lane' (YASRS 12: 18–19).

It is noticeable that by the later Middle Ages more non-combustible materials were being used in the building of houses – brick and flag infill to timber frames, brick or stone ground floors, the use of flat tiles or flag for roofs. But this could scarcely be said to have been effective, since fires continued. Nor did the use of non-combustible materials arise out of the specific aim of reducing fires, for as I have already suggested architectural fashion probably had as much to do with the changing use of building materials.

Price also had to be taken into account; and not only price, but probably what was considered appropriate to social station – part-timber and stone houses with flag or tile roofs might be suitable for wealthy burgesses, but the urban poor could scarcely expect, let alone afford, luxury of this sort even on a smaller scale. If municipal authorities and landlords were serious about reducing the risk of fire they were at the same time caught by this social/cash nexus. At Selby, for example, account rolls for the repair of houses belonging to the abbey show a distinctly divergent approach to the materials used. In 1403, for instance, houses in Ousegate, one of the principal streets, were being roofed with tile, while those in other streets were being thatched. The explanation may be connected with the social standing of the occupiers of the properties and the rents obtainable. Certainly properties described as the mill cottages were roofed with thatch. But this does not explain the repair of a malt house and its ovens in Micklegate at the heart of the town with timber walls daubed with mud and a thatched roof: this seems to have been asking for trouble (Tillotson 1988: 98, 106–7). Hull was perhaps one of the first corporations to start to insist on non-combustible materials being used in the construction of new houses, although it was not until the 1570s that they began to insist on the use of tile rather than thatch.

Some town authorities might wish to rid towns of fire risks by pushing dangerous industries out to the suburbs, as we shall see at Beverley with regard to brick-making. But other authorities appear to have taken little action of this sort. Nor could it have been possible to eliminate all risk of fire in what was a high-risk urban environment. Collections of timber and thatched outbuildings to the rears of houses where activities requiring fire – metal-working, baking, brewing – were carried on were a hazard, especially where whole streets were built in this way. It simply was not possible to relegate all town trades requiring fire to the outskirts since the small-scale activities of many occupiers were the very economic life of the town. Thus, given the poor firefighting technology available and the impossibility of eradicating all risks, fires remained a potential source of destruction within the medieval urban environment.

CONCLUSION

The view of the medieval town as a place in which filth and disease abounded is one in need of some alteration. Both the archaeological and documentary records can be interpreted to show that the condition of towns was taken seriously by those in authority. If little action was taken over one of the greatest risks to the environment, fire, works were carried out to prevent flooding at vulnerable towns, and measures were taken to provide or safeguard pure water supplies, to remove sewage and public nuisances, and to pave and cleanse the streets. What is more, some privileged groups – urban religious communities, for instance – enjoyed a high standard of sanitation.

However, the evidence must not be pushed too far. For one thing, most of it relies on the records of larger towns; whether the same concerns were given equal attention at the small towns is less easy to assess. Perhaps with their smaller populations the problems encountered in small towns were not of the same magnitude or urgency as those in the large ones with their greater density of residence, although there were surely some similarities of approach. Also, descriptions of the conditions of towns and the obnoxious habits of some inhabitants suggest that there were at least unwholesome quarters within all large towns. Furthermore, the very fact that municipal bodies consistently had to order people to comply with town ordinances and desist from practices such as fouling water courses with offal or hides suggests that these were continuing problems and were not eradicated even over long periods despite municipal bans. In other words we should view attempts at the reform of public health as taking place against a background of squalor and recalcitrance. The more traditional view should not, therefore, be ditched but modified. The chief problem with it is that it arises from an attitude of confident modernity which contrasts the evils of the past with the progress made today.

One aspect of the medieval urban environment and its ills that is neglected is the effect of dense human residence in the vicinity of commercial and industrial activity. This is a relevant question to raise, if one accepts the view of many historians that the eleventh–fourteenth centuries (roughly speaking) were a period of economic expansion, much of it taking place within towns. What was the effect, for instance, of living in overcrowded dwellings on the medieval psyche? Or of walls in timber-framed and partitioned dwellings where only a few inches of lath and plaster separated neighbour from neighbour? Or what was the effect of noise pollution in an environment where production was being stepped up? A great deal has been written about the effect of disasters such as the Black Death on medieval society (Platt 1996, for example), but very little on the effects of town life and the stresses, tensions or day-to-day irritations it might have imposed on individuals because of its very differences from rural life.

We rarely find these issues raised in the usual records, and as a result we have a tendency to assume that they did not exist. Occasionally, however, we are given a flash of insight, as at York in 1520 when the municipal body ordered that 'no man from hensfurth . . . shall suffre ther chyldren to go with clapers [rattles] uppon Shere [Maunday] Thursday and Good Friday' (Palliser 1982: 104), presumably because of the annoyance caused by possibly large numbers of children in a city like York. A similar, although more specific, injunction can be found at Bradford in 1412 when two men were fined by the court there for going about the streets at night dressed in linen sheets and with 'lez Ratyls in their hands as if they might be malignant spirits' (BMC IV), while in 1572 – admittedly a late example – the Doncaster court forbade the playing of 'gytterons'[1] in the street after 9.00 p.m. (Theobald 1943: 288). Finally, John Trevisa's poem 'The Blacksmiths' should make us realise that medieval town-dwellers might suffer just as much in the fourteenth century from noisy neighbours as their twentieth-century counterparts:

Swarte smeked smithes smatered with smoke
Drive me to deth with din of here dintes,
Swich nois on nightes ne herd men never:
What knavene cry and clatering of knockes!

NOTE

1. Probably a cittern, a lute-like instrument.

CHAPTER ELEVEN

Outside the Town

TO THINK OF THE medieval town as a tightly built environment, densely populated, with inward-looking residents encircled by walls or ditches is mistaken. Several historians (Hilton 1982a, for example) have commented on how the town and its surrounding fields, villages and countryside – its region – were connected. Villages were often dependent on towns for markets, not only as places where produce could be sold, but also as places where goods and services unobtainable in the village might be bought. Towns had their own fields and pastures used by townspeople – pasture for horses, pastures where graziers and butchers might fatten cattle, fields where crops might be grown. This was particularly important at some small towns where a dual economy might operate between trade and agriculture, and it was also important at seigneurial boroughs where there might also be manorial/agricultural tenants. Manor might be legally distinct from borough, but the business of both seems to have become mixed at several places – Bradford, as we have seen. The existence of an open-field system of agriculture on the doorstep of the town must, nevertheless, have represented a real spatial difference, a difference given further definition where agricultural tenants lived on the outskirts of town or even in suburbs, common in several towns, called 'bondgate' or something similar. Thus, while there were links between town and countryside, there were also spatial distinctions which should not be forgotten.

A further difference ought to be emphasised. Although the image of the medieval town set amid countryside may be one we wish to believe in, the closer one looks at documentary records of towns the more one comes to realise that numbers of urban structures were located outside the town. Hospitals, mills or tileries could be found close to and dependent on some towns; small industrial suburbs had grown up outside others. In places the gallows might be situated on the high road into town, a harsh reminder that some municipal bodies had the power of life and death over townsfolk. The separateness of the town and the power of its authorities might be expressed in other ways, too. A great bridge across a river into a town or the town gates themselves might have been built to magnify in the mind of the visitor the image of municipal power and civic pride.

TOWN WALLS AND DEFENCES

The town walls or other defences are a good place to start since, whatever the links between town and country, walls conveyed a definite sense of corporate identity and formed a clear boundary between inside and outside. But such boundaries took several forms – ditches, moats, ramparts, walls. Even towns which lacked walls often had gateways across the principal roads leading into the town. At York the most comprehensive system of walls and defences survive. They are largely a rebuilding of earlier timber defences with limestone walls and gateways (bars) in the twelfth and thirteenth centuries, although work continued until the fifteenth in the section near Walmgate. There were four bars all with barbicans or outer defences originally, but only the barbican at Walmgate Bar survives. All of the bars could be defended and could be closed with gates and portcullises. Further defences were added in the form of towers, and a deep ditch also ran around the outside. This left York vulnerable to attack only by water, along the Ouse. Thus at Skeldergate and Lendal, where the river ran through the defences, chains which could be raised or lowered hung across the river, suspended between towers on opposite banks so that the river too could be closed off.

A section of the walls at York.

Micklegate Bar, from an early nineteenth-century engraving taken before its barbican was demolished.

A view from inside the barbican at Walmgate Bar,
now the only barbican at York.

Lendal Tower. This was one of a pair of towers from which chains were suspended across the Ouse.

There were other walled towns in the county besides York – Hull, New Malton, Scarborough and Richmond, for example. Virtually nothing now exists of these walls except at Richmond where two much remodelled bars survive at Cornforth Hill and Friars' Wynd, while at New Malton what looks like a postern gate from the defences has been incorporated into the wall of a later building near to the market place. The most impressive town walls other than York's, however, were those of Hull. The town appears to have been enclosed by a ditch and rampart before 1321 after which date the construction of brick walls with towers and bars had begun, eventually enclosing the town on three sides. A moat was an additional defensive feature. The River Hull formed the eastern boundary of the town defences and, as at York, a chain was used to close the mouth of the Hull where there was a battery to defend it from at least the sixteenth century.

Not all towns were encircled by walls. Even some large and prosperous towns such as Beverley never acquired them, despite attempts to obtain a licence and grants from the crown in 1322 (Turner 1971). Beverley does appear to have had system of ditches around it which probably also served as drains together with three substantial bars of which only one remains. These were built of brick between 1405 and 1410. There were also a number of timber bars across the minor roads into Beverley and almost certainly a chain to close off Beverley Beck, mention of which is made in the borough records in 1391 (Leach 1900: 31). Bars could be found at several of the county's towns, and it seems likely that they were elaborate works at some, of which we have little or no record. We have lost four bars at Doncaster, for example, a town which had defences similar to those of Beverley: ditches and bars, but no walls. Doncaster also stood at a crossing of the River Don to the north of the town, and the bar by the bridge there seems to have been particularly striking, being described by Leyland as a 'great tourid Gate of Stone' (Toulmin-Smith 1907: 238).

At other towns defences consisted of ditches usually with earth thrown up in the form of a bank or rampart. A ditch and rampart once surrounded Knaresborough, for instance, and may also have been part of the outer defences of the castle while at the same time enclosing the town around the market place. Although it has disappeared today, it can still be traced to the north of the High Street by a rise in the ground. Bars, probably of simple construction, could also be found at several towns such as Leeds or Wakefield.

The picture that emerges of defences, whether walls and bars or just simply ditches, is more complicated than at first meets the eye. They undoubtedly played a defensive part at some towns, especially in the north of the county where Scottish raids became a serious and recurrent threat after Bannockburn in 1314, although it was generally castles or fortified houses which held out rather than town defences. At other places defences were too open to provide protection, as at Beverley where the town did not withstand the assaults made on it by both Lancastrian and Yorkist forces in 1460. Many bars seem to have been no more than places where traffic into the town could be stopped and tolls taken for the upkeep of the fabric of the town or from foreigners who wished to use the markets. Town walls at many towns were more a mark of status, for even where little in the way of defences existed, a grand gateway might enhance the image of the town. Beverley and Doncaster are the outstanding examples that we know about, and if the principal bars there *were* intended for defence, decorative elements also entered into the design – crow-stepped battlements, ogee-headed niches and the civic arms at North Bar, Beverley. Castellated styles of architecture, furthermore, suggested not just protection, but that there was something *to* protect. Town walls said a great deal about civic pride.

BRIDGES AND BRIDGE CHAPELS

Bridges formed part of the approaches to some towns especially in a county like Yorkshire where several were located on river crossings.

Little remains of Richmond's walls except this heavily reworked bar at Cornforth Hill and a similar one at Friars' Wynd.

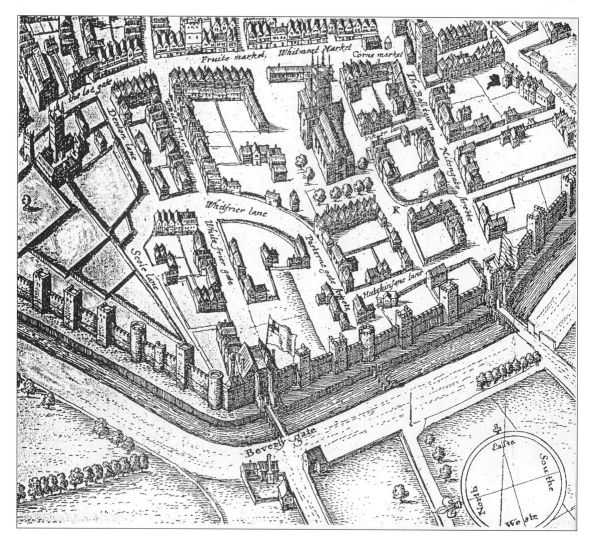

Part of Hull's walls and the Beverley Gate taken from Hollar's prospect of 1640. The walls were removed in the 1770s to make way for the expansion of the town and its docks.

Boroughbridge, Doncaster, Leeds, Otley, Ripon, Rotherham, Sheffield, Tadcaster, Wakefield, Yarm and York are the principal ones. Documentary records suggest that many early bridges were of timber and little is known of their construction. However in the fourteenth and fifteenth centuries most timber bridges were being replaced by stone bridges. The reason for this may well

be wear and tear as much as anything else, for anecdotal evidence suggests that there were a number of collapses. A spectacular and early example is the collapse of Ouse Bridge at York in 1154 which is said to have occurred when Archbishop William and his followers were crossing. The weight of people and horses was too much for the old bridge and all fell into the Ouse but were saved from injury and death by William's intercession. A more earthly reason for the rebuilding of some bridges was probably civic pride, for like the great gateway, a bridge might be the introduction to a town.

Bridges also had a religious dimension and became the places where chapels and shrines

North Bar, Beverley, constructed of brick around 1409.

The bridge chapel at Rotherham dates from the 1480s.

The other surviving bridge chapel in the county is on this long-span bridge across the Calder at Wakefield. The chapel dates from after 1350, and was refronted during the nineteenth century.

might be situated. Several Yorkshire bridges had chapels built on them, and two – at Rotherham and Wakefield – retain their chapels, now a rarity in England. Wayside shrines, especially to the Virgin, were popular and could also be found on bridges – the description of that on Otley bridge has already been given on p. 88. And similarly, hermitages might be situated near bridges as at Snaith where a field continued to be called Le Hermytage at Le Turnbrigge during the sixteenth century (Calendar of Patent Rolls 1566–9: 162).

Such chapels and shrines were places where prayers might be said for a safe journey or thanks given for a safe return. Here also wayfarers might be more easily persuaded to make charitable donations, donations that in part might be used for the upkeep not only of the chapel, but the bridge and highway – roads that gave access not only to the wider world, but also to the chapel itself. As we have seen, bequests for the maintenance of bridges became popular in the later Middle Ages. A generous provision, for example, was that made by John le Gras, canon of Beverley before 1279 in endowing a chapel on the bridge at Hull (YASRS 111: 11). Morris (1989: Chapter 9) has also suggested that bridges, in crossing a river, might symbolise another crossing, a passing from life to death, and hence a further reason for the chapel or shrine and its endowment. Duffy (1992: 367) has carried this line of argument further suggesting that bridges also symbolised the Christian life and communication of charity, as well as signifying Christ himself, the bridge between earthly life and paradise.

Most medieval stone bridges showed a high degree of engineering skill and many stand today, although seldom in use for heavy traffic unless reinforced and widened. Long-span stone bridges were frequently constructed on a series of pointed arches. On the underside of each arch it is common to find masonry ribs supporting the deck of the bridge, thus allowing masons to build an extremely strong structure. Bridges with arch-ribs in their construction were undoubtedly developed from vaulting in the great churches, yet while rib vaults were developing in churches from the twelfth century (*pace* Durham), the

technique seems to have been used little for bridges until the fourteenth century, perhaps because so many earlier bridges did not need to be rebuilt until this later date. When earlier timber bridges were replaced with stone, the technology of the rib vault was well understood. It is interesting to note that arch-rib bridge construction was largely abandoned by the eighteenth century, but was to return in the hands of nineteenth-century engineers using cast iron arch-ribs for railway and other bridges.

RELIGIOUS BUILDINGS

Bridge chapels were not the only religious buildings to be found outside towns. Some urban monasteries and friaries were located on the outskirts of towns, especially the friaries which were built later than most monasteries. These have already been examined in Chapter 4, but it is as well to remind ourselves of the locations of some, and that although they may have been beyond the ditch or walls of the town, they were nevertheless intimately bound up with urban life.

One other religious institution mentioned only obliquely above was the leper hospital. It is easy to mistake the reasons why leper hospitals were built well out of town. It does seem obvious that a disease such as leprosy, for which there was no cure, should be isolated to prevent infection. While this was one motivating factor, we should also be mindful of others. Leprosy was viewed as a visitation of God's displeasure, and the corruption of the flesh by leprous nodules betokened the corruption of the soul. The Church's teaching in this matter followed Levitical law:

> All the days wherin the plague shall be in him he shall be defiled; he is unclean: he shall dwell alone; without the camp shall his habitation be. (Leviticus 13: 46)

But there was more to this, for the leper house was a means of ridding the town not only of a disease, but of what had come to be seen as the embodiment of sin, especially carnal sin.

Arch-ribs beneath the medieval bridge at Rotherham.

Common law as well as ecclesiastical law required lepers to live outside towns, and lepers could be forcibly removed by writ (*de leproso amovendo*). The leper was thus an outcast for several reasons, and was defiled and rejected. The statutes of the leper hospital of St Julian near St Albans stated this position clearly:

> Since among all infirmities the disease of leprosy is held in contempt, those who are struck down with such a disease ought to show themselves only at special times and places, and in their manner and dress more contemptible and humble than other men. (Richards 1977: appendix)

However, if the leper was compelled by law to live outside town, there was no contingency upon the town to provide shelter. The leper hospital was thus a charitable institution and infraction of the rules could lead to expulsion. The charitable nature of such hospitals is probably the reason why so many were built. Prelates, nobility and magnates generally – all founded them, and most towns of any size possessed at least one, the dedication often being to St Mary Magdalene. There are documentary references to leper hospitals at Beverley, Doncaster, Hedon, Pontefract, Ripon, Scarborough, Tadcaster, Whitby and York, all located outside these towns, and there may have been others for which records no longer exist. Yet although leprosy was prevalent, it was probably never a disease of epidemic proportions and by the mid-fourteenth century appears to have been declining. A visitation of the Ripon leper hospital in 1341 revealed that the leper house had been taken down between 1317 and 1329 (SURTEES 74: 225). By the Reformation surveys of leper hospitals carried out for the crown show that they contained no lepers. Probably as a result, no leper hospitals have survived complete in the county. Either they fell into disuse and were cleared away or they were rebuilt as almshouses.

One other religious building – if it can be properly called a building – was the hermitage. Few hermitages remain, many being perhaps flimsy constructions while others were little

more than caves. It is the latter that have survived. St Robert's Cave at Knaresborough on the banks of the River Nidd consists of a cave, stone bench and the remnants of a chapel of perhaps the late twelfth century. Robert Flower became a famous hermit said to have been visited by King John, and although never cannonised he was recognized as a saint during the Middle Ages. Beneath the present-day Pontefract General Infirmary is the cell of another medieval hermit. It is a two-roomed cell cut from the rock and dating probably to 1386, when it is said to have been inhabited by Adam de Laythorpe. Documents also inform us of other hermits at different towns – Howden where a hermitage was recorded just to the north of the town in 1284 (Butler and Powls 1994: 13), Richmond where a hermitage or anchorage existed to the northeast of the town and Snaith as we have seen (above, p. 180).

INDUSTRY AND INDUSTRIAL SUBURBS

The outskirts of towns were places where industries might also be situated, but usually particular types of industries such as brick-making. Locating such industries on or near their source of raw materials – clay in the case of brick-making – saved both labour and transport costs; there was also space for storage and for industrial development on land not available within towns. Pollution from smoke was another reason for an out-of-town site, a location sometimes forced on the proprietors of obnoxious industries, as the Beverley borough records make clear in 1467:

> Also it was wholesomely ordered, on account of the stink and badness of the air to the destruction of fruit trees and other disadvantages which may arise therefrom, that no-one henceforth dare to build any kiln for burning bricks in the aforesaid town of Beverley, or nearer the same town than brick-kilns are now built, under penalty of 100s. (Leach 1900: 58)

Medieval brick-yards were sometimes called tileries; this did not necessarily imply that tiles

*The chapel building at the former leper hospital of St
Mary Magdalene at Ripon, now a rare survival.*

The cave of St Robert of Knaresborough – the entrance to the cave with a stone bench to the left. The picture is taken from the site of the chapel, only the foundations of which exist.

were made there, although they might have been. In the Beckside and Grovehill districts of Beverley to the east and south of the town several tileries once existed. Recent archaeological investigation (Evans 1990b) has revealed that both brick and tile-making were carried on in this area, flat tiles, sometimes glazed, being made. Large brick-yards could be found at Beverley and also at Hull, while York had a Tile House on Bishop's Fields to the southwest of the city.

The getting and converting of building materials generally was a job relegated to the outskirts of towns. Where it occurred within towns it was often made illegal, since it could cause severe problems. At Bradford, for instance, in 1411 the court brought the rector to task for digging for stone in the highway within the town near to the church (BMC IV: 28). Stone was an important building material in Bradford, and at Manningham, about a mile out of the town, we learn that in 1340 John Le Litster had been digging stones without licence of the court 'for covering houses' (BMC I: 10). This was probably for roofing flags, although it may have been flags used to fill the interstices of timber studding.

The big consumer of stone, however, was the church. In the construction of so many churches, not to mention the great urban and monastic churches which required constant maintenance, large quantities were needed, and where good stone occurred near towns whole areas might be turned over to quarrying. The outstanding area of such operations in Yorkshire was around Tadcaster where the fine magnesian limestone had been quarried for several churches including the abbeys of Drax and Selby, as well as Howden and York Minster. Charters preserved in monastic day books show that Thievesdale to the southwest of Tadcaster contained quarries belonging to different religious institutions abutting onto one another (YASRS 10: 317–18). Once quarried the stone could be moved along the river system of Yorkshire – by sled to Tadcaster then via the Wharfe and the the Ouse. At other towns religious institutions were not so fortunate – the monks of Bridlington Priory were granted a quarry, but at Filey some miles away along the

coast (Farrer 1915: 466). But Tadcaster was far from the sole area of good building stone and quarries existed around Doncaster and Pontefract, for example. Nor was the stone always for local use. Stone from these quarries made its way to Westminster to be used on churches there (Salzman 1952: 131). Sometimes the church itself, where it was a quarry owner, sold stone to outside interests. Thus a fabric roll of Beverley Minster shows that in 1445–6 stone roofing flags and fifty-eight tons of stone as well as many other worked products were sold from the minster's quarries (Leach 1899: 55).

One other building material should be mentioned and that is lime. Apart from agricultural uses, lime was the basis for mortar and plaster. There were lime pits outside Bradford on the wastes, for example (BMC IV: 96) – presumably there were lime kilns also. Certainly around Hull there were lime kilns, as there were at Beverley in the Grovehill area near to the brick-yards.

An industry that had similar requirements to the brick and tile-making industry was the pottery industry. Potteries had been established in several Yorkshire towns, but notably at Beverley, Doncaster, Hedon and Scarborough. At Beverley potteries were located along with the tileries in Beckside and Grovehill, and at Doncaster and Hedon too they seem to have been located largely away from the town. Scarborough is unusual in this respect, since its pottery appears to have been within the town and adjacent to the fortifications of 1135 on the edge of the old borough. Potteries were established where suitable clays could be found, but the point about the above potteries is that they seem to have fulfilled more than a purely local need – wares from the kilns at Scarborough, for example, have turned up in other parts of England and may well have been exported to Northern Europe (Farmer 1979).

Finally one further specialised building that could be found outside towns was the mill. Corn mills were the most prevalent, but from the thirteenth century the the scope of milling increased. A process important to the wool textile industry was fulling, that is the cleansing and thickening of cloth after it comes from the loom. The traditional way of effecting this was by trampling and beating the cloth in water – hence the medieval trade name Walker. But from the thirteenth century water-power had been applied to the process, and many water mills were to be rebuilt to incorporate fulling stocks as well as mill stones. While the textile industry could be found in most parts of Yorkshire, there seems to have been a tendency to build fulling mills in the north and west of the county. At Richmond, for instance, mills were located on the River Swale, and at least two were fulling mills built shortly after 1268 (Tyler 1979). A similar fulling mill existed at Whitby. In the west, fulling mills were built at Bradford, Doncaster, Knaresborough, Leeds and Wakefield, and by the fifteenth century at Halifax. It also seems likely that water-power was being harnessed to turn grindstones in the vicinity of Rotherham and Sheffield.

Windmills were also important in corn milling. Documents and maps indicate that numbers were located in fields around the peripheries of several towns. With due heed taken of cartographic convention, Speed's plans of York and Hull depict windmills outside the town walls, as there were at other towns from Guisborough in the north to Wakefield in the west. These mills are likely to have been post mills, whose bodies could be rotated around a post so that the sails could be turned into the wind, and was a type of mill that had begun to appear in Europe probably from the twelfth century.

In examining medieval urban-based industry it becomes clear that it was largely potteries and the building materials and milling industries that were located outside towns. This may seem an obvious point – clay fields and quarries had to be worked on site where they occurred. The milling industry had its own spatial needs – water for motive power, or a large enough and exposed enough site suitable for a windmill. While this is correct, matters are not quite so straightforward. There was nothing to prevent a windmill or a water mill from being built within a town where there was a suitable site or flow of water, but this rarely happened. Potteries also could be located inside the town, but again they rarely were, although Scarborough was an exception. And the same could be said of quarries. That the majority of such industrial locations were outside towns suggests that restrictions were imposed by town authorities relegating certain industries to the limits of or outside town, as indeed we have seen at Beverley, while as we have seen at Bradford penalties were imposed for the obstruction of the highways by quarrying. Obstruction of roads, the risk of fire and the polluting effects of smoke seem to have been the principal reasons for pushing out these industries, other than a purely geographical determinant. Nevertheless, we should not neglect to take into account the locations of raw materials and sources of motive power. The point is that industries did not somehow simply grow up at certain places. They were the direct result of decisions taken by both individuals and municipal bodies, and as such represent a further element of town planning, of urban controls affecting the spatial distribution of industry in the countryside outside the town.

CHAPTER TWELVE

The Urban Legacy

THERE ARE TWO OBVIOUS WAYS in which we continue to feel the effects of the Middle Ages on our surroundings today. First there are the medieval buildings themselves, whether the great monuments such as Beverley or York Minster or simply a timber-framed house. Despite destruction or disfigurement in past centuries, including our own, medieval urban architecture survives. This is especially true of the north and east of Yorkshire, where, with the exceptions of Hull and Middlesbrough, nineteenth-century industrialisation has been far less intense or even non-existent. That medieval architecture should have survived the onslaughts of the centuries at all says a good deal about the vigorous forces that brought it into being and the esteem in which some buildings have been held by succeeding generations.

The second influence is that of medieval design. The greatest impact here was on the Gothic Revival of the nineteenth century, whether on architecture, or the fine or decorative arts. Between about 1830 and 1900 many new buildings in Gothic styles, new churches or scholarly restorations of existing medieval buildings, took shape, appearing in town centres or the growing suburbs.

While the above comments are worth making, there is a third, more subtle and more profound way in which the medieval urban legacy has controlled urban development and continues to exercise some influence, and that is the medieval division of space. The pattern of the county's medieval towns, for example, has been discussed in Chapter 3, but it is worth further comment, for once the pattern had emerged, it changed little until the nineteenth century and

remains recognisable today. If some medieval towns never became flourishing centres of trade, few failed. Only Ravenserodd and perhaps Drax were lost in natural disasters; possibly Almonbury, Bingley, Brough, Harewood and Skipsea never developed an urban impetus sufficient to sustain them as towns in the Middle Ages. Despite changes in the county's economic structure – the relocation of the wool textile industry largely in the west was the biggest – the pattern of towns remained pretty much as it was in the late Middle Ages until 1750.

While many aspects of life changed dramatically during the next 100 years, the urban pattern did not alter radically, although its hierarchy did. If massive population increase and urbanisation had occurred in the west by 1850, especially around Leeds and Bradford, and if by 1900 it is possible to see a West Yorkshire conurbation and a city system around Rotherham and Sheffield, yet at their cores these were all medieval towns. Few new towns had been added in the eighteenth century – Huddersfield, Keighley and Thorne being really the only ones, and these were already showing urban characteristics in the early modern period. Industrialisation in the nineteenth century, however, led to the period of greatest urbanisation when several villages became industrial towns – Batley and Dewsbury in the west, Middlesbrough in the north, Goole in the east, together with the resorts of Harrogate, Ilkley and Saltburn. During the twentieth century, it is true to say that a more complex urban structure has developed, but this is principally in the west, while in the north and east the medieval pattern continues to hold good.

The medieval planning of the central areas of these towns similarly holds good. If many towns expanded in the period between 1600 and 1800, those in the north and east grew generally at a lesser rate rate than the industrial towns of the south and west with the exceptions of ports such as Hull and Whitby. It is the market towns in these more rural parts of the county that retain much of their medieval planning. While Chapter 3 deals with planning and street layout in the medieval town, a further point to be considered here is how long-lived such street patterns and plans were, even when the buildings fronting them had been rebuilt several times in the succeeding centuries.

A clue to former influences on the planning of the urban landscape can sometimes be found by the ways in which roads take a sudden turn for no apparent reason, or streets follow winding routes rather than direct ones. The explanation is often to be found in the medieval layout where buildings such as monasteries or defensive features such as town walls once occupied important spaces but have now disappeared. At New Malton, for example, a quite definite arc is followed by Market Street, Greengate and Finkle Street, corresponding to the medieval town wall, only fragments of which survive incorporated into the rears of later buildings. What little completely new building occurred in the central Middle Ages and later took place outside this arc of the walls as the medieval name Newbiggin testifies.

The same development can be seen at Richmond – hence the semi-circular market place within an area that was perhaps once part of the outer defences of the castle and continued to be known as the Baille in the fifteenth century (YASRS 39: 142). At Bawtry the street plan presents a different puzzle. Here the old Great North Road makes a sudden turn to the east through the town before it resumes its course. This was almost certainly a deliberate diversion in order to reroute traffic through the market place. A similar course of events is probably responsible for the strange plan of Snaith, where the present A645 – an important east–west route – has apparently been diverted to the north and through the market places.

Towns like these continue to display medieval influences over large parts of their plans. They are also towns which, for differing reasons, never became centres of industrial growth in the nineteenth century. But what of the towns and cities of the south and west where it is generally assumed that industrialisation brought about transformative changes? Bradford, Leeds, Rotherham and Sheffield all grew into mighty industrial cities in the nineteenth century, while towns such as Doncaster and Halifax lagged only a little way behind. None of them conjure up much of a medieval feel today, and our image of them is one of Victorian cities redeveloped in the twentieth century with shopping centres and office blocks. This is true to a large extent of Sheffield, where the loss of important medieval features – the castle, for example – had taken place in earlier centuries, and where the building of steel and cutlery works along the river in the nineteenth century together with the redevelopment of central areas in the twentieth has led to a loss of earlier sites and planning. While a similar development has taken place in other towns, the medieval *influence* is more readily deduced, even sensed. Bradford and Rotherham retain much of their medieval plan, and until recently so did Doncaster.

Most remarkable in this respect is Leeds. As a medieval town Leeds was of little account, but it expanded during the sixteenth and seventeenth centuries to become by the eighteenth the most important market centre for wool textiles in the north of England, and by about 1800 the fifth largest town in the country. In the nineteenth century there was further commercial, industrial and population growth, and the city was a communications centre for road, rail and water transport. Yet the planned urban unit added to the village of Leeds during the Middle Ages remained: Briggate is recognisable even today as

---

Medieval gateway built into the rear of a building bordering the market place at New Malton. It perhaps represents a postern in the circuit of walls.

A bird's-eye view of central Richmond shows the medieval semi-circular market place, which was probably contained within the outer defences of the castle from which this shot was taken. The only recognisable medieval building here, however, is the chapel centre right.

the heart of the city. This street was never cut across or realigned. New building in the seventeenth and eighteenth centuries appeared in the streets and fields adjacent. While street widening was carried out in the nineteenth century when the toll booth was removed, and while street frontages were rebuilt, the essentials of the medieval plan have endured.

Another element of medieval town plan can be found in shop and house fronts. The plots of land allotted in burgage or other forms of tenure for the building of houses and shops have tended to have a formative influence on the appearance of central streets. Over time plots may have become subdivided or a couple of plots may have been combined, but plot boundaries established in the Middle Ages have continued to dictate frontage boundaries in many towns. As Slater (1987) has suggested in relation to medieval Lichfield and Stratford-upon-Avon, some large plots may have been offered at the time on the basis that they might be subdivided by a prospective developer, so that the subdivision often occurred during the Middle Ages rather than as a later modification of medieval spatial organisation. This seems to be supported by the charter given to Leeds, for example, by Maurice Paynell around 1207 which stated that the owners of part of a plot would have the same rights as if they owned the whole, while an extent of Leeds in 1341 reveals that several burgesses owned fractions of a burgage, suggesting that subdivision had indeed occurred (Le Patourel 1957: 32, 69).

Whether narrow or wide such boundaries are in evidence in street fronts throughout the county, from industrial and commercial centres to market towns or resorts. At some towns long plots have survived where there has been little disruption in the nineteenth and twentieth centuries – Helmsley and Snaith, for example. At others, plots to the rears of shops have become developed with buildings of different dates, from terraces of cottages to warehouses and small industrial buildings – Skipton and Yarm prove typical examples.

Even a city such as Leeds retains narrow passages along Briggate which once gave access to rear plots, although now mostly developed with eighteenth- and nineteenth-century buildings and with their frontages masked by nineteenth- and twentieth-century buildings.

Although the division or amalgamation of plots for building was a process which continued into later centuries, it is probably true to say that large numbers had been altered by 1500, and that few or no new areas of plots were created in most towns. This had implications for what was to follow, especially in the eighteenth century, for what later generations of townspeople were to inherit was a heterogeneous pattern of tenure especially in the large urban centres, so that few large-scale and uniform redevelopments were ever carried out. Even in towns where just one or two landed or commercial families predominated they never gained quite the same control over building development as aristocrats had over estate villages because of this tenurial diversification. In eighteenth century Richmond, for example, if the Dundas family owned much of the town and had made it their deliberate policy to acquire as many burgages as they could to further their political ends, nevertheless substantial numbers were owned by the Yorke family, and numbers of others remained in the hands of several small proprietors. While this did concentrate political power in the hands of Sir Lawrence Dundas as the owner of the majority of the burgages, spatially his power was limited. Had he desired to do so, it meant that the town could not, without the agreement of all parties, be rebuilt in that rational style of planning we perhaps too readily associate with Georgian towns.

Some commentators view the eighteenth century as the great age of urban improvement when order and elegance ousted medieval and post-medieval urban disorder. Streets were rebuilt in classical styles and whole districts were systematically redeveloped. Recently the case has been forcefully made by Peter Borsay (1989) who has taken pains to show how the upper social groups might regard the town as an arena for social display and the pursuit of leisure, the rebuilding of houses and public buildings in classical styles being of great importance

Developed burgage plot behind High Street, Skipton.

Lambert's Yard, Leeds – sixteenth(?)-century
development to the rear of building fronting Briggate,
probably the only surviving building of this date in
this part of the city.

to the process. This is true. But in other respects Borsay and others push the argument too far. While the ideal of some architects and designers and their patrons may have been to create rationally planned classical houses set within greater schemes of planning, the reality was different. Witness, for instance, the failure of early attempts at the overall planning of a classical city such as Wren's plans for the rebuilding of London. Some large-scale planning projects were carried out, however, and gave a semblance of this total rationality of approach – Bath, Warwick and Whitehaven, for example – resulting in replanned towns built in mostly classical styles, but they were outnumbered by the exceptions. More typical were the additions of new streets and squares at the edges of towns or on vacant sites close to town centres. Even the straightening and rebuilding of existing streets in a uniform classical style, if not a rare occurrence, was one effected with some difficulty. The medieval division of urban space into streets with plots which in themselves might be subdivided and in different tenures hampered any process of wholesale redesign. In other words, the planning of English towns until the nineteenth century remained what it had mostly always been: the piecemeal addition of planned units.

The only occasions when large areas within an existing town might be completely replanned were after fire disasters, which is what happened at Warwick in 1694, so that Daniel Defoe could observe above twenty years after:

> Warwick was ever esteemed a handsome, well-built town, and there were several good houses in it, but the face of it is now quite altered; for having been almost wholly reduced to a heap of rubbish, by a terrible fire about two and twenty years ago, it is now rebuilt in so noble and so beautiful a manner, that few towns in England make so fine an appearance. (Rogers 1989: 145)

Rebuilding campaigns like this, however, affected very few towns indeed, and none in Yorkshire. Although some rebuilding after fires in York took place, this was restricted to small sections of street, rather than large areas of the city.

The division of streets into plots had yet further implications, especially for classical rebuilding. Although it might have been possible to obtain two or even three plots in order to build, say, a small symmetrical terrace, this was as far as things went in many town centres. Larger compositions were usually situated on greenfield sites adjacent to the town or where land along roads leading into the town could be obtained. Far more common in central areas of the town was the rebuilding of individual houses and shops, new terraces and villas appearing in suburbs.

The keynote of the classical facade was symmetry in combination with careful proportion. Large virgin sites allowed design of this sort to proceed with relative ease, but single, halves or thirds of a burgage plot did not. Facades became of necessity a travesty of classical principles. Since narrow frontages allowed for perhaps two windows across the house, the doorway had to be placed to one side rather than in a central position, thus marring the symmetry. Such blemishes occurred in even the best terraces, but in long, uniformly designed streets it scarcely mattered, since the lack of symmetry was hidden by the register of the fenestration along the terrace, or by accenting the middle or by the addition of pavilions to the ends. In this way an overall impression of symmetry was maintained. In a slim shop or house front, however, the lack of symmetry was all too obvious, and individuals rebuilding on a central site hemmed in by the property of their neighbours could not resort to the architectural sleight of hand of the terrace builder on a clear site.

The rebuilding of some detached houses even where plots were relatively large and lacking in restrictions did not always guarantee an ideal result. Much, of course, depended on the architect, but as much depended on the nature of the rebuilding, for the refronting and internal redecoration of an earlier house might place constraints on the occupier or designer. The reordering of rooms behind the front was often difficult because of the structural evolution of the premises. Thus, medieval houses three cells long with an entrance located between the first and second cell often became classical houses with off-centre doorways, because of the structural difficulties likely to be encountered if entrances were to be moved to a central position. This can be seen in market towns especially, where there appears to have been a greater number of houses around the periphery and at the outer ends of main streets where three-celled farm houses of medieval or post-medieval origins had sometimes been located. But it also occurs along Micklegate in York, for example, where the facades of several large classical houses are sometimes symmetrical and sometimes not, suggesting the replacement or refronting of earlier houses with passageways to the rears of plots.

Some sites imposed further restrictions on facades, leading to compromises in the setting out of openings and the detailing. Windows, for instance, should have followed a careful gradation through perhaps three stages from ground to second floor – rectangular openings on the first two floors to square openings on the third, the openings being set in vertical alignment. But the proportion of individual window-levels and their relation to the whole facade might all be thrown awry because of the need to fit a new front to a pre-existing structure whose room heights did not correspond to the principles of proportion required by classical designs. We should not forget that multi-storeyed construction was of medieval origins in English towns and not a later introduction, so that the designs of some earlier houses influenced not only the width but also the height of the house with consequent implications for its vertical proportioning.

It is not surprising that the occupiers of some town centre properties, either because of slender means or an acceptance that a medieval house could not satisfactorily be adapted to classical designs, seem to have allowed the older structure to determine the proportions, and simply added a scheme of classical decoration to a house or shop front. The house in New Market, Pontefract, illustrated on p. 129 has been thus 'Georgianised'

– in other words the front has not been altered to give a single vertical plane; the jettying has been retained, but has been dressed with Tuscan columns and an eaves cornice, the detailing being arranged to give a semblance of symmetry and sash windows.

The importance of the effects of this medieval division of space cannot be overemphasised. When in turn many eighteenth-century urban buildings came to be rebuilt or replaced in nineteenth-century reconstructions of central streets, some plot boundaries continued to be respected, even in the expanding towns of the south and west where a large amount of new building was taking place. The exceptions were the sales of large urban estates – rare in central areas – or municipal schemes of improvement which tended to become more common in the second half of the nineteenth century after several enabling acts aimed at clearing slum property. In Bradford, for example, although several centrally located new streets were built, not to mention two railway stations, ornate warehouses, shops, chambers, churches and chapels, the medieval core of Ivegate, Kirkgate and Westgate remained mostly intact. While some plots may have been amalgamated here and there, others were not. Some vacant pieces of ground existed around the edges of the town, and some were developed with long, unified designs for shops, warehouses and chambers.

But medieval field divisions remained influential in some instances either because land was in the hands of different owners, or because of the preference of some Bradford speculators for selling land close to the town in small, expensive parcels. Towns which were not great centres of expansion, such as the market towns of the north and east where populations either remained stable or rose gently, continued to develop as they had traditionally – by small-scale additions

Shops and chambers built in the second half of the nineteenth century in Westgate, Bradford. The widths of their frontages are determined by medieval plot widths in a street which had contained the medieval market place.

Market Place, Knaresborough. The nine-teenth-century town hall to the right occupies the site of and has replaced the toll booth; the shops and offices stand on land once owned by the Trinitarian Priory of St Robert. Their widths represent the division of the plots.

and refrontings, but in nineteenth-century architectural styles.

Town and city centres in the county today create one of two impressions. Either they seem Victorian cities and industrial towns with all that this implies in terms of civic pride, or they are old-fashioned market towns, small and full of eighteenth- and nineteenth-century houses. Added to this the twentieth century has left its mark in areas of glass and concrete high-rise buildings, especially in the cities of the south and west. Where medieval buildings exist they have usually become tourist attractions. Most commonly they are churches and castles, for,

with the exception of York, standing timber structures in towns are rare and sometimes only scraps remain. In a paper given in 1966 to the conference of the Urban History Group, G. H. Martin (1968) spoke of 'the town as palimpsest' to be read and reread as the history of successive building phases as one age reworked and wrote across the lines of another. Yet matters are more subtle even than this, for the medieval page was written in the master cypher. If the points raised in the above discussion are valid, then plots, boundaries, streets, street names, the proportions of some buildings and the heights of others are all encoded in this medieval hand.

Bibliography

Abrams, Philip (1978) 'Towns and economic growth', in Abrams and Wrigley (1978).

Abrams, Philip and Wrigley, E. A. (1978) *Towns in Societies: Essays in Economic History and Historical Sociology*, Cambridge.

Abulafia, David et al. (1992) *Church and City 1000–1500: Essays in Honour of Christpher Brook*, Cambridge.

Addyman, P. V. (1989) 'The archaeology of public health at York, England', *World Archaeology* 21(2): 244–64.

Atkinson, W. A. (1938) 'The Castle and the tolbooth. A sixteenth century dispute in Knaresborough', *YAJ* 33: 175–95.

Aylmer, G. E. and Cant, R. (1977) *A History of York Minster*, Oxford.

Ballard, Adolphus and Tait, James (1923) *British Borough Charters 1216–1307*, Cambridge.

Barley, M. W. (1975) *The Plans and Topography of Medieval Towns in England and Wales*, CBA Research Report No. 14.

Bartlett, J. N. (1953) *Lay Poll Tax Returns for the City of York in 1381*, vol. 30, East Riding Antiquarian Society.

Beresford, Maurice (1967) *New Towns of the Middle Ages*, London.

Biddle, M. (1976/86) 'Towns', in Wilson (1976/86).

Bond, E. A. (1868) *Chronica Monasterii De Melsa*, vol. III, London.

Borsay, Peter (1977) 'The English urban Renaissance: the development of provincial urban culture *c*1680–*c*1760', *Social History* 2(2).

Borsay, Peter (1989) *The English Urban Renaissance: Culture and Society in the Provincial Town 1660–1770*, Oxford.

Boyle, J. R. (1895) *The Early History of the Town and Port of Hedon*, Hull.

Braudel, Fernand (1981) *Civilization and Capitalism 15th–18th Century: The Structures of Everyday Life*, London.

Braudel, Fernand (1983) *Civilization and Capitalism 15th–18th Century: The Wheels of Commerce*, London.

Bridbury, A. R. (1975) *Economic Growth: England in the Later Middle Ages*, Hassocks.

Bridbury, A. R. (1981) 'English provincial towns in the later Middle Ages', *Economic History Review*, 2nd ser., XXXIV(1).

Brunskill, R. W. (1997) *Houses and Cottages of Britain*, London.

Buckland, P. C. et al. (1989) *The Archaeology of Doncaster 2: The Medieval and Later Town*, BAR British Series 202(i).

Butler, Susan and Powls, Ken (1994) *Howden: An East Riding Market Town*, Howden.

Clark, Helen (1979) 'The archaeology, history and architecture of the medieval ports of the East Coast, with special reference to King's Lynn, Norfolk', in McGrail (1979).

Clay, C. T. (1935 and 1949) *Early Yorkshire Charters*, Leeds.

Cleveland & Teeside Local History Society (1989) *A Timber-Framed Building at Yarm*, Bulletin No. 56.

Clough, Cecil H. (1982) *Profession, Vocation and Culture in Later Medieval England*, Liverpool.

Cooke Taylor, W. (1891) *The Modern Factory System*, London.

Cooper, T. P. (1913) 'The medieval highways, streets, open ditches and sanitary conditions of the city of York', *YAJ* 22: 270–86.

Crosfield, A. (Miss) (1791) *The History of North-Allerton*, York.

Dobson, R. B. (1977) 'Urban decline in late medieval England', *Transactions of the Royal Historical Society* 27.

Dobson, R. B. (1992) 'Citizens and chantries in late medieval York', in Abulafia et al. (1992).

Drage, C. (1987) 'Urban castles', in Schofield and Leech (1987).

Drake, Francis (1736) *Eboracum*, York.

Duffy, Eamon (1992) *The Stripping of the Altars*, London.

Dyos, H. J. (1968) *The Study of Urban History*, London.

Earnshaw, J. R. (1976) *A Reconstruction of Bridlington Priory*, Bridlington.

Ellis, S. and Crowther, D. R. (1990) *Humber Perspectives: A Region through the Ages*, Hull.

Evans, D. H. (1990a) *Blayde's Staith, High Street*, CBA Forum.

Evans, D. H. (1990b) 'The archaeology of Beverley', in Ellis and Crowther (1990).

Evans, D. H. and Heslop, D. H. (1985) 'Two medieval sites in Yarm', *YAJ* 57: 43–78.

Farmer, P. G. (1979) *An Introduction to Scarborough Ware and a Reassessment of Knight Jugs*, Hove.

Farrer, William (1914) *Early Yorkshire Charters*, vol. I, Leeds.

Farrer, William (1915) *Early Yorkshire Charters*, vol. II, Leeds.

Faulkner, P. A. (1966) 'Medieval undercrofts and town houses', *Archaeological Journal* 123: 120–35.

Faull, M. and Moorhouse, S. (1981) *West Yorkshire: An Archaeological Survey to AD 1500*, Wakefield.

Fieldhouse, R. and Jennings, B. (1978) *A History of Richmond and Swaledale*, Chichester.

Furnivall, F. J. (1868) *The Babees Book*, Early English Text Society.

Garside, Maurice (1921) 'The Halifax Piece Hall', *TRANSHAS*: 169–208.

Gillet, E. and MacMahon, K. A. (1989) *A History of Hull*, Hull.

Gilmour, B. J. J. and Stocker, D. A. (1986) *St Mark's Church and Cemetery*, CBA/Trust for Lincolnshire Archaeology.

Girouard, Mark (1990) *The English Town*, London.

Goldberg, P. J. P. (1992) *Women, Work, and Life Cycle in a Medieval Economy: Women in York and Yorkshire c.1300–1520*, Oxford.

Goodchild, John (1991) *Aspects of Medieval Wakefield and Its Legacy*, Wakefield.

Goodman, A. E. (1981) 'Responses to requests in Yorkshire for military service under Henry V', *Northern History* 17: 240–52.

Graham, Rose (1901) *St Gilbert of Sempringham and the Gilbertines*, London.

Grenville, Jane (1997) *Medieval Housing*, Leicester.

Hall, T. Walter (1913) *Sheffield 1297 to 1554*, Sheffield.

Hanson, T. W. (1917), 'The evolution of the parish church, Halifax, from 1455 to 1530', *TRANSHAS*: 181-204.

Harvey, J. H. (1977) in Aylmer and Cant (1977).

Hayfield, Colin and Slater, Terry (1984) *The Medieval Town of Hedon*, Hull.

Heighway, C. M. (1972) *The Erosion of History: Archaeology and Planning in Towns*, London.

Hillery, G. A. (1955) 'Definitions of community', *Rural Sociology*, 20(2).

Hilton, R H. (1982a) 'Towns in English medieval society', *Urban History Yearbook*, Leicester.

Hilton, R H. (1982b) 'Lords, burgesses and hucksters', *Past and Present* 97: 3–17.

Horrox, Rosemary (1988) 'The urban gentry in the 15th century', in Thomson (1988).

Horrox, Rosemary (1994) *Fifteenth Century Attitudes*, Cambridge.

HMC (1900) *Report on the Manuscripts of the Corporation of Beverley*, London.

James, John (1967) *The History and Topography of Bradford*, Queensbury (original 1841).

Jennings, Bernard (1970) *A History of Harrogate and Knaresborough*, Huddersfield.

Jervoise, E. (1931) *The Ancient Bridges of Northern England*, London.

Jones, E. L., Porter, S. and Turner, M. (1984) *A Gazeteer of English Urban Fire Disasters 1500–1900*, Historical Geography Research Series, No. 13.

Jones, John (1859) *The History and Antiquities of Harewood*, London.

Keen, M. (1990) *English Society in the Later Middle Ages*, Harmondsworth.

Keene, D. J. (1975) 'Suburban growth', in Barley (1975).

Keene, D. J. (1985) *Winchester Studies 2: Survey of Medieval Winchester*, vol II, Oxford.

Klapisch-Zuber, Christiane (1990) 'Women and the Family' in Le Goff (1990).

Knottingly Civic Society (1979) *Knottingley: Its Origins and Industries,* Knottingley.

Lancaster, W. T. (1912) *Chartulary of the Priory of Bridlington,* Leeds.

Laslett, Peter (1965) *The Past We Have Lost,* London.

Leach, A. F. (1896) 'The building of North Bar, Beverley', *East Riding Antiquarian Society Transactions* 4: 26–37.

Leach, A. F. (1899) 'A fifteenth century fabric roll of Beverley Minster', *East Riding Antiquarian Society transactions* 7: 50–83.

Leach, A. F. (1900) *Beverley Town Documents,* London.

Le Goff, Jacques (1977) *Pour un autre Moyen Age: Temps, travail et culture en Occident,* Paris (trans. Goldhammer, A. (1980) *Time, Work and Culture in the Middle Ages,* Chicago).

Le Goff, Jacques (ed.) (1990) *The Medieval World,* London.

Le Patourel, J. (1957) *The Manor and Borough of Leeds, 1066–1400,* vol. 45, Thoresby Society, Leeds.

Lilley, Jane (1994) 'North Bridge Road, Doncaster', *Interim* 19(4): 4–12.

McGrail, Sean (1979) *The Archaeology of Medieval Ships and Harbours in Northern Europe,* National Maritime Museum Archaeological Series, No. 5.

Martin G. H. (1968) 'The Town as Palimpsest', in Dyos (1968).

Mauchline, Mary (1972) 'Medieval society', in Ripon Civic Society (1972).

Maxwell, Sir H. E. (1913) *The Chronicle of Lanercost, 1272–1436,* Glasgow.

Morrell, W. W. (1867) *The History and Antiquities of Selby,* Selby.

Morris, Richard (1989) *Churches and the Landscape,* London.

Mumford, Lewis (1938) *The Culture of Cities,* London.

Owen, N. H. (1966) 'Thomas Wimbledon's sermon: "Redde racionem villicacionis tue"', *Medieval Studies* 28: 176–97.

Owst, G. R. (1961) *Literature and Pulpit in Medieval England,* Oxford.

Palliser, D. M. (1982) 'Civic mentality and the environment in Tudor York', *Northern History* 18: 78–115.

Palliser, D. M. (1988) 'Urban decay revisited', in Thomson (1988).

Palliser, D. M. (1992) 'Yorkshire boroughs', *Medieval Yorkshire* 21: 29–30.

Pantin, W. A. (1963a) 'The merchants' houses and warehouses of King's Lynn', *Medieval Archaeology* 6–7: 173–81.

Pantin, W. A. (1963b) 'Medieval English town house plans', *Medieval Archaeology* 6–7: 202–39.

Parker, J. H. (1853) *Some Account of Domestic Architecture in England,* vol II, Oxford.

Peck, William (1813) *A Topographical History and Description of Bawtry and Thorne,* Doncaster.

Pickering, Danby (1762) *The Statutes at Large,* Cambridge.

Pirenne, Henri, (1972) *Economic and Social History of Medieval Europe* (trans. of 1936 edn), London.

Platt, Colin (1996) *King Death: The Black Death and Its Aftermath in Late-Medieval England,* London.

Pontefract and District Archaeological Society (n.d.) *Historic Buildings in Pontefract at 7–9 Corn Market and Swales Yard,* Pontefract.

Postan, M. M. (1972) *The Medieval Economy and Society,* London.

Postan, M. M. (1973) *Essays on Medieval Agriculture and General Problems of the Medieval Economy,* Cambridge.

Poulson, George (1841) *The History and Antiquities of the Seigniory of Holderness,* Hull.

Raine, Angelo (1955) *Medieval York,* London.

Ramm, H. G. (1968) 'A case of twelfth-century town planning in York?' *YAJ* 42.

Ramm, H. G. (1972), 'The growth and the development of the city to the Norman Conquest', in Stacpoole (1972).

RCHME (1981) *The City of York: Central Area,* vol. 5, London.

RCHME (1982) *Beverley: An Archaeological and Architectural Study,* London.

RCHME (1987) *Houses of the North York Moors,* London.

Reynolds, Susan (1977) *An Introduction to the History of English Medieval Towns,* Oxford.

Richards, Peter (1977) *The Medieval Leper and his Northern Heirs,* Frome.

Rigby, S. H. (1995) *English Society in the Later Middle Ages: Class, Status and Gender,* London.

Ripon Civic Society (1972) *Ripon: Some Aspects of its History,* Clapham.

Rogers, Pat (ed.) (1989) *Daniel Defoe: A Tour Through the Whole Island of Great Britain*, London.

Rosser, Gervase (1984) 'The essence of medieval urban communities: the vill of Westminster 1200–1540', *Transactions of the Royal Historical Society* 34.

Rossiaud, Jacques (1990) 'The city dweller and life in cities and towns', in Le Goff (1990).

Rubin, Miri (1992) 'Religious culture in town and country: reflections on a great divide', in Abulafia et al. (1992).

Rubin, Miri (1994) 'The Poor', in Horrox (1994).

Saltmarshe, Col P. (1920) 'Ancient drainage of Howdenshire', *Transactions of the East Riding Antiquarian Society* XXIII: 28–33.

Salzman, L. F. (1952) *Building in England Down to 1540*, Oxford.

Schofield, John and Leech, Roger (eds) (1987) *Urban Archaeology in Britain*, CBA Research Report 61.

Schofield, John and Vince, Alan (1994) *Medieval Towns*, Leicester.

Shelby, L. R. (1967) *John Rogers, Tudor Military Engineer*, Oxford.

Short, Philip (1980) 'The fourteenth-century rows of York', *Archaeological Journal* 137: 86–136.

Simmons, T. F. (1879) *The Lay Folks Mass Book*, London.

Sjöberg, Gideon (1960) *The Preindustrial City Past and Present*, New York.

Slater, T. R. (1987) 'Ideal and reality in English episcopal medieval town planning', *Transactions of the Institute of British Geographers* 12: 191–203.

Slater, T. R. (1989) 'Doncaster's town plan: an analysis', in Buckland et al. (1989).

Speight, Harry (1902) *Lower Wharfedale*, London.

Stacpoole, A. (1972) *The Noble City of York*, York.

Storey, R. L. (1982) 'Gentlemen-bureaucrats', in Clough (1982).

SURTEES:

2:	*Wills and Inventories . . . of the Northern Counties* Durham, 1835.
30:	*Testamenta Eboracensia*, Durham, 1865.
45:	*Testamenta Eboracensia*, Durham, 1865.
53:	*Testamenta Eboracensia*, Durham, 1865.
56:	*Archbishop Gray's Register*, Durham, 1872.
74:	*Memorials of the Church of SS Peter and Wilfred, Ripon*, Part 1, Durham, 1882.
79:	*Testamenta Eboracensia*, Durham, 1884.
81:	*Testamenta Eboracensia*, Part 3, Durham, 1888.
85:	*English Miscellanies*, Durham, 1890.
91 & 92:	*Certificates of . . . Chantries, Guilds, Hospitals etc., in the County of York*, Durham, 1894.
120:	*York Memorandum Book*, Part I, Durham, 1912.
123:	*The Register of Archbishop John Le Romeyn*, Durham, 1886.

Swanson, Heather (1989) *Medieval Artisans: An Urban Class in Late Medieval England*, Oxford.

Tann, Geoff (1992) 'True Lovers' Walk, Yarm', unpublished report, Cleveland County Archaeology Section.

Theobald, C. H. (1943) *Extracts from a Doncaster court roll of the sixteenth century*, YAJ 35: 288–310.

Thomson, J. A. F. (1988) *Towns and Townspeople in the Fifteenth Century*, Gloucester.

Tillotson, J. H. (1988) *Monastery and Society in the Late Middle Ages*, Woodbridge.

Toulmin-Smith, Lucy (1907) *The Itinerary of John Leland in or about the years 1535–43*, vol. I, London.

Toulmin-Smith, Lucy (1909) *The Itinerary of John Leland in or about the years 1535–43*, vol. IV, London.

Turner, Hilary (1971) *Town Defences in England and Wales*, London.

Tyler, A. (1979) *Richmond: An Archaeological Study*, n. p.

Vance, J. E. (1971) 'Land assignment in pre-capitalist, capitalist and post-capitalist cities', *Economic Geography* 47: 101–20.

VCH (1913) *Yorkshire*, vol. III, London.

VCH (1914) *Yorkshire North Riding*, vol. I, London.

VCH (1923) *Yorkshire North Riding*, vol. II, London.

VCH (1961) *The City of York*, London.

VCH (1969) *Yorkshire: The East Riding: The City of Kingston-upon-Hull,* vol. I, London.

VCH (1989) *Yorkshire: The East Riding: The Borough and Liberties of Beverley,* vol. VI, London.

Whitaker, T. D. (1805) *The History and Antiquities of the Deanery of Craven,* Leeds.

Williams, David (1981) *Medieval Skipton,* Skipton.

Williams, R. (1973) *The Country and the City,* London.

Wilson, Christopher (1994) *The Gothic Cathedral,* London.

Wilson, D. M. (ed.) (1976/86) *The Archaeology of Anglo-Saxon England,* Cambridge.

Wilson, P. R., Jones, R. F. J. and Evans, D. M. (1984) *Settlement and Society in the Roman North,* Bradford.

YASRS:

6:	*Index of Wills in the York Registry,* Leeds, 1922.
10:	*The Coucher Book of Selby,* Leeds, 1891.
12:	*Yorkshire Inquisitions,* Leeds, 1892.
25:	*Chartulary of St John of Pontefract,* Leeds, 1899.
31:	*Yorkshire Inquisitions,* Leeds, 1902.
39:	*Yorkshire Deeds,* Leeds, 1909.
44:	*Three Yorkshire Assize Rolls,* Leeds, 1911.
48:	*Yorkshire Monasteries, Suppression Papers,* Leeds, 1912.
59:	*Yorkshire Inqisitions,* Leeds, 1918.
80:	*Miscellanea: A Selection of Monastic Rentals and Dissolution Papers,* Leeds, 1931.
98:	*York Civic Records,* vol. I, Leeds, 1939.
103:	*York Civic Records,* vol. II, Leeds, 1941.
111:	*Yorkshire Deeds,* Leeds, 1946.
120:	*Yorkshire Deeds,* Leeds, 1953.

Name Index

Page numbers in *italic* refer to illustrations.

Subject Index

Page numbers in *italic* refer to illustrations

see also spatial divisions; urban pattern;
    urbanism

urban pattern, 20–7, *26*
    decline, 65–7
    growth and development, 187–8, 192, 195

medieval planning, effect of, 196–200, *197,
    198–9*
urbanism, 4

walls and defences, 169–74, *170, 171, 172, 173, 175,
    176, 177*
warehouses, 116–18, *117, 147*